THE TRAVELER'S ATLAS
EUROPE

THE TRAVELER'S ATLAS
EUROPE

MIKE GERRARD

BARRON'S

First edition for North America published in 2009 by
Barron's Educational Series, Inc.

A QUARTO BOOK

All inquiries should be addressed to:
Barron's Educational Series, Inc.
250 Wireless Boulevard
Hauppauge, New York 11788
www.barronseduc.com

ISBN-13: 978-0-7641-6176-6
ISBN-10: 0-7641-6176-8

Library of Congress Control No.: 2008939662

QUAR.TAE

Conceived, designed, and produced by
Quarto Publishing plc
The Old Brewery
6 Blundell Street
London
N7 9BH

Senior editor: Katie Hallam
Co-editor: Ruth Patrick
Copy editor: Clare Hubbard
Art director: Caroline Guest
Designer: Sunanda Kashyap
Cartographers: Julian Baker, Malcolm Swanston
Design assistant: Saffron Stocker
Picture research: Sarah Bell

Creative director: Moira Clinch
Publisher: Paul Carslake

Color separation by PICA Digital Pte Ltd.,
    Singapore
Printed in Singapore by Star Standard Pte Ltd.

9 8 7 6 5 4 3 2 1

CONTENTS

"FRANCE, AND THE WHOLE OF EUROPE, HAVE A GREAT CULTURE AND AN AMAZING HISTORY. MOST IMPORTANT THING, THOUGH, IS THAT PEOPLE THERE KNOW HOW TO LIVE!"

JOHNNY DEPP

When I was twelve years old my parents packed me off on a school trip, my first-ever visit to continental Europe. We left Liverpool train station at midnight, and the next day we were crossing the English Channel, headed for Ostend. Unfortunately there was a bad storm in the Channel, the crossing took twice as long as it should have, and I spent most of it being violently ill. However, the reward was a journey down the Rhine to see the impressive castles and the kind of scenery we were a bit short of back home. It was the start of a life spent traveling, much of it in Europe.

At the age of seventeen I fell in love—with a country. It was my first visit to Greece, done the hard way by driving through Europe and ending up in Athens. Home was a campsite in the northern suburb of Kifisia, but the highlight was finding my way up through the back streets of the Plaka to see the Acropolis. You could still walk into the Parthenon then, and touch those ancient stones, and feel some of the magic, a contact with craftsmen and artists who lived 2,500 years ago.

When he was asked why he read so much, Ernest Hemingway once said that it was because it enabled him to live other people's lives. It's the same with travel. On my many other visits to Greece I've imagined the lives of monks in the monasteries at Meteora, and wondered what it was like to consult the Oracle at Delphi.

My curiosity and wanderlust turned me into a travel writer, so I've been lucky enough to see a lot more of Europe than I otherwise would have. I've stood on its very edge, in Istanbul, and ventured inside the Arctic Circle in Finland in winter. "When does the sun rise?" I asked the airport check-in clerk when it was still dark at 9 A.M. "February," he said.

Author Mike Gerrard doing his homework in front of the Tower of the Winds at the Ancient Agora in Athens.

I've cycled from Prague to Vienna, visiting Bohemian castles on the way, and walked in the Tatra Mountains in Slovakia. There I woke up early one morning and went for a walk in the woods in Starý Smokovec, remembering the story the hotel receptionist had told about a bear with her cubs crossing the main street in town recently. It was quiet in the woods, misty and dank, and rather eerie. The path disappeared into the pine trees ahead. From somewhere just off the trail ahead of me I heard something move, and the bellow of a beast. I walked back to the hotel and attempted to mimic the noise, only to be told it was a roe deer.

Europe isn't just about its extremes, or its more adventurous side. It's also about the centuries of culture in its great cities like Paris, Budapest, Athens, London, and Istanbul. It's about indulging yourself in the vineyards of Bordeaux, the Scottish distilleries, and in the sherry bodegas in Jerez. This book is about fifty places that, to me, are special in some way. It could easily have been five hundred. Europe is a never-ending story.

Mike Gerrard.

1 BELGIUM: BRUGES
PAGES 12-15

2 ENGLAND: LONDON
PAGES 16-19

3 ENGLAND: LAKE DISTRICT
PAGES 20-23

4 STONEHENGE AND AVEBURY
PAGES 24-27

5 THE CORNISH COASTAL PATH
PAGES 28-31

6 FINLAND: LAPLAND
PAGES 32-35

7 ICELAND: NATURAL WONDERS
PAGES 36-39

8 IRELAND: SOUTHWEST
PAGES 40-43

9 NORTHERN IRELAND: ANTRIM
PAGES 44-47

10 THE NETHERLANDS: AMSTERDAM
PAGES 48-51

AT A GLANCE: **EUROPE**

Get your bearings: all the places visited in this book are plotted on the map, so you can find where to go next.

11 NORWAY: FJORDS
PAGES 52-55

12 THE SCOTTISH HIGHLANDS
PAGES 56-59

13 THE SCOTTISH ISLANDS
PAGES 60-63

14 EDINBURGH
PAGES 64-67

15 SWEDEN
PAGES 68-71

16 WALES: SNOWDONIA
PAGES 72-75

17 CROATIA: DUBROVNIK
PAGES 78-81

18 CROATIAN ISLANDS
PAGES 82-85

19 GREECE: ATHENS
PAGES 86-89

20 SANTORINI AND THE GREEK ISLANDS
PAGES 90-93

21 DELPHI
PAGES 94-97

22 METEORA
PAGES 98-101

23 ITALY: VENICE
PAGES 102-105

24 THE CINQUE TERRE
PAGES 106-109

25 ROME
PAGES 110-113

26 RENAISSANCE ITALY
PAGES 114-117

27 TURKEY: ISTANBUL
PAGES 118-121

28 ROMAN EPHESUS
PAGES 122-125

29 ANDORRA: THE PYRENEES
PAGES 128-131

30 FRANCE: PARIS
PAGES 132-135

NORTHERN EUROPE

"We live in a wonderful world that is full of beauty, charm, and adventure."

Jawaharlal Nehru, Indian prime minister, 1889-1964

THE HISTORIC BUILDINGS OF BRUGES

Bruges is one of the most popular tourist destinations in Europe, and justifiably so, as a walk around the city center will quickly show.

The best time to visit Bruges' Markt is on a Wednesday morning, when the market is held there, or in December for the traditional Christmas market.

IT WAS IN BRUGES IN ABOUT 1473 that the printer William Caxton is believed to have published the world's first book in English. If he returned today to the city in which he lived for thirty-three years, he could probably still find his way around what is regarded as the best-preserved medieval city in Europe. The whole of the city center is a UNESCO World Heritage Site.

When the English poet William Wordsworth visited Bruges, he wrote that he felt "a deeper peace than in deserts found." In fact, the city, which is the capital of the West Flanders province of Belgium, was almost too perfect for the novelist Arnold Bennett, who visited in 1896 and wrote that whereas in most cities you seek out the picturesque, "in Bruges, assailed on every side by the picturesque, you look curiously for the unpicturesque, and don't find it easily."

Bruges' Oldest Building

The oldest building in Bruges is the Sint-Janshospitaal (St. John's Hospital), which was founded in the twelfth century. There are numerous medieval buildings in the center, from the grandest of churches to humble cottages, and it is this contrast that makes Bruges so special. It retains the feel of a complete medieval city, unlike some where only the largest and most important buildings have survived. Bruges is a city where you can see that ordinary people lived, not just the wealthy and influential.

Of course, many wealthy people lived here, for Bruges was one of the most important cities in Europe. This was the reason Caxton was here in the first place. Many rich European noblemen lived in Bruges, and this gave Caxton access to their libraries. They were here because in medieval times

The canals of Bruges are beautiful at any time: winter, summer, day, or night.

-> FACT FILE

POPULATION 120,000

CURRENCY Euro

CLIMATE Bruges has a temperate climate, with pleasant summers that never get too hot, and though it gets cold in winter, it seldom snows. It can rain at any time of the year, and is slightly wetter in summer.

WHAT TO TAKE Your camera; also be prepared for wet weather.

BEST TIME Any time is a good time, but summer gets crowded, so spring and fall are good bets if the weather cooperates. You want to see Bruges in the sunshine.

NEAREST AIRPORT Most flights for Bruges will go to Brussels Airport, from where you need to take a train into Brussels and then change to the Bruges trains, which are frequent.

ACCOMMODATION Bruges has some wonderful, characterful hotels in the city center, but it is hugely popular, so you need to book ahead.

Bruges went through a Golden Age, like the Golden Age of Athens in the sixth and fifth centuries B.C.

City Charter

Bruges received its city charter in 1128, and for the next few hundred years it flourished as a great European commercial and cultural center. It had easy access to the sea, and this enabled trading to thrive, especially the wool trade. Later, trade routes were established with the Mediterranean ports, and then even further with the lucrative spice trade in the Far East. It developed as a financial center, too.

And then, just as its wealth had slowly built up, in the early sixteenth century it slowly began to decline. The channel that connected it to the sea began to silt up. Other northern European cities, particularly Amsterdam and London, quickly exceeded Bruges in importance. It was not until the nineteenth century that its fortunes began to change again, and it was through the very thing for which it remains famous today—tourism.

Bruges became one of the first cities in Europe to attract visitors from other countries for recreational purposes. It still had its reputation, and it still had the beautiful buildings that had been constructed during its Golden Age. Not everything is quite as it seems, though. Not every building is as old as it looks. Many modern buildings have been added to the cityscape, but have been built to replicate the medieval style and so blend in and preserve the feel of the city.

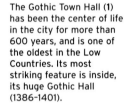

The Gothic Town Hall (1) has been the center of life in the city for more than 600 years, and is one of the oldest in the Low Countries. Its most striking feature is inside, its huge Gothic Hall (1386-1401).

Markt

Any visit to Bruges takes in, at some point, the Markt. This cobbled market square is at the very heart of the city, and has been since its beginnings, but even this is not what it seems. Many of the medieval-looking buildings were built in the nineteenth and twentieth centuries—but the effect is still stunning.

The Markt is dominated by the Belfort, or Belfry, and this 272-foot (83-m) high tower is certainly the real thing. However, it is not the original, which was a wooden belfry that was struck by lightning and burned to the ground in 1280, only forty years after it had been built. The present brick replacement was constructed between 1482 and 1486, and visitors can climb to the top to see the forty-seven bells that ring out the carillon around the city.

Even these notes, heard all over the center, are a reminder of the medieval past. At a time when people did not have their own clocks or watches, the Belfort's bells were a timepiece, signaling the end of the working day, or when it was time for a break. Everyone knew the different bell sounds, and knew if there was good news or bad news being proclaimed, or if they were being summoned to the Markt for an important announcement.

Town Hall

These announcements would have been drafted in one of Bruges' other significant buildings, the Stadhuis, or Town Hall. This stands on the Burg, the city's other main square, and its vast and imposing

façade was built in 1376. The interior is equally impressive, especially the Gothic Hall that dates to 1400 and has been sympathetically restored. Next door to the Stadhuis is the Civiele Griffie, the Records Office, built in 1537.

These are some of the most impressive buildings, but the true joy of the city is to be found by wandering its streets and discovering the less grand buildings, especially the quaint cottages and houses that line the canals. Look closely at the bridges over the canals, too, especially the Augustijnenbrug, the city's oldest. It was built in 1391 to help Augustinian monks from a nearby monastery get into the city center more quickly. It has survived for more than six hundred years, and looks as if it could survive for as long as visitors still come to see the marvelous old buildings of Bruges.

St. John's Hospital (**2**) dates back to at least 1188 and provided shelter for pilgrims and travelers as well as medical care. It's one of the oldest surviving hospitals in Europe.

This view of Bruges' Markt shows the Gothic towers and spires. Its Provincial Court (**1**) was rebuilt in neo-Gothic style after the original building was demolished.

Bruges' Belfry Tower (**1**) was once even higher. Its wooden spire was destroyed by fire in 1741 and never replaced.

Once heavily used for commercial purposes, the canals of Bruges are now restricted to tourist boats.

LONDON: OLD FATHER THAMES

London grew around the River Thames, and its banks and bridges tell much of its history, from Roman times to Nelson's navy and today's modern Docklands.

Albert Bridge (between Chelsea Harbour **3** and Cadogan Pier **4**).

THAMES PIERS IN
CENTRAL LONDON

1   Putney
2   Wandsworth Riverside
3   Chelsea Harbour
4   Cadogan
5   Millbank Millennium
6   Westminster Millennium
7   Waterloo Millennium
8   Embankment
9   Savoy
10 Festival
11 Blackfriars Millennium
12 Bankside
13 London Bridge City
14 Tower Millennium
15 St. Katharine's
16 Canary Wharf
17 Hilton Docklands
18 Greenland
19 Greenwich
20 QE II

⊖ Underground station

ON THE BANKS OF THE RIVER THAMES in Wapping, east London, is a historic and popular riverside pub called the Mayflower. That is not its original name, as it acquired it only in 1957, but the name was changed to commemorate the fact that it was at this very spot in 1620 that the Pilgrim Fathers first boarded a ship called the *Mayflower*. They sailed from London to Plymouth, then to Southampton, before setting sail on a historic journey across the Atlantic to find themselves a new life in America.

There's death here too, as nearby is another pub, the Captain Kidd, in an area that was known as Execution Dock. There was a gallows here where pirates, including Captain Kidd, and other criminals were put to death, until the last hanging took place here on December 16, 1830.

Isle of Dogs

Follow the Thames downstream a short way and you reach the Isle of Dogs. It is an area so old that no one knows for sure where its down-to-earth name came from. It may have been a place where there were once royal kennels. It may even have been called the Isle of Ducks, after the wildfowl that lived in the marshes here. One of the most popular explanations is that it was originally called the Isle of Dykes, because Dutch engineers built dykes here to try to keep back the floodwaters of the Thames—a natural problem that still occurs, and required the opening of the Thames Flood Barrier in 1984. The world's rising water levels mean that the barrier is used increasingly.

The Millennium Bridge (between **11** and **12**) crosses the water between St. Paul's Cathedral and Tate Modern art gallery.

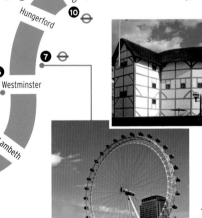

The Glo▮ (above) ▮ based ▮ Shakespear▮ original Glo▮ theat▮

Westminster Bridge and the Houses of Parliament.

The London Eye on the south bank is a stunning way to see the sights.

London's history is inseparable from the River Thames. You could walk its banks for a year and not hear all the stories there are to tell. In fact, you could stay in one place for a year and immerse yourself in the different layers of history, of everything that has happened there to shape the city of London.

Take the Isle of Dogs as one example. From being a marshy area where no one went except to go hunting, it became London's docklands where ships would sail to and from places like the West Indies and the Canary Islands. The Canary Islands boats docked in Canary Wharf, and that name is still in use even though the area has been transformed into London's financial headquarters. Work began on Canary Wharf Tower in 1988, and two years later it was Britain's tallest building.

Greenwich

Opposite the Isle of Dogs on the south bank of the Thames is the part of London that has more maritime links than any other—Greenwich. To the rest of the world Greenwich is probably best known as the home of Greenwich Mean Time, and the place where zero degrees longitude was established, the longitude equivalent of the equator.

Visitors from all over the world come to be photographed astride the meridian line, at Greenwich Observatory. The Observatory no longer looks out at the stars, because of the light pollution caused by the growth of one of the world's biggest cities. But from the hill on which it stands you can still look down on Old Father Thames, and on the Old Royal Naval Hospital, too, which became the Royal Naval College. Here also is the National Maritime Museum, and the last resting place of the *Cutty Sark*, one of the world's most famous sailing ships, the last tea clipper in existence.

-> FACT FILE

POPULATION 7,400,000

CURRENCY Pound sterling

CLIMATE London has a temperate climate, with few extremes. Summers are warm, and winters can be cold but are seldom freezing for long. Despite its reputation among foreign visitors for being foggy, this has not been true for several decades. Nor is it all that rainy, although rain can fall at any time of year.

WHAT TO TAKE Plenty of money, as London is one of the most expensive cities in the world.

BEST TIME Summer is the most reliable time for good weather, and it can be glorious despite the crowds.

NEAREST AIRPORT London has several airports nearby, but the closest to the city is Heathrow, 15 miles (24 km) west of the center. There are underground and overground trains, and buses and taxis into the city.

ACCOMMODATION London has everything, but prices are on the high side, especially in the West End. Stay farther out, but near a tube station, if you want to save money.

WHAT TO READ Peter Ackroyd's *London: The Biography* is a magnificent, epic, and readable account of London's history.

You could see Tower Bridge opening, one of the most famous London sights.

Canary Wharf, the financial center of Britain, hosts some of its tallest buildings.

Pleasure cruises and freight barges continue to use the river daily (left).
Looking west from Tower Bridge (below), with the Tower of London on the right and the curved City Hall on the left. The contrast between the two buildings is an example of what makes London so visually exciting.

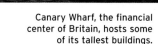

Tower Bridge

It was in the glorious Painted Hall at the Royal Naval College in 1806 that the body of England's great maritime hero, Admiral Lord Nelson, who had died in victory at the Battle of Trafalgar, lay in state for three days while the nation paid its respects. The architect Christopher Wren had not only designed the Royal Observatory and the Royal Naval College, but of course created his masterpiece, St. Paul's Cathedral. It was to here that Nelson's funeral barge was taken from Greenwich, and where he was buried with a full state funeral—normally given only to a member of the royal family.

Nelson's funeral barge would have passed under two bridges to reach St. Paul's, though today there are three bridges on the route. The third, Tower Bridge, now a very potent symbol of London and the river, was added only in 1894, the first bridge to be built east of London Bridge. Tower Bridge opens up to admit river traffic through, which was one reason no bridge had been built there before; boats needed to get to the Port of London, more convenient for the city center than the commercial docklands area.

It was near Tower Bridge that the city of London began. The first known settlement was made here by the Romans in A.D. 43. They came up through Kent and settled near where Tower Bridge now stands. They found the first fordable point on the River Thames, and here they built the first bridge across the river. It was the start of a city that would one day grow to be the largest in the world, and whose river, Old Father Thames, still keeps rolling along, down to the mighty sea.

Once the world's largest Ferris wheel, the London Eye stands at 443 feet (135 m) high and is situated on the south bank of the Thames, between the Westminster and Hungerford Bridges.

–> Lord Nelson

Vice-Admiral Horatio Nelson is one of Britain's greatest seafaring heroes. He was born in Norfolk, England, in 1758, the son of a vicar, and joined the Royal Navy at the age of twelve. He rose quickly through the ranks, not hampered by the fact that he suffered from seasickness all his life! His finest hour was also his final hour, when he died while defeating Napoleon's navy at the Battle of Trafalgar.

ENGLAND'S LAKE DISTRICT

Home to the highest mountain in England, and inspiration for the nation's best-loved poem, the Lake District contains some of the finest scenery in the British Isles.

Scafell Pike (1) is 3,205 feet (977 m) high, making it the highest mountain in England.

William Wordsworth wrote his famous poetry while living in Dove Cottage (2).

ALTHOUGH IT IS SCARCELY 35 miles (56 km) from one side to the other, the Lake District contains some of England's most dramatic scenery, and some of its best-loved landmarks. It is home to England's highest mountain, Scafell Pike (3,205 feet/977 m), and its natural beauty inspired the Romantic poets, notably William Wordsworth. Wordsworth's poem "Daffodils" was chosen recently as Britain's best-loved poem, and it is a sign of the timeless nature of parts of the English countryside that you can still visit in spring today and see the same daffodils that thrilled Wordsworth in 1804.

William Wordsworth

It was in April 1804 when Wordsworth wrote his poem, also known by its opening line of "I wandered lonely as a cloud," though the actual incident took place two springs earlier near Ullswater. His sister Dorothy recorded the event in her own journal, and Wordsworth acknowledges his debt to her own descriptions of the daffodils.

It was part of Wordsworth's talent that he saw the beauty in the detail. He saw that the joy of the Lake District was not only in its grandeur, its rugged mountains, and its vast lakes, but in its flowers and its animals, too. People respond to his poems because he can capture in words what we all feel but few can express—the utter delight in the vivid yellow of a swath of daffodils spread before us.

Wordsworth wrote "Daffodils" while living at Dove Cottage, near Grasmere. It was his home in the Lakes from 1799 to 1808, at first with his sister Dorothy, and from 1802 also with his new wife, Mary, and Mary's sister. If it was crowded already, the arrival of three children meant they eventually had to find a larger home, although when they

Derwent Water (3) in Borrowdale is one of the major lakes in the Lake District, and certainly one of the most popular and beautiful.

-> FACT FILE

POPULATION 42,000

CURRENCY Pound sterling

CLIMATE The mountains and the location on the west side of England make the Lake District one of the wettest parts of the country. It can rain at any time. Some snow is normal in winter, and summers are usually warm but never really hot.

WHAT TO TAKE Wet-weather clothing, good walking shoes, and a cell phone if going walking in quieter areas. The weather can change very quickly when you get up high.

BEST TIME Late spring/early summer is beautiful, as is the fall. Try to avoid weekends, as they are busy.

NEAREST AIRPORTS Manchester International Airport is about 80 miles (129 km) south of the southern lakes. Newcastle International Airport is about 90 miles (145 km) east.

ACCOMMODATION Plenty of options all over the Lakes, from vacation rentals and inexpensive guesthouses to luxury spas and hotels.

moved out of Dove Cottage, another writer, Thomas de Quincy, moved in. Today about 70,000 visitors a year pass through the door of Dove Cottage, which is kept much as it was when the Wordsworths lived there, and it is one of the most popular sights in the Lake District.

One of the few negative things you can say about the Lake District is that it is too popular. In high summer and on holiday weekends it is more difficult to wander lonely as a cloud, but it can still be done. You just need to plan a little, and avoid the tourist hot spots–towns such as Windermere, Bowness, Kendal, and Keswick.

The Lakes

The lakes of the Lake District are so big, and there are so many of them, that it is possible to escape the crowds. One curious fact is that only one of the lakes in the National Park has the word *lake* in its name: Bassenthwaite Lake. The others all use the word *water*, as in Derwent Water, or just a single name, such as Grasmere or Windermere. As the word *mere* means "a lake that is big but not deep," it does not need another *lake* to go with it.

Windermere is the best-known lake of them all, as it is the largest natural lake in England. It is a long thin lake, some 10 ½ miles (16.9 km) from north to south, but in places only a few hundred yards across. It is probably best appreciated from up high, away from the crowds that cluster its shores, and the leisure crafts that make good use of it.

From up on one of the peaks surrounding Windermere, those leisure crafts look more like water boatmen, the little insects that skate across the surface of the water. From up high you also get a better sense of the scale of the lake, and of the beautiful rugged hills and the thick woods that line its banks in places. It is also a better place to get a perspective on the way this landscape was carved out, by glaciers cutting between the peaks during the Ice Age.

One of the prettiest lakes is Derwent Water, or Derwentwater, which is surrounded by trees and hills, and has several islands (one of them inhabited) that sit picturesquely in it. It is only 3 miles (4.8 km) long and about 1 mile (1.5 km) at its widest, but it is surrounded by good walks to take you up into the hills and away from the crowds, if that is what you want.

Ullswater is the second-biggest of the Lake District lakes, at 9 miles (14.5 km) long, but only ³/₄ mile (1.2 km) wide at its widest. It is arguably

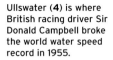

Ullswater (**4**) is where British racing driver Sir Donald Campbell broke the world water speed record in 1955.

the most beautiful of the lakes, having a swirling S-shape to it, as it cuts through lush green hills and woodland that is bright green in summer, and golden in its fall colors. It is also where William Wordsworth and his sister Dorothy went in April 1802, to Gowbarrow Park. From here they walked, as you can today, to see the hillsides covered in butter-yellow daffodils. And crowded or not, these beautiful flowers will lift your spirits.

There are five islands in Derwent Water (3), the largest named Vicar's Island, as it once belonged to monks from Fountains Abbey, in Yorkshire.

Colwith Force on the River Brathay in Ambleside (5) has several different falls along the river, a popular spot for walking.

Skelmergh or Skelsmergh Church (6) is typical of the Lake District in having more than one version of its name.

Windermere (7) has been a popular tourist destination since the middle of the 19th century, when the railroad arrived here.

STONEHENGE AND AVEBURY

From Arthurian tales to the legend of Robin Hood, England is a land of mystery, but nothing is as mysterious as Stonehenge and the nearby stone circles at Avebury.

IN AN AGE WHEN WE OFTEN THINK there are fewer and fewer mysteries left in the world, a visit to Stonehenge and Avebury will remind you that England has always been a land of mysteries. And there are some that the scientists may never explain. It is why we are drawn to the standing stones at Stonehenge, and the stone circles at Avebury nearby–to wonder at how and why they were built. We want to know, and yet it is far more important not to know.

The site at Avebury is believed to be even older than Stonehenge, going back almost five thousand years, and is just as mysterious. Although both places have circles of standing stones, the two sites could not be more different. Part of Avebury's charm is that the main stone circle is in the middle of the Wiltshire village–or rather the village is in the middle of the stone circle.

Even without its strange stones, Avebury would be a picturesque English village, where old cottages line the main street, and a pub lies at the heart of it. There are a few village stores, but many of these exist only because of the visitors who come to see the stones. There is a large parking lot on the edge of the village, too. Mystery does have its drawbacks if you live in the middle of it.

Beer and Theories

For the visitor, though, there is something utterly magical about being able to sit outside the traditional English pub, in the middle of a vast stone circle, and enjoy a beer while weighing up the different theories about the building of the stones.

Although the Avebury stones are much smaller than Stonehenge, the main circle, or henge, within which the stones are contained is a massive

This aerial view of Avebury (1) shows how the Wiltshire village and its ancient stone circles intertwine.

POPULATION 500, Avebury

CURRENCY Pound sterling

CLIMATE The temperate climate makes this part of England a little milder but rather wetter than the rest of the country. Rain can occur any time. Summers are usually pleasant but seldom hot, whereas winters can find freezing temperatures and frost, and often a little snow.

WHAT TO TAKE One of many fascinating books about the building of Avebury and Stonehenge.

BEST TIME Any time of year. The stones look wonderful in the height of summer or in a wintry landscape.

NEAREST AIRPORTS Bristol airport is the closest; London's Heathrow Airport is about 70 miles (113 km) northeast of Stonehenge and Avebury.

ACCOMMODATION There are a few rooms in Avebury, at the Red Lion pub or in the village, but the nearest larger place with hotels and other accommodation options is the small town of Devizes, 7 miles (11 km) away. Salisbury is 10 miles (16 km) south of Stonehenge.

The sun shining on Stonehenge (**2**) emphasizes the site's astronomical significance to the people who built it.

1,400 feet (427 m) in diameter. Within this earthwork is the largest prehistoric stone circle in existence, and that is 1,100 feet (335 m) across. Within this are two further smaller circles, and leading off from them are two long stone avenues. One of these is still partially standing, and traces of the other have been found.

It is a complex site, and its purpose is not known. One theory is that it was a burial site, perhaps used for ancestor worship, as human bones have been found near and beneath some of the stones. It may be that the taller stones represent men, and the shorter stones women. It may also be that the site has some astronomical purpose, in the same way that other ancient civilizations built structures to record or salute the sun and the stars. Whatever its function, no one visiting the more famous Stonehenge should miss coming to Avebury, too.

Stonehenge
About 17 miles (27 km) due south of Avebury stands Stonehenge. Like Avebury, it is a UNESCO World Heritage Site, but unlike Avebury, it stands alone and magnificent on the Salisbury Plain. It too is

surrounded by a man-made ditch, thought to be about 3,100 years old, but those startling stones are more recent, and more recent than Avebury's, too, having been dated to about 2500–2200 B.C.

As with Avebury, the purpose of Stonehenge is simply not known, although there are just as many theories. Not knowing why they are there, though, is for many people one of their main attractions. To stand in awe of something inexplicable is not an experience we commonly have in the modern world.

The area was certainly used as a burial ground, as human bones have been found that date from about the time the first-known ditch was built. But then, almost a thousand years later, the stones themselves were probably added. The site itself may have been used for several thousand years, as there is evidence that wooden posts were sunk here as long ago as about 8000 B.C. It seems likely these were in an east-west alignment, and so did have some special significance and were not merely foundation posts for domestic dwellings.

The stone circle at Avebury (1) is here photographed on the morning of the spring equinox, an important date in what was, among other things, possibly a calendar of the heavens.

Construction

What is just as intriguing as why Stonehenge was built is how it was built. The first stones here came in about 2500 B.C. from the Prescelli Mountains in Pembrokeshire, South Wales, about 245 miles (394 km) by land from Stonehenge. The stones–each of which weighs up to five tons–are thought to have been taken over land, at first to the coast, then floated on huge rafts up the River Avon, then brought here by hauling them over the ground before standing them upright.

About three hundred years later, though, the stones were rearranged, and the larger stones that today dominate the site were brought from the Marlborough Downs, a mere 20 miles (32 km) away. Trying to imagine the scenes here when this was being done is only part of the magic of both these breathtaking sites. Although the time gap between now and then is vast, it is still possible to feel that by being here you are making some kind of contact with our fascinating ancestors.

-> Get Up Close

It is not possible to get close to the Stonehenge stones during normal visiting hours. However, it is possible to get right into the center circle by arranging a special personal visit, though this will need to be done well in advance because of the demand.

Silbury Hill, near Avebury, is the largest man-made earth mound in Europe, but its purpose has yet to be discovered (1).

The Stonehenge site extends far beyond the major stones, though not everything is obvious to the visitor seeing things at eye level.

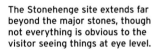

Avebury Manor (1) dates from the 16th century, a modern building in comparison with the ancient stone circles.

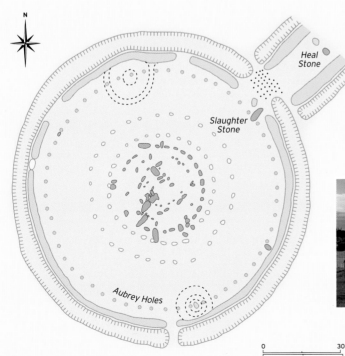

Heal Stone

Slaughter Stone

Aubrey Holes

0   30 meters
0   100 feet

The stones at Avebury (1) provide useful shelters for the local sheep when the weather is bad.

27

THE CORNISH COASTAL PATH

The southwest stretch of Britain's longest long-distance footpath provides some of the most memorable walking in England, with the sea always at your side.

The Coastal Path goes right through St. Ives (1), at one time a prosperous fishing port and now a much-visited holiday resort. Its picturesque houses and narrow back streets have made it popular with artists, and a branch of London's Tate gallery is based here.

CORNWALL IS A WORLD APART. When you cross the border from Devon, it is as if you leave England behind long before you get to Land's End. The Cornish people held on to their Celtic culture when it was wiped out in the rest of the country by the Saxon invaders. Scotland and Wales remain Celtic nations, but in England only Cornwall has that fiery independent spirit. The dramatic landscape reflects this, too, and nowhere more so than around the coast, with its cliffs and its tales of smuggling, a coast that can be walked in its entirety, a distance of 258 miles (415 km), along the Cornish Coastal Path.

The path is a part of the longer South West Coast Path, which at 630 miles (1,014 km) is the longest of Britain's long-distance footpaths. Using public rights of way, the path runs around the coasts of Devon and Cornwall, and on into Dorset on the south coast and Somerset on the north coast. Large parts of it use the old paths once trodden by customs officers as they patrolled the coasts looking for smugglers, who made use of the many concealed bays—especially in the more remote parts of Cornwall—to bring goods into the country illegally.

Climbing the Coast

Despite the fact that it follows the coast, the Coastal Path is no easy amble along level ground. The coast in this corner of England is rugged, and riddled with rivers, inlets, coves, and cliffs, which cause the path to rise and fall, often quite steeply. It was estimated by the South West Coast Path Association, an independent charity that was founded to help people get the most from the Coastal Path, that walking its complete length once would involve you in climbing 114,931 feet (35,031 m), which is almost four times the height of Mount Everest.

The fishing port of Mousehole (2) is pronounced "Mowzal," and its strong character makes it an essential stopping-off point when walking the Coastal Path.

-> FACT FILE

CURRENCY Pound sterling

CLIMATE Its southerly location makes Cornwall one of the warmest parts of the British Isles, with many sunny days. Its setting also brings plenty of rain, however, but most rain falls from October to February. Winters are mild, with only occasional snow and frost, and most of this is inland.

WHAT TO TAKE Sturdy walking shoes, good maps, cell phone, wet-weather clothing, and sunscreen.

BEST TIME Early summer and early fall are good times. Midsummer gets better weather but can be crowded.

NEAREST AIRPORTS Newquay, Bristol, and Plymouth.

ACCOMMODATION Cornwall is a popular vacation area, with a wide range of accommodation. However, if you are walking the path and need to be in a particular place on a particular night, you must book ahead. Some of the places it passes through are quite small, and some of the accommodation is in vacation rentals, rented only by the week.

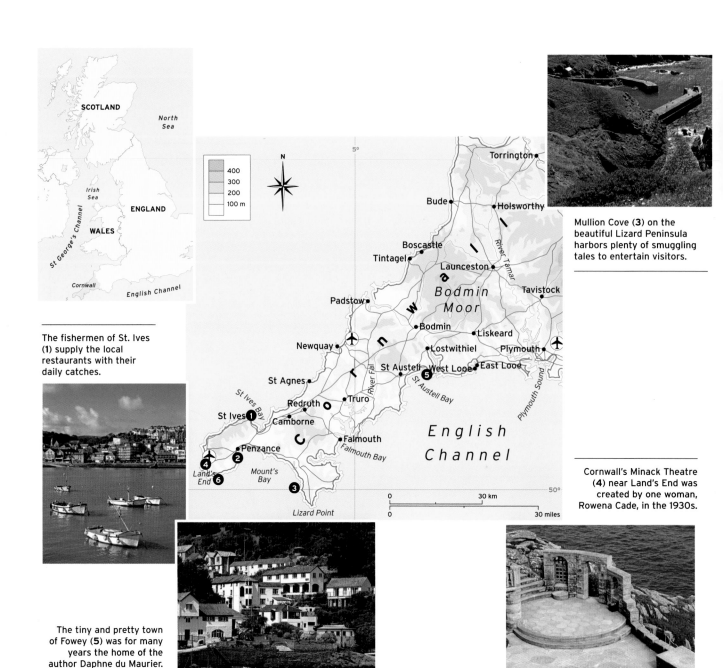

Mullion Cove (**3**) on the beautiful Lizard Peninsula harbors plenty of smuggling tales to entertain visitors.

The fishermen of St. Ives (**1**) supply the local restaurants with their daily catches.

Cornwall's Minack Theatre (**4**) near Land's End was created by one woman, Rowena Cade, in the 1930s.

The tiny and pretty town of Fowey (**5**) was for many years the home of the author Daphne du Maurier.

Shipwrecks and Smugglers

Not to diminish the beauty of the rest of the walk, but in Cornwall it takes on another dimension. Stuck out on a limb at the very edge of England, thrusting out into the Atlantic Ocean and squeezed between the Celtic Sea and the English Channel, the Cornish coast can be both the most beautiful and the most dangerous in Britain. It is an area renowned for shipwrecks, and the villagers here were not slow to reap the benefits of claiming the wrecked cargoes and making some use of them, as they were no longer of use to their previous owners.

Cornwall has always had a lawless spirit, and if the cargoes would not come to them, they would often sail out to find their own cargoes, making rendezvous with smuggling ships out in the wind-tossed seas, and struggling home in the dark with their booty. It was then that the customs men would patrol the cliffs, looking for the slightest glimpse of a lonely boat, and then trying to figure out where it would come ashore, and how best they could get there to intercept it. But the smugglers knew the cliffs and the coves and the paths every bit as well as the customs men, and a fine cat-and-mouse game would follow.

World Heritage Sites

The South West Coast Path takes walkers through two World Heritage Sites. One is found on the East Devon and Dorset stretch—the Jurassic Coast. The other is in Cornwall—the combination of man and landscape that is the Cornwall and West Devon

Mining Landscape. The mining here was mainly of tin and copper, although in some places arsenic was also mined for a time. As you walk the coast, the ghostly relics of tin and copper mines can be seen: towers in the sky, and the evidence of shafts underground.

In combination with the tales of smuggling and the tough life of the Cornish fishermen, the mining history narrates a tale of not just a stunningly beautiful landscape, but a harsh one, too, that had to be fought.

Walking the Coastal Path

Walking at an average speed and for up to eight hours a day, the entire Cornish Coastal Path could be walked in ten-eleven days. They would be hard days, though, and taking no account of delays, bad weather, or just the wish to stop off and swim, or relax in a pub for an hour or two. Allow two weeks and the walk becomes less of an endurance test, and three weeks would be ideal if you can spare the time. That way a day off here and there to explore the places on the route is also possible.

It is not a journey to undertake lightly or on the spur of the moment. It needs some planning, and fortunately there are several books and web sites that can help you do this. There are companies that will organize it all for you, and guesthouses along the way are used to help walkers transport their luggage on to the next port of call—though this option obviously is not cheap.

Sunrise at Porthcurno Bay (6) portrays some of the mystery and dramatic grandeur of the Cornish coastal scenery.

FINNISH LAPLAND

Finnish Lapland is an appropriate home for Santa Claus, as it is a place that fills everyone with a childlike wonder, and an area that is both innocent and wild.

THIS PLACE IS NOT EUROPE as most people imagine it. It is at the other end of the continent from the Mediterranean beaches and more than 1,000 miles (1,600 km) from cities like London and Paris. It is way north of Moscow and, unlike Iceland, is mostly inside the Arctic Circle. It is cold, and scenic, and a reminder that Europe does still have its wild and remote areas. Welcome to Lapland.

Although Lapland as a general term spreads across Sweden as well as Finland, it is the Finnish province of Lapland that is most associated with the name. It is an area that is the size of Switzerland, Belgium, and the Netherlands combined, and yet it has no mountains, only undulating fells.

The remote Finnish landscape can be eerie and surreal, as if from a fantasy world.

Land of Extremes

To many it has a wholesome image as the home of Santa Claus (see page 34), and the place where you can take your children for a treat just before Christmas. But that image does not do justice to its grandeur, and its wild and rugged nature. Get yourself lost here in midwinter and you will not see Christmas again. It is a bitter and harsh environment, as well as a breathtakingly beautiful one. Literally so, as the sudden shock of stepping into a temperature of well below zero can chill your lungs. At the same time, the sights here will also stop you in your tracks. It is like walking into a Christmas card, seeing the kind of scenery you associate more with Alaska, Canada, or Siberia than with Western Europe.

Rovaniemi

Rovaniemi is the capital of Finnish Lapland, where about 60,000 people (one-third of the Lapland population) live. Roughly 10,000 of these are students in Rovaniemi, giving the city a youthful

Reindeers' antlers are grown afresh every year, and their outer fur conceals a thick additional coat beneath, to keep them warm in such harsh conditions.

–> FACT FILE

POPULATION 190,000

CURRENCY Euro

CLIMATE Summers are surprisingly warm, with daytime temperatures in the upper 70s°F (mid-20s°C), though winters are bitterly cold—the January average is 7°F (-14°C). Snow is common from late September till early May.

WHAT TO TAKE Warm clothing, your camera, and a sense of wonder.

BEST TIME Visit Santa Claus in December, though to see Lapland in summer is a whole other experience.

NEAREST AIRPORT Rovaniemi, the main city in Lapland.

ACCOMMODATION A good choice of comfortable hotels in the main towns, but renting a wilderness cabin is also popular, and family-run guesthouses are also available. There is a Clarion Hotel Santa Claus in Rovaniemi.

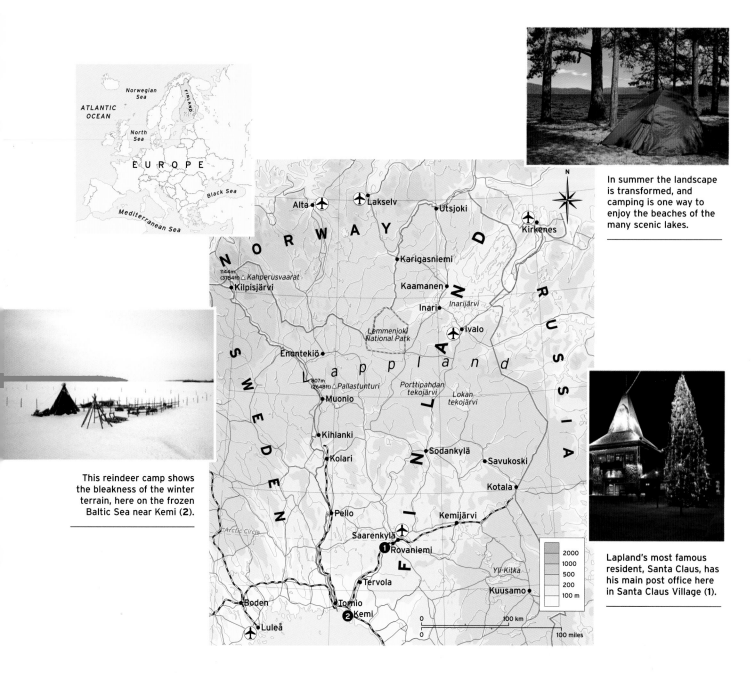

In summer the landscape is transformed, and camping is one way to enjoy the beaches of the many scenic lakes.

This reindeer camp shows the bleakness of the winter terrain, here on the frozen Baltic Sea near Kemi (2).

Lapland's most famous resident, Santa Claus, has his main post office here in Santa Claus Village (1).

-> Santa Claus

How Santa Claus ended up living in Lapland is a bit of a mystery. The original Saint Nicholas was born in southern Turkey. Over the centuries the stories have merged with myth and legend, especially that of the Germanic pagan god Odin, to somehow produce a commercialized avuncular man in red robes. He lives either at the North Pole or, as most countries believe, in Finnish Lapland.

and lively feel, far removed from its Santa Claus image. Despite the fairly small population it is one of the biggest cities in the world in terms of its area, as it sprawls over 3,095 square miles (8,016 sq km). There have probably been people living here where two major Lapp rivers—the Ounasjoki and the Kemijoki—merge for at least eight thousand years, but it was in the nineteenth century that Rovaniemi prospered when Lapland's natural resources of gold and timber were in demand all over the world.

The city might be the home of Santa Claus, but it is just as good to visit in the summer, when the sun never sets. Then you can enjoy outdoor activities like hiking and cycling, and head for the nearby Arctic Circle and find a land where the air is so clean and fresh that every breath seems to increase your feeling of well-being. In winter the winter sports take over and the adrenaline rush increases, though even if you are not an avid cross-country skier you can enjoy hiking using snowshoes, or taking a wildlife safari, or a sleigh ride pulled by huskies—exhilarating enough for some people.

The Sami

The indigenous people of Finnish Lapland, and of the Lapp area, are the Sami. There are only about seven thousand in Finland, out of an overall population estimated at up to one hundred thousand, but Sami is an officially recognized Finnish language and the people are an important part of the culture here. There were, however, long periods when the Sami culture and language were threatened by the state, as also happened in Russia when minorities were persecuted and forced to either speak Russian or face extinction.

The Sami have lived in this land for at least 2,500 years and possibly as long as 10,000 years. Their past is still, in part, a mystery. The Sami traditionally lived by the migration paths of the reindeer, supplementing their diet by fishing, and by trapping other animals. They would trade furs and meat for necessities, though from the sixteenth century onward many of the Sami abandoned their nomadic life and become farmers and fishermen.

Reindeer

The Sami depended on reindeer, and it can be a surprise to some people to discover that some of them are wild animals, not solely kept in a corral for Santa's use at Christmas. There are about two hundred thousand reindeer in Lapland, and there is a mix of wild, domesticated, and semidomesticated—their owners let them range free but they always know where they are!

These deer—known in North America as caribou— have adapted in fascinating ways to the extreme temperatures in which they live. They have two layers of fur, the outer layer being made up of hairs that are hollow inside, giving the animal more warmth. Their noses, too, are unusual, and quite large inside. This enables the cold air being breathed in to be warmed before it reaches the reindeer's lungs. Some of the heat and moisture is retained from the expelled air, to warm and dampen the cold, dry, winter air being taken in. Their hooves also change with the seasons, to adapt to the different ground conditions and to enable them to dig in the snow for food in winter. It is little wonder that Santa Claus chose them to help him deliver presents in the depths of the Finnish winter.

Cross-country skiing is a popular pursuit for all the family in Lapland, and sometimes is simply the best means of getting about.

ICELAND'S NATURAL WONDERS

Iceland is a world of its own, a country of lakes and fjords, glaciers and volcanoes, mountains and hot springs, sitting independently between Europe and North America.

ICELAND IS A ONE-OFF. The closest neighbor to this aptly named country is Greenland, which is usually included as part of North America even though it is a Danish province. Iceland is considered part of Europe although it is 603 miles (970 km) to Bergen in Norway, the closest point on the mainland of Europe. On the way you would pass by the Faroes and the Scottish Shetland Islands, two other places that do not fit easily into any particular cultural boxes.

Despite its name and image, Iceland is not actually within the Arctic Circle, which only passes through the island of Grimsey, 25 miles (40 km) north of the Icelandic mainland. It is also not as fiercely cold in winter as you might expect, with temperatures hovering around freezing point. It is not exactly warm either, which is why the country's hot springs are so popular, but there are far colder places on the planet. It is in summer when you really notice the lack of heat, and you are more likely to need an umbrella than sunscreen.

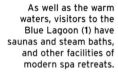

As well as the warm waters, visitors to the Blue Lagoon (1) have saunas and steam baths, and other facilities of modern spa retreats.

The Blue Lagoon

There are certain sights you have to see when visiting any destination, even if thousands of other people are heading there at the same time. Just as in Paris you must see the Eiffel Tower, in Iceland everyone visits the Blue Lagoon. This geothermal spa has been formed within the lava fields of southwestern Iceland, and its deep blue color and the steam that rises from the surface, in this volcanic setting, make for an unusual and slightly surreal experience. Even when you are expecting to set foot in a hot spring, the natural temperatures of the lagoon can still startle—the water temperature remains at about 104°F (40°C). When the air temperature is below zero, stepping into this steaming bath with hundreds of other bathers around you is a very Icelandic experience.

Geysers and Glaciers

If the Blue Lagoon is an indulgence, then seeing some of Iceland's geysers and glaciers is a more

More water flows over the Dettifoss Falls than over any other waterfall in Europe (2).

-> FACT FILE

POPULATION 316,000

CURRENCY Icelandic króna

CLIMATE Iceland's subpolar climate is moderated by the mild Gulf Stream, which means that winters are not as cold as many people expect them to be. In the coldest months, December–January, the temperature in Reykjavik averages around freezing point. On the other hand, summers are colder than many people expect, with a July-August maximum of 57ºF (14ºC). In Reykjavik it also rains on two days out of three, with May-June being the driest months, October and January the wettest.

WHAT TO TAKE Warm clothes, despite the Gulf Stream.

BEST TIME May-June, when it is driest and summer is on the way.

NEAREST AIRPORT Reykjavik

ACCOMMODATION All kinds of accommodation, at all prices, though the cost of living in Iceland is high and that is reflected in the cost of hotels and other accommodation.

Jökulsárlón (3) is the largest glacial lake in Iceland, although it came into existence only in 1934–35 because of glacial melting.

humbling experience. Vatnajökull is, at 3,127 square miles (8,100 sq km), the largest glacier in Europe. In places the ice is almost 3,300 feet (1,006 m) thick, and underneath it are several active volcanoes. This produces the strange phenomenon of a volcano occasionally erupting underneath the dense ice of Vatnajökull. When the volcanic eruption bursts through the ice, it forms something called a tuya. This is a very rare, steep-sided, and flat-topped volcano, looking something like a dark version of the mesas you see in the deserts of the American Southwest—and in many old cowboy movies.

Another phenomenon Iceland shares with the United States is the geyser, though Iceland can claim the original—the Great Geysir. This erupting hot water spout gave the world the English word *geyser*, from the Icelandic word *gjósa*, which means "to erupt." Accounts of geyser activity here go back to the twelfth century, and the Great Geysir is immensely impressive when it performs, shooting a spout of hot water up to 200 feet (61 m) into the air. However, nature's artist is temperamental and can be quiet, even for years at a time, before returning to then blow off steam several times a day. More reliable is the nearby Strokkur geyser, which explodes to less than half the height of the

Great Geysir, but does it regularly every five to ten minutes throughout the day.

Waterfalls

To see really powerful water forces at work you must travel to the Dettifoss waterfall in northeast Iceland. Iceland is covered in waterfalls, one consequence of the steady rainfall here, and Dettifoss is said to be the most powerful falls in Europe, for the volume of water that plunges over them. It is about 328 feet (100 m) wide and 89 feet (27 m) high, and to approach its thundering power after heavy rains is to really be in awe of the capabilities of nature—and why humans are always seeking ways to harness and use that power. Dettifoss is in the Jökulsárgljúfur National Park, which has been described as a miniature version of the Grand Canyon in the United States, and there are two other smaller but still powerful falls nearby: Hafragilsfoss and Selfoss. *Foss* is an Old Norse term for a waterfall or a force, and is also still in use in northern England, where there are falls like Janet's Foss in the Yorkshire Dales.

World Heritage Sites

Iceland also has two UNESCO World Heritage Sites, showing both the old and new faces of this strange land. The Thingvellir National Park was created in 1928, and apart from its natural beauty it is also where, in 930, the Icelandic Parliament, the Alping, was founded. It is one of the oldest parliaments in the world. In total contrast, Iceland's other UNESCO site is the island of Surtsey, which is a brand new island formed as the result of underwater volcanic eruptions that began in 1963 and continued for four years. There are now fascinating ongoing scientific studies of the island to see how seeds, plants, animals, birds, and bacteria manage to colonize a new island, which is now the most southerly point of Iceland. So even today this intriguing island is still in a process of change.

The island of Surtsey (4) is a new addition, as it started to be formed only in 1963.

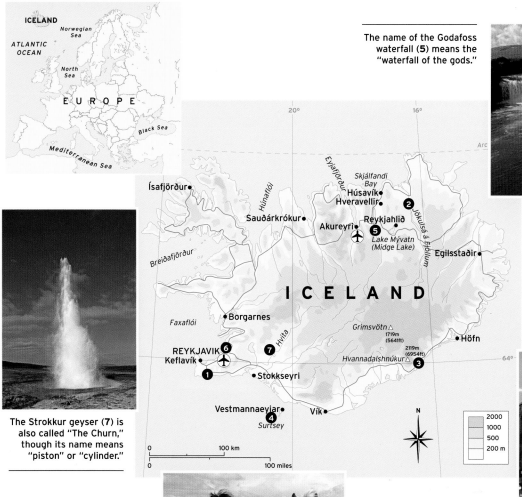

The name of the Godafoss waterfall (**5**) means the "waterfall of the gods."

The Strokkur geyser (**7**) is also called "The Churn," though its name means "piston" or "cylinder."

Reykjavik is thought to have been established in about A.D. 870 and is the most northerly capital city in the world (**6**).

Horses were brought to Iceland by the Vikings in about the 9th century and still roam wild today.

ICELAND

Norwegian Sea

ATLANTIC OCEAN

North Sea

EUROPE

Black Sea

Mediterranean Sea

20° 16°

Arc

Ísafjörður

Húnaflói

Eyjafjörður

Skjálfandi Bay

Húsavík

Hveravellir

2

Jökulsá á Fjöllum

Saudárkrókur

Akureyri

Reykjahlið

5

Lake Mývatn (Midge Lake)

Egilsstaðir

Breiðafjörður

ICELAND

Borgarnes

Grimsvötn △ 1719m (5641ft)

Höfn

Faxaflói

Hvíta

2119m (6954ft)

REYKJAVIK **6**

7

Hvannadalshnúkur △ **3**

64°

Keflavík

1

Stokkseyri

Vestmannaeyjar

4

Vík

Surtsey

N

2000
1000
500
200 m

0   100 km
0   100 miles

IRELAND'S GEM: THE SOUTHWEST

The Irish counties of Kerry and Cork capture all that is wonderful about Ireland and are the kind of places where you immediately want to go and live—and many visitors do!

EVERY NATION HAS ITS FALL GUYS, the countries whose people are supposed to be stupid. The Americans make jokes about the Poles, and the British make jokes about the Irish. The Irish in their turn make jokes about the Kerry man. "How would you get a Kerry man to climb on the roof of a pub? Tell him the drinks are on the house." To which the Kerry man no doubt gives a weary smile, confident in the knowledge that he cannot be so stupid if he lives in the most beautiful part of Ireland.

> ─> **Reeks**
>
> *Reeks* is a common word used for mountains in Ireland, and is thought to come from a rick, or a stack of things, like a hayrick or haystack.

Carrantuohill (1) in the distance is the highest mountain in Ireland and not to be tackled lightly.

The two counties of Kerry and Cork in the extreme southwest are picture-postcard Ireland. They are the Ireland of green fields, friendly faces, traditional music in welcoming pubs, great food, and simply one of those special parts of the world that creates a feeling of well-being every time you breathe in a breath of its air.

Down here you also seem to get more scenery for your money. The coastline is jagged with inlets, rivers, and bays, creating some dramatic cliffs, pretty harbors, Ireland's highest mountains, and several long peninsulas, each of which has its own character and attractions.

Ring of Kerry

The best known and most visited of these peninsulas is the Iveragh Peninsula, although it is more recognizable by its unofficial name: the Ring of Kerry. The Ring is a road that runs for 110 miles (177 km) right around the peninsula.

-> FACT FILE

POPULATION County Cork 480,000, County Kerry 140,000.

CURRENCY Euro

CLIMATE The mountains bring with them some of the highest rainfall in Ireland, although by contrast the Atlantic Gulf Steam also means that this is the mildest part of the country. Summers never get too hot, and winters never too cold, but you have to be prepared for the possibility of all four seasons in one day.

WHAT TO TAKE Wet-weather clothing, good walking shoes, a healthy appetite.

BEST TIME Any time of year is good, summer the best, though it is most crowded then.

NEAREST AIRPORT Cork International Airport.

ACCOMMODATION All kinds, all prices, all over the place.

St. Colman's Cathedral in Cobh (2) was started in 1868 and, with its tall spire and high position overlooking the harbor, can be seen from afar.

The harbor at Kinsale (**3**) attracts yachts from all over the world, their owners drawn by the town's reputation for gourmet Irish food.

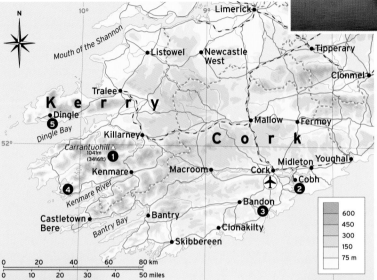

If you never get out of your car when driving around the Ring of Kerry (**4**), you may never discover some of the finest beaches in Ireland.

The lighthouse that guards Dingle harbor (**5**) was built in 1885 to help guide boats around the treacherous rocks.

These traditional musicians at the Bullman Pub in Kinsale (**3**) are typical of many you'll meet when traveling around the southwest of Ireland.

It is considered one of the most beautiful drives in Ireland, if not the most beautiful. It is so popular that coaches can drive it only in a counterclockwise direction, to prevent them from meeting each other along the narrow roads and around blind corners, and holding up the traffic while one of them reverses. Motorists therefore find it better to travel clockwise around the Ring, to avoid spending time looking at the back of a slow-moving coach rather than the splendid scenery.

And what scenery it is! The road weaves its way through mountains, past lakes, and gives views of the sea and bays, such as Dingle Bay. It passes through pretty little towns and villages, and there are stopping points where you can step out and admire the view, and take in a breath of the air that is still fresh, despite the constant traffic. One of the classic stopping points is at Ladies' View, where the land and lakes just seem to go on forever, dropping away into the distance.

At the eastern end of the Iveragh Peninsula, and adding to its grandeur, is Ireland's highest mountain range, the strangely named Macgillycuddy's Reeks.

The Macgillycuddys were a clan that lived in this part of Ireland, and the mountains were named after them in the eighteenth century. The range runs for more than 12 miles (19 km) and includes not only Ireland's highest mountain, Carrantuohill (3,416 feet/1,041 m), but Ireland's only two other mountains that are more than 3,281 feet (1,000 m) high, and over a hundred peaks that are more than 2,000 feet (610 m) high.

Dingle Peninsula

North of the Iveragh Peninsula and Macgillycuddy's Reeks is the Dingle Peninsula, another achingly beautiful part of this corner of Ireland. At the eastern end as you enter the peninsula you pass the Slieve Mish Mountains, farther along is Mount Brandon, which is Ireland's highest peak outside of Macgillycuddy's Reeks, and at the very end of the peninsula you will have reached the most westerly point of the Irish mainland. Beyond are only the Blasket Islands, and then it is next stop North America.

Cork

Not all of the region's attractions are in Kerry. Cork has its own beauty, and has become renowned in recent years for its good food. It is not just in the main town of Cork, either, as the harbor town of Kinsale is now known as Ireland's food capital. The Kinsale Food Festival each October is a huge event, and certainly a good time to visit the area. But all along the coast there are fine restaurants, with fresh seafood naturally being one of the attractions. The county is also the home of Ballymaloe House, rated as one of the country's best hotels and with what most people regard as the finest restaurant in Ireland.

So with the country's finest restaurant, its highest mountains, most beautiful drive, and far too many other attractions to find room to mention, there is no doubt that this southwest corner of Ireland is one of the loveliest parts of Europe. And if you travel around, you will hear the accents of people from all over Europe, who came to visit and ended up staying. You have been warned.

Kinsale (3) has colorful buildings that add to its appeal, alongside its reputation for food and drink.

ANTRIM COAST: IN GIANT'S FOOTSTEPS

The Antrim coast of Northern Ireland can take the breath away with its long stretches of natural beauty, including the Giant's Causeway.

MUCH OF THE IRISH COAST IS MAGNIFICENT, but there are some stretches that have a special beauty and a character all their own. This is true of the North Antrim Coast, which has a wide range of contrasting attractions. These include the UNESCO World Heritage Site at the Giant's Causeway, the wildlife on the offshore Rathlin Island, the unusual Carrick-a-Rede rope bridge, the oldest legal distillery in the world, and mile upon mile of beautiful white sand beaches.

The Giant's Causeway

The most famous place along the coast is the Giant's Causeway, which became a UNESCO World Heritage Site in 1986. It is a strange and eerily beautiful place, and most people would not agree with the British writer Dr. Samuel Johnson, who said that it was "worth seeing, yes: but not worth going to see."

In 2007 more than seven hundred thousand people did go to see the Causeway, making it Northern Ireland's most popular visitor attraction. It has been visited since 1740, when a Dublin woman first sketched the odd rock formations and brought them to public attention. They started to be formed about 60 million years ago, when a series of volcanic eruptions forced lava into a depression in the ground. As the lava cooled and hardened into

The columns that make up the Giant's Causeway (1) are as much as 36 feet (11 m) high, and some rare plants are hidden among their nooks and crannies.

-> FACT FILE

POPULATION Northern Ireland 1,700,000.

CURRENCY Pound sterling

CLIMATE Although the climate is temperate, the old Irish saying about being able to experience all four seasons in one day is just as true in Northern Ireland. Be prepared for rain any time. It seldom gets hotter than the upper 80°sF (30°C) in summer, but temperatures can fall below freezing in winter.

WHAT TO TAKE Clothes for all seasons. Binoculars and camera.

BEST TIME Any time is good, for different reasons, although the depths of winter are probably best avoided.

NEAREST AIRPORT Belfast International Airport is about 40 miles (64 km) south of Bushmills and the Giant's Causeway.

ACCOMMODATION There are plenty of hotels and good guesthouses all along the North Antrim Coast. Homey bed-and-breakfasts are renowned for their warm welcomes, and generous breakfasts!

The rope bridge at Carrick-a-Rede (2) carries a quarter of a million people a year across to the little offshore island, and sways 75 feet (23 m) above the water.

Rathlin Island (**3**) is Ireland's closest point to Scotland and home to tens of thousands of seabirds that gather together in big colonies like this.

rock again, it created the forty thousand or so strange hexagonal columns that make up the Giant's Causeway—though not all of them are in fact hexagonal.

That's a canned version of what the geologists say, but a more enjoyable tale also reveals how the Causeway got its name. A legendary Irish giant named Finn MacCool once roamed the northern coast, and he could see from here across the narrow strait to Scotland and the home of his bitter rival, Benandonner. Finn built the Causeway and challenged Benandonner to a fight, but as his rival strode toward him, Finn saw that the Scottish giant was much bigger than him, and he ran to his wife for advice. Finn's wife then disguised her husband as a baby, and she showed the baby to Benandonner as Finn's child. Benandonner raced back to Scotland fearing for his life: If this was the baby, how big must the father be? He tore up the Causeway behind him, which is why today only part of it appears off the coast before disappearing beneath the surface.

There is much more to see here than just the Causeway. The area is also a National Nature Reserve, and there are miles of walking trails, many of them along the Causeway coastline, where there

are almost 4 miles (6.5 km) of sheer cliffs that rise to 295 feet (90 m) in places. It is certainly a coastline of giant proportions.

Carrick-a-Rede
Just east of the Causeway off the shore is Carrick-a-Rede island, the name meaning "rock in the road." This little offshore island is on a salmon migration route, so there were rich pickings for the local fishermen at the right time of year. To make it easier to get to the island they built a rope bridge, which is still in use, although these days mainly as a tourist attraction. You might see salmon in the season from June to September, and fishermen, too, but it is no longer the lucrative trade it once was because of a depletion in the stocks. The bridge is taken down in winter, when it could become dangerous to use.

Rathlin Island
From Carrick-a-Rede you can see Rathlin Island on the skyline, with Scotland beyond on a clear day. It is 6 miles (10 km) to Rathlin from here, and it can be a choppy crossing to get there. It can be a stimulating one, though, as the island's coastline cliffs start to appear dramatically through the mist.

The island is a huge magnet for birds, and therefore for bird-watchers: the Royal Society for the Protection of Birds (RSPB) has a large nature reserve on the island. There is accommodation on Rathlin, and some ancient sites as well as wonderful walks. As the only inhabited island off the Northern Irish coast, it also has a character and culture all its own.

Bushmills

Ireland also has a drink that is all its own: Irish whiskey. It is not only spelled differently from Scottish whisky, but tastes different, too, and different again from American bourbon.

On the edge of the tiny town of Bushmills stands the oldest legal whiskey distillery in the world. It was legalized in 1608, although it is believed that whiskey was being produced here for at least four hundred years before that. It is only 2 miles (3 km) from the Giant's Causeway, and the water that goes into Bushmills whiskey flows over the same rocks that made the Causeway. The distillery is old, but it probably does not go back all the way to the time of Finn MacCool, although after a glass or two no doubt the Irish will have you believing it does.

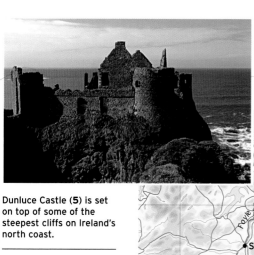

Dunluce Castle (5) is set on top of some of the steepest cliffs on Ireland's north coast.

There are unusual formations all around the Giant's Causeway site, such as these (1) on the nearby cliffs.

The North Antrim Coast (4) has some fine bays with wide sandy beaches, often deserted.

AMSTERDAM: WALKING ON WATER

Amsterdam, like Venice, was built on water, and wherever you walk in the city there are layers of history beneath your feet.

WHEN YOU WALK IN AMSTERDAM, you are walking on water, for this Dutch city is a man-made miracle. Amsterdam is like no other city, as it grew out of swamps and water. It combines the shimmering beauty of its canals with the vigor of an old European port, and the unique freethinking of its people. Freewheeling, too, as they bump over the cobbles on their bone-shaker bikes and cycle by the canals. They are often walking or cycling over water as well, and not just when crossing the canals. Many of the city's main streets were once waterways, its magnificent huge train station is built over water, and even its Royal Palace rests on boggy marshland. It is a city that should not even exist.

Centraal Station

Most visitors arrive at the Centraal Station, which is the city's main transport hub and brings travelers in from Amsterdam's international airport, Schiphol.

But when you arrive like this in Amsterdam, you should tread carefully, because you are walking over 8,687 wooden stakes that support the station, which stands on three artificial islands. Where the station now is was once water, where clippers returned from the Dutch East Indies carrying cargoes of nutmegs and cloves. It was where fishermen from along the coast came into the city and up the canals, to tie up their boats and sell their catch.

But in 1876 the Dutch government, along the coast in Den Haag, decided that the city's new station would be built here, and not in the south of the city as the Amsterdam City Council wished. Work began in 1882, and it took seven years to complete, the biggest building project in Amsterdam in the whole of the nineteenth century. The design was by the Dutch architect Pierre Cuypers, who by then was finishing work on his other Amsterdam masterpiece, the Rijksmuseum.

Amsterdam's Centraal Station (1) is aptly named, as it's the hub for trains, trams, taxis, and ferries— and of course bicycles.

Throughout the city, canals provide a convenient means of getting about (2).

–> FACT FILE

POPULATION 750,000

CURRENCY Euro

CLIMATE Warm but not hot summers, mild and seldom freezing winters, but there are often periods of damp chilly weather. Possible rainfall all year-round.

WHAT TO TAKE Umbrella or raincoat, good walking shoes.

BEST TIME April-May are the driest months, July-August the warmest.

NEAREST AIRPORT Schiphol, 11 miles (17.5 km) southwest of the city, with good train connections.

ACCOMMODATION A shortage of hotel beds means you should book ahead. Lots of characterful canalside houses, but often with lots of stairs and no elevators.

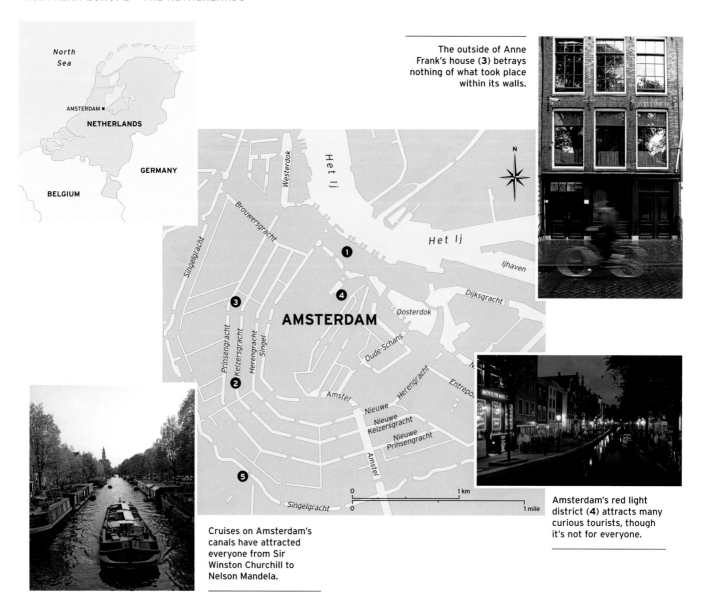

The outside of Anne Frank's house (**3**) betrays nothing of what took place within its walls.

Cruises on Amsterdam's canals have attracted everyone from Sir Winston Churchill to Nelson Mandela.

Amsterdam's red light district (**4**) attracts many curious tourists, though it's not for everyone.

The prominent Dutch journalist Geert Mak described the station as "the city's greatest planning blunder ever. The wonderful panorama of the city, the two miles of shimmering masts, spires and merchant houses, was destroyed for ever."

Whether it was appreciated or not, everyone wanted to see this exciting new creation, and fourteen thousand people bought platform tickets on the morning it opened. Sail had given way to steam. Canals were about to give way to more streets to cater to the growing population.

Dam Square

If you walk out of the station and down the main street ahead of you, the Damrak, you are still walking on water. In the late thirteenth century this was a water channel through which the Amstel River flowed out to the sea. When you reach Dam Square, the busy main square of the city and where the Royal Palace stands, you are at the spot where a few fishing families lived, on the banks of the

Amstel, living off the fish that they caught. But the Amstel was unpredictable and would often change its course through the soft marshy land that was here in those days. So the fishing families got together and built the dam that would give this remarkable city its name: the Amstel Dam.

Living here presented its challenges, though, and in the middle of the seventeenth century the now flourishing city of Amsterdam needed a new town hall. The existing building had burned to the ground, a surprisingly common occurrence down the years in this watery community. But to build the grand new town hall, which would be the biggest in Europe at the time, the builders needed first to sink no fewer than 13,659 wooden piles deep into the marshes to act as supports. In 1795 the French invaded Amsterdam, and in 1808 Louis Bonaparte decided the town hall would make rather a handsome Royal Palace—which it has been ever since.

Hauling Horses from the Canals

South from the square is the busy shopping street of Kalverstraat, and if you find walking through the crowds difficult, just remember that at one time you would have needed to swim to get here. Along here is the Amsterdam Historical Museum, which stands on what was once an island, and here is where you will learn a great deal about the watery nature of Amsterdam. One exhibit in particular reminds us of some of the hazards of canalside living.

A man with the appropriate name of J. C. Sinck invented a hoist for fishing horses out of the canal.

Falling in was a common enough occurrence, and it is in the nature of canals that it is not easy to get out once you are in. It is even harder for horses. With his creation of a crane on the back of a cart, Sinck made a fortune in the days when one horsepower was all that most people could afford, and no one could allow their most valuable asset to go to a watery grave. These days not many horses fall into the canals. But people do, usually after a drink or two, and some of them never get out again.

The Rijksmuseum (5) has been only partially open since renovations started in 2003. It is due to open fully again in 2013.

NORWAY'S WEST-COAST FJORDS

The awe-inspiring fjords along Norway's west coast were once described by *National Geographic* magazine as "the world's best travel destination."

IT TAKES THREE MILLION YEARS to make a fjord, and just one second to have your breath blown away by its majestic beauty. The west coast of Norway has some of the most dramatic fjords in the world, where the sea digs deep into the land in steep-sided valleys, as if trying to reach the mountains beyond. Imagine some of the world's deepest gorges, then half submerge them in the sea, add waterfalls, put some villages, orchards, and green pastures on each side, add blue skies and white clouds above, and a few snowcapped peaks to top it all off, then breathe in the cool fresh air, and

there will be no place in the world you would rather be.

The formation of fjords may be slow, but it is a simple process. Glaciers moving down toward the sea cut U-shaped valleys, and when the glaciers eventually melt, the sea rushes in to fill those valleys. An unusual feature of fjords is that they are often deeper than the seas nearby. Glaciers gouged out very deep valleys, but deposited a great deal of sediment as they reached the sea, so the entrances to fjords are sometimes shallow, but farther in they can be extremely deep. Norway's Sognefjord, to

Norway's fjords, like the Hardangerfjord (1) shown here, are almost too perfect to be true when conditions are clear.

CURRENCY Norwegian krone

CLIMATE The west coast is warm (for Scandinavia) and wet. The rain is consistent throughout the year, but worst in winter. Typical summer temperatures along the coast are in the mid-60sºF (18ºC).

WHAT TO TAKE Umbrella and raincoat, binoculars for the wildlife.

BEST TIME Summer, when the weather is best and the days are long.

NEAREST AIRPORTS Bergen Airport is 12 miles (20 km) south of the city center. There is also an airport at Ålesund.

ACCOMMODATION Plenty of options in the towns along the way such as Bergen, Flora, and Ålesund.

There is no need to explain how the Seven Sisters Falls in the Geirangerfjord (**2**) got their name.

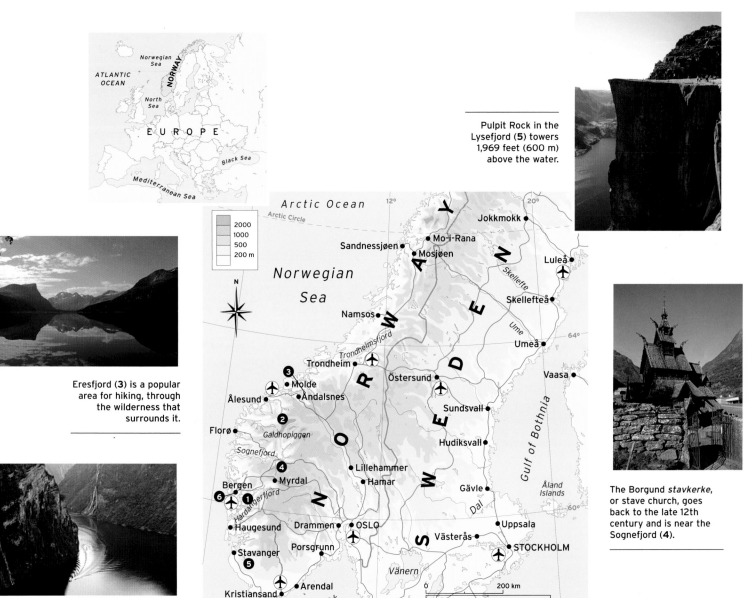

Pulpit Rock in the Lysefjord (**5**) towers 1,969 feet (600 m) above the water.

Eresfjord (**3**) is a popular area for hiking, through the wilderness that surrounds it.

Even cruise ships are dwarfed by the scale of the Geirangerfjord (**2**), one of the most popular and beautiful in Norway.

The Borgund *stavkerke*, or stave church, goes back to the late 12th century and is near the Sognefjord (**4**).

the north of Bergen (main gateway for the west-coast fjords), has a maximum depth of 4,292 feet (1,308 m)—three times deeper than Lake Superior, the deepest of North America's Great Lakes.

The Greatest

To the north of Bergen, Sognefjord is Norway's biggest fjord, and the second longest in the world after Greenland's Scoresby Sund. Sognefjord is also one of the most spectacular, as it cuts from the sea inland for some 127 miles (204 km). Although it does have that maximum depth of 4,292 feet (1,308 m), this is reached at its upper levels, and as it approaches the sea, there is one part where it is less than 328 feet (100 m) deep.

But the Sognefjord is not about statistics; it is about the sheer majestic beauty of the place. As you sail its waters or walk along its shores, it seems to retreat away from you in both directions forever, weaving in and out of the peaks like a snake of the deepest blue. Either side of the water the steep slopes are in some places covered in greenery, in others showing the harsh bare rock. Here and there are the communities who live by the fjord, mostly connected by boat, living in what are unbelievably stunning settings for most of the year, though the fjords can be rain lashed and bitterly cold.

As if the Sognefjord on its own were not almost too unbearably beautiful, off it runs the Nærøyfjord, one of two of the west-coast fjords to have been put on UNESCO's list of World Heritage Sites. The Nærøyfjord may be only about 10 1/2 miles (17 km) long, but these, along with the Geirangerfjord, are said by UNESCO to be archetypal fjord landscapes, among the most beautiful in the world. Waterfalls splash and thunder their way down the steep sides of both fjords, and rivers run from them to glacial lakes, creating a scenery that makes you thrilled to have seen it at least once in your life.

The Geirangerfjord is the other fjord on UNESCO's list, though the protection offered by the United Nations is threatened from two directions— one natural and one man-made. The threat from humans is the proposal to run power cables across the fjord, an act that would see the Geirangerfjord removed from UNESCO's list. The natural threat is even more worrying, as it could see the complete destruction of a large part of Geirangerfjord. The Åkerneset mountain is on the verge of collapsing into the fjord, which would destroy some of the landscape, raise water levels, and cause a tidal wave that would destroy some of the nearby settlements. It is a reminder that the kind of powerful forces that created the fjords are still around.

South from Bergen is the Hardangerfjord, Norway's next biggest fjord after Sognefjord,

running for 111 miles (179 km). For much of its length it runs alongside the Folgefonn peninsula, which carries the three glaciers that together are known as the Folgefonna glaciers. The largest of the three, the Søndre Folgefonna, is 5,446 feet (1,660 m) above sea level, making for a spectacular sight if you are cruising along the Hardangerfjord in a boat. The three glaciers together make up the Folgefonna National Park, considered the most beautiful in Norway, stretching as it does from fjord to the glacial peaks.

Bergen

The start and end point for many people wanting to explore the western fjords is Bergen, Norway's second city. It is here that cruise ships call in, picking up passengers to go and explore the fjords, and there is a big fishing industry here, too. In fact, the open-air fish market is one of its attractions, whereas the Bergen Aquarium is one of the finest in Europe and also shows the creatures beneath the sea. But a city is still a city, and after a day or two, knowing what is close by, you are sure to want to get out and visit the fjords, "the world's best travel destination."

The old wharf of Bergen (6) dates from the 14th century and is a UNESCO World Heritage Site.

THE SCOTTISH HIGHLANDS

Described as one of the most beautiful areas in Europe, the Highlands are the place for those who really want to get away from it all.

A proud piper adds the unique tone of the bagpipes to the Highland atmosphere.

Ullapool (1) may have a population of fewer than 1,500, but it is still the largest settlement in this part of the remote Scottish Highlands.

THE HIGHLANDS MAKE UP about half the Scottish mainland, lying to the north and west of the Highland Boundary Fault. This runs from Arran on the west coast to Stonehaven in the east, dividing the country into the southerly Lowlands and the northerly Highlands. There are various opinions on the exact geographical boundaries, but there is no arguing that the Scottish Highlands are one of the most beautifully dramatic and fascinating parts of Europe.

The Highlands are the oldest mountains in Europe, with some of the rocks dating back 3,000 million years–some of the oldest on earth, in fact. They were first formed during a period known as the Caledonian Orogeny, which happened about 400 million years ago and created the mountains of northern Britain, Ireland, and western Norway. It took its name from the Latin name for Scotland– *Caledonia*.

Later the Ice Age came and carved out the glens and shaped the mountains, which were further molded by winds and rain over millions of years, to produce the stunning landscape that we see today.

Ben Nevis

The Scottish Highlands are not particularly high, even by European standards. Their highest point, Ben Nevis, is the highest mountain in Britain, but at 4,411 feet (1,344 m) it is a mere pimple compared with Mount Elbrus in the Caucasus, the highest in Europe at 18,510 feet (5,642 m). Indeed, more than one hundred thousand people make it to the summit of Ben Nevis every year, and although some of them tackle the sheer north face, the vast majority take the Pony Track that weaves up the south side of the mountain. That is not to say it is an easy climb–when the weather turns bad, all these mountains can take lives.

Where Mountain Meets Sea

Although it is the mountains that naturally dominate, the Highlands region also includes vast stretches of beautiful coast. One of the most glorious areas is Wester Ross, the west coast of Ross-shire, where the Highlands march right up to the coastline and loom over sandy beaches. Here too are beautiful towns like Ullapool, which began

Ben Nevis (2) is the rooftop of the British Isles, and a much tougher climb than it looks, as many inexperienced hikers discover every year.

–> FACT FILE

POPULATION 270,000

CURRENCY Pound sterling

CLIMATE The Western Highlands is one of the wettest parts of Europe, though less rain falls in the east of the region. It can fall at any time, though summers are drier. This is also the coldest part of Britain, with the temperature never getting too hot in summer, but the winters can be bitterly cold, with plenty of snow.

WHAT TO TAKE Insect repellent for the persistent midges, wet-weather gear, walking boots.

BEST TIME June–August has the best chance of good weather, with long days and lots of events taking place. Many places close outside the Easter–October tourist season, and winters are only for skiers and the hardiest of travelers. Roads often get closed during the worst of the winter.

NEAREST AIRPORT There is an international airport at Inverness, in the east.

ACCOMMODATION A wide range of choice, with homey bed-and-breakfasts and guesthouses offering good value, but some luxury retreats, too.

At 110 miles (176 km)
the River Spey (**3**) is the
second-longest river in
Scotland, 10 miles (16 km)
shorter than the River Tay.

life in 1788 as a herring port and is still an active
fishing port today, more than 200 years later. Now
it is popular with walkers and wildlife lovers, with
readers for its book festival, and with musicians for
its active support of all kinds of traditional music.

Ullapool, like most of the Highlands, is in the part
of Scotland known as the Gàidhealtachd. This is the
region where the Scottish Gaelic culture still
thrives, which includes the Scottish Gaelic language,
although it is not actively spoken everywhere.
Generally speaking, the farther north and west you
go, the stronger the traditions and the more you
are likely to hear Gaelic spoken. In fact, if you head
far enough west, to Newfoundland, you will hear
Scottish Gaelic spoken there, too.

It is all part of a strong and proud traditional
culture that makes traveling in the Highlands a
whole different experience than being in the
Lowlands, and certainly far removed from the
Sassenach English, over the border. Sassenach itself
is just a modernization of the Gaelic word
for a Saxon: *Sasunnach*.

Highland Lochs

Wester Ross is also where you will find Loch Maree,
which at 12 ½ miles (20 km) long is the biggest loch
north of Loch Ness. Scattered across its vast surface
are more than 30 islands, many of them covered in
pine trees, a reminder of the huge coniferous forests
that once covered the whole of the Highlands. Loch
Maree is also one of the most beautiful sights in the
whole region—and that's saying something, as the
region is full of beautiful sights.

Of course the best known of all the countless
Highland lochs, and monstrously popular you might
say, is Loch Ness. Loch Ness runs southwest from
Inverness, the unofficial capital of the Highlands,
and extends 23 miles (37 km) through part of the
Great Glen. The loch is more than 750 feet (229 m)
deep in places, and certainly has a brooding
atmosphere that is well suited to tales of myths
and monsters.

The Whisky Way

You might find it easier to see a monster in Loch
Ness if you have been sampling one of the
Highland's most popular and tasty products—whisky.
The Speyside Way is a long-distance footpath that
stretches 65 miles (105 km) as it follows the River
Spey from Buckie down to Aviemore, though you
can add a few side trails to it as well. Not only does
it take you through some wonderful riverside
scenery, but you will see some names on the way
that are familiar to whisky lovers worldwide:
Macallan, Glenfiddich, and Glenlivet among them.

The Cairngorms

The River Spey flows through one of the most impressive parts of the whole Scottish Highlands–the Cairngorms National Park. It is the biggest national park in Britain, covering an area of 1,467 square miles (3,799 sq km), and there are plans in hand to extend it even farther. It is hugely popular for skiing in winter, especially around Aviemore, and it contains much that is best about the Highlands: mountain scenery, lochs, rivers, walking, whisky, and wildlife. The Highland Wildlife Park is home even to wolves, which roamed wild here till the eighteenth century. And who is to say they will not roam here again one day? This is the wild Highlands, after all.

It's said that you will have to climb Ben Nevis (**2**) several times before you can be sure of a view as clear as this.

The smell of a distillery cellar is distinctive, and an incentive to sample one of the finest products from the Scottish Highlands.

Ullapool (**1**) stands on Loch Broom and is unusual in that it was founded only in 1788 and was designed by the English architect Thomas Telford.

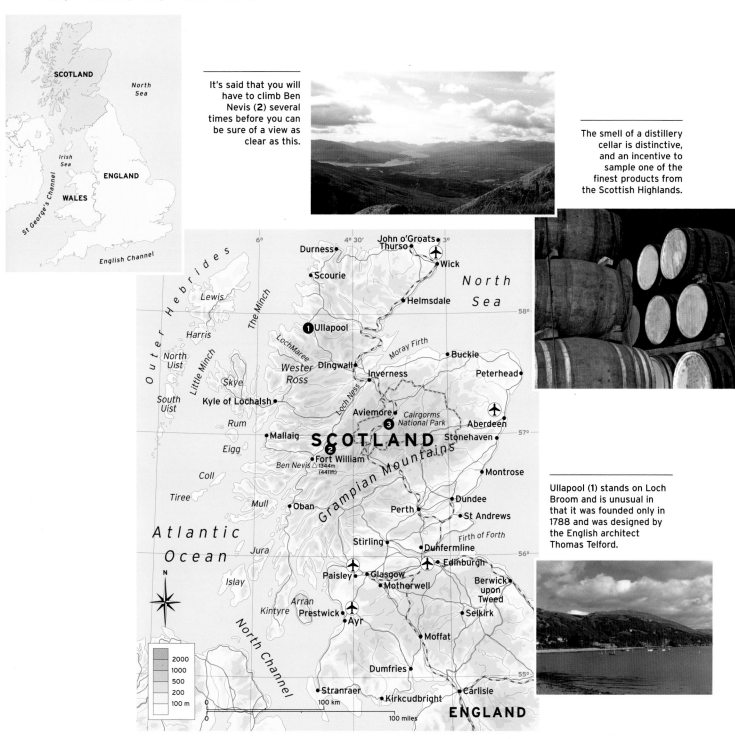

59

THE SCOTTISH ISLANDS

Scotland has almost eight hundred islands—from the vastness of Lewis and Harris to tiny specks like Eilean Donan in Loch Duich.

IT IS THE SHEER VARIETY of the Scottish islands that makes them so fascinating for travelers. About 130 of them are inhabited, and they range from the most southerly island, Arran, which is actually farther south than Berwick-upon-Tweed in England, to the island of Unst in the Shetlands, the most northerly of all the inhabited islands. About 300 miles (483 km) and the entire country of Scotland stand between the two.

The Shetlands

The Shetlands are one of the best known and popular of the island groups, sitting out off the northeast tip of Scotland between the North Sea and the Atlantic Ocean. They are actually closer to Norway than they are to the Scottish capital, Edinburgh, and the people here definitely see themselves as Shetlanders first, and Scottish second. When Shetlanders talk about the mainland here, they are referring to their own biggest island, Mainland, not to Scotland.

And the island is big. At 374 square miles (969 sq km), it is the third-largest Scottish island and the fifth largest in all of the British Isles, and that includes the islands of Britain and Ireland.

The Shetlands are islands for walkers and wildlife lovers, as nature thrives in this remote place. Here are seals, otters, puffins, whales, dolphins, porpoises, petrels, polecats, mountain hares, and many other creatures that are impossible to see elsewhere.

There are ancient settlements here, too, as Shetland has been inhabited since at least 1500 B.C. In just one place, Jarlshof, you will find remains from the Bronze Age, the Iron Age, the Picts, the Vikings, a medieval farmhouse, and a seventeenth-century manor house. It is a reminder of just how many layers of history lie beneath the skin of the present.

The Orkneys

Between the Shetlands and the Scottish mainland, and visible from John O'Groats, stand the Orkney Islands, or just plain Orkney. There are ancient remains here, too, including Skara Brae, the most complete Neolithic village in Europe. This World Heritage Site comprises ten dwellings, showing us what it was like in a village of farmers and fishermen back in about 3000 B.C.

Five thousand years later and many Orkney people are still farmers and fishermen.

−> FACT FILE

POPULATION 100,000

CURRENCY Pound sterling

CLIMATE Varies widely across the different island groups, but expect rain at any time of year. Summers can be glorious but not necessarily hot–even in southerly islands like Islay the average August temperature is only 61ºF (16ºC). The Shetlands have subzero temperatures in winter, but it is unusual for frost and snow to linger.

WHAT TO TAKE All-weather gear, as conditions can change several times a day.

BEST TIME Summer sees the islands at peak activity and provides the best chance for warm dry weather–but it is not guaranteed even then.

NEAREST AIRPORT There are direct flights to Shetland, Orkney, and the Hebrides from most Scottish cities and from London.

ACCOMMODATION In many of the islands accommodation tends to be homey and simple, in pubs and guesthouses, with small hotels in many of the main towns. Planning ahead is essential, especially at busy times, as space is limited.

Storr Rock (**2**) reaches a height of 2,358 feet (719 m) above Loch Fada, with the pinnacle known as the Old Man of Storr visible here, slightly to the right.

Visitors can go more quickly over the sea to Skye on the Skye Bridge (far left, **1**), opened in 1995.

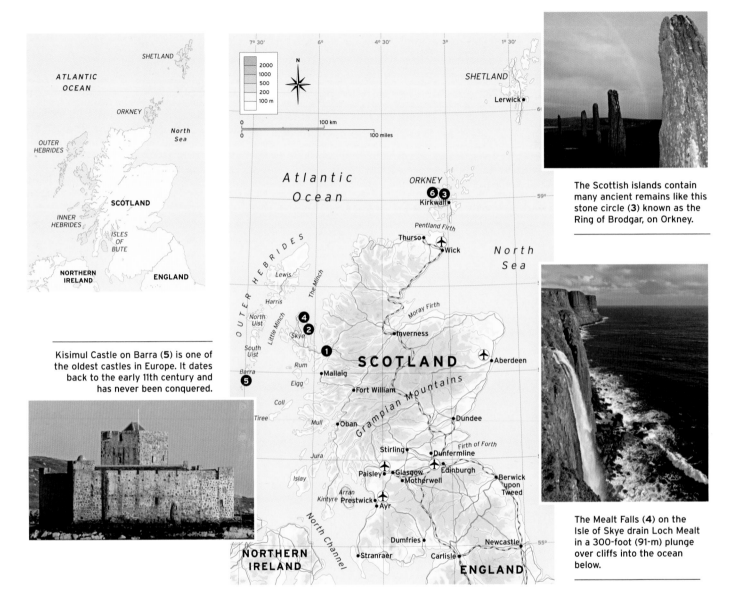

The Scottish islands contain many ancient remains like this stone circle (3) known as the Ring of Brodgar, on Orkney.

Kisimul Castle on Barra (5) is one of the oldest castles in Europe. It dates back to the early 11th century and has never been conquered.

The Mealt Falls (4) on the Isle of Skye drain Loch Mealt in a 300-foot (91-m) plunge over cliffs into the ocean below.

Musical traditions are strong here too, as they are in all the islands, where communities had to entertain themselves, and passed songs and stories down the generations.

Skye

Off the west coast of Scotland is a whole other string of stunning islands, coming with their different traditions and landscapes. Less isolated than the Shetlands, or even Orkney, Skye is now connected to the mainland by the controversial Skye Bridge, just 623 yards (570 m) long. This closeness to the mainland means that Skye is much more used to visitors, as they have been coming here since 1897, when the train network reached the Kyle of Lochalsh and made it easier for city dwellers to get here. It is a big island, though, second largest of all the Scottish islands, and escaping the crowds is quite easy. A ferry ride away

are four smaller islands, each with fewer than one hundred inhabitants: Canna, Rum, Eigg, and Muck.

Big and Small

North of Skye in the Outer Hebrides is the biggest island of them all, so big it needs two names: Lewis and Harris. The northern part of the island is Lewis and the southern part is Harris, which can lead to some confusion. Harris is the hillier half of the island, and has more than thirty peaks that are above 1,000 feet (305 m) high, and the island is big enough to even have a proper town, Stornoway, where about 8,000 people live—almost one third of the population of the whole Western Isles.

By contrast the island of Barra has just 1,300 inhabitants, and is a mere 8 miles (13 km) from north to south. But even within that compact space it manages to pack many features that make this group of islands so attractive—high and dramatic

mountain peaks, sandy beaches, ancient remains, traditional music, and warm-hearted people.

Queen of the Hebrides

Farther south and only 25 miles (40 km) from the Irish coast is Islay, known as the Queen of the Hebrides, again, a very different island. It is renowned for one thing above all else—its whisky distilleries. There are eight at the time of writing, with another one planned, and they include such world-famous names as Bowmore, Ardbeg, Bruichladdich, Lagavulin, and Laphroaig, said to be the favorite drink of Prince Charles. There is much more to the island than whisky, though, with Celtic crosses in remote churchyards, sandy beaches, golden eagles, and other wildlife. Stroll along the shore and you may see seals or sea otters lounging around or foraging for food.

Islay's neighbor, Jura, is smaller and quieter, with only about 180 people sharing the island with 6,000 deer. This magical retreat for walkers and wildlife lovers is dominated by its three rounded mountain peaks known as the Paps of Jura. The names of the mountains capture some of the mystery of this, and the other Scottish islands. The smallest, Beinn a' Chaolais, means the Mountain of the Kyle, a kyle being a strait of water. Next highest is the Holy Mountain, Beinn Shiantaidh, and the biggest of them all at 2,576 feet (785 m) is Beinn an Òir, or the Mountain of Gold. The names have a lyrical quality about them, a singing sound, and a beauty that comes from the people and the land. It is a beauty you find everywhere throughout the Scottish islands. It is a beauty like nowhere else in the world.

The Neolithic site of Skara Brae on Orkney (**6**) takes visitors back to see the lives of the people who dwelled there more than 5,000 years ago, including an authentic re-creation of one of their homes.

EDINBURGH DURING THE FESTIVAL

Scotland's historic capital is transformed every summer by the largest arts festival in the world, making it the perfect time to enjoy the city, both ancient and modern.

FROM THE HISTORIC QUARTER around Edinburgh Castle to the elegant New Town, Scotland's capital city buzzes with energy. It has a reputation for being "genteel" when compared with Scotland's other big city, Glasgow, but then most cities would be genteel compared with Glasgow. For the visitor, Edinburgh is a happy meeting ground of tradition and the avant-garde, as evidenced by the pomp of the Military Tattoo on the one hand, and the famous Fringe arts festival on the other, both held in August.

Edinburgh was once called the Athens of the North, thanks to its progressive and cultured nature, similar to the Golden Age of Athens. The much-loved Scottish author Sir Walter Scott, whose memorial stands along Princes Street, described the city as the Empress of the North. It became the capital of Scotland in 1437, and its new Scottish Parliament Building, home of the Scottish Assembly, is a striking, modern city landmark.

The Parliament Building stands opposite the Palace of Holyroodhouse, the queen's official residence in Scotland, and they face each other as a constant reminder of the uneasy relationship between the British monarchy and the wish of many Scots for at least some kind of independence.

Arts Capital

Edinburgh is the country's arts capital, too, with many fine galleries, museums, performing arts venues, and a strong literary legacy. The city's Writers' Museum celebrates the works and lives of Scott, Robert Louis Stevenson, and Robert Burns. The first two were born in Edinburgh, and Burns was a regular visitor. The Museum naturally features strongly in the Festival, which is in fact several festivals all taking place at the same time, including the Edinburgh International Book Festival. There are so many events going on in the city in

The Edinburgh Military Tattoo began in 1950 and is a popular part of the Edinburgh Festival, selling out well in advance (1).

-> FACT FILE

POPULATION 450,000

CURRENCY Pound sterling

CLIMATE Despite its northern latitude, Edinburgh enjoys a mild climate. The temperature will fall below freezing some days in winter, but bitter cold and snow are infrequent. Even in the middle of summer the temperature only occasionally gets above 65ºF (18ºC). Rain can fall at any time of year, although the city enjoys a below-average rainfall for Scotland.

WHAT TO TAKE Umbrella, even in summer, and something for chilly evenings.

BEST TIME If going for the Festival you must book a long way in advance, as every bed will be taken. Otherwise there is really no bad time to visit.

NEAREST AIRPORT Edinburgh has its own international airport 9 miles (14 km) west of the city center.

ACCOMMODATION All types of accommodation, from luxury hotels to homey guesthouses, which often offer the best value and warmest welcome.

Edinburgh's Princes Street was named for the sons of King George III, who was on the British throne when the street was laid out in the late 18th century (**2**).

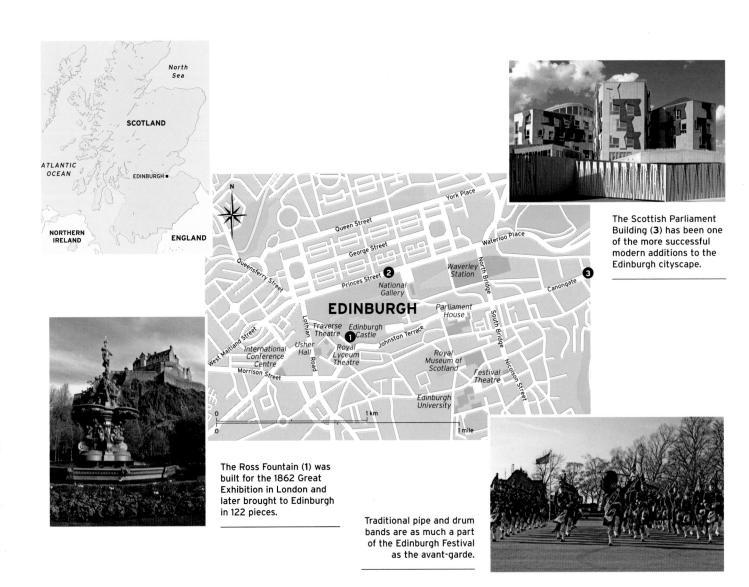

The Scottish Parliament Building (3) has been one of the more successful modern additions to the Edinburgh cityscape.

The Ross Fountain (1) was built for the 1862 Great Exhibition in London and later brought to Edinburgh in 122 pieces.

Traditional pipe and drum bands are as much a part of the Edinburgh Festival as the avant-garde.

late August and early September that a visit needs planning with the precision of the Military Tattoo.

In addition to the Book Festival and the official Edinburgh International Festival, there is also the famous Fringe festival that, like the main Festival, began in 1947. Then there's the Jazz and Blues Festival, the International Television Festival, and the Edinburgh Art Festival, which is different from, but a part of, the overall Edinburgh International Festival. This raises the costs of venue rental and can actually work against the serious business of getting people to your events when there is so much happening. It is no surprise that visitors often wander around looking bemused, clutching maps and programs and peering at street signs.

Top Comics

Walking the streets during the Festival you never know what you will encounter, and that is all part of the fun. It might be musicians or magicians, poets or performance artists, trying to lure you to a gig,

passing the hat around, or just performing for the sake of it. If you go without booking, you are likely to find the hot tickets all sold, although often it is not till things kick off that anyone knows what the hot tickets will be. Often it is the rising new comedy stars who attract attention, but you may also get to see some more established acts.

When the sun shines, as it often seems to do at Festival time, there is no finer city to be in. In fact, there is no finer city at any time of year. It has more than 4,500 listed buildings in the city center, two parts of which–the Old Town and the New Town–have been jointly designated as a UNESCO World Heritage Site. And yet despite this, there is no feeling of being in a city preserved in aspic.

Old Town, New Town

The Old Town centers around the Royal Mile, the long street that stretches from Edinburgh Castle standing high at one end, down to the Palace of Holyroodhouse and the Scottish Parliament at the other. Edinburgh Castle perches on top of Castle

Rock, plainly visible from many parts of the city. The Rock is a volcanic crag nearly 400 feet (122 m) high, and within the castle walls is the city's oldest building—tiny St. Margaret's Chapel, built in the twelfth century.

Edinburgh's other main thoroughfare is Princes Street, and it is around here that you will find the New Town. It is only "new" in comparison with the Old Town, as it was mostly laid out and built between the mid-eighteenth and mid-nineteenth centuries. When the New Town was started, there were already about eighty thousand people living in the Old Town and more space was needed. The result was a series of elegant streets and buildings, including the landmark Balmoral Hotel, the Scott Monument, the National Gallery of Scotland, and the Royal Scottish Academy (RSA). It is the function of the RSA to promote contemporary Scottish art, and that is a job that the Edinburgh International Festival does very well too, every summer.

-> Sir Walter Scott

Sir Walter Scott was born in Edinburgh in 1771, and achieved worldwide fame for novels such as *Waverley*, about the Jacobite Rebellions; *Ivanhoe*, set in twelfth-century England; and *Quentin Durward*, the tale of a Scottish mercenary working for Louis XI. Scott also wrote poetry, including *The Lady of the Lake* and *The Lay of the Last Minstrel*, and is one of the best known and best loved of all Scottish authors.

Street performances are what the Fringe festival is all about, in the tradition of gathering a crowd and entertaining them.

SWEDEN: LAND OF THE MIDNIGHT SUN

In summer the sun never sets on this magical landscape, as if wanting visitors to grasp every moment of their time in one of Europe's last true wildernesses.

THE LAND OF THE MIDNIGHT SUN refers to a band across the northern area of the globe, within the Arctic Circle, including Alaska, Canada, Greenland, and parts of Scandinavia and Russia. It is in Sweden, though, where some of the most stunning scenery is to be found, and where you have some of the continent's last remaining wilderness areas.

Access to Sweden's Land of the Midnight Sun is through the country's most northerly city, Kiruna, which is 91 miles (146 km) north of the Arctic Circle. It has road and rail links with the rest of the country, and its airport is the most northerly in Sweden. It sees the Midnight Sun for about six weeks of the year, from the end of May onward; the opposite phenomenon, the Polar Night, when the sun never rises, is a rather less popular time to visit.

Kiruna is the capital of the Kiruna region, Sweden's largest, which is almost as big as the whole of Slovenia. The region is popular with lovers of the outdoors, as there are six rivers and about 6,200 lakes to enjoy, and it is also where you will find Sweden's highest mountain, Kebnekaise (6,903 feet/2,104 m), and beautiful silver birch forests. Here you can experience the thrill of skiing under the Midnight Sun, jogging across ice-covered lakes, hiking in silvery forests, or even playing golf at midnight on one of the most northerly courses in Europe.

The southern peak of Kebnekaise is unusual in that although it is currently the highest peak in Sweden, it may not be for much longer. There are two major peaks in the Kebnekaise massif, and the southern peak is the higher because it is covered permanently by a glacier. However, that glacier is shrinking because of global warming, and if it continues at its present rate, then the northern peak, which is glacier-free, will soon be the highest in the country.

Sunrise and sunset merge at Paittasjärvi Lake (1): The sun dips to the horizon as if to set, only to begin its journey back up again into the sky.

The Northern Lights dance in the sky over Kiruna (2), the most northerly city in Sweden.

—> FACT FILE

CURRENCY Swedish krona

CLIMATE Despite its latitude most of Sweden is surprisingly mild for most of the year, thanks to the Gulf Stream. In northern Sweden, however, the average high temperature in July, the warmest month, is only 63ºF (17ºC), and in the coldest month, January, the average daily *high* temperature is 14ºF (-10ºC). Here it will also start snowing in September, and snow might remain on the ground until May. Rain usually falls by way of heavy storms, even in summer.

WHAT TO TAKE Warm and waterproof clothing!

BEST TIME From May until the middle of July is when the sun never sets, and you can truly see the sun at midnight.

NEAREST AIRPORT Kiruna is the most northerly city in Sweden, and its airport is the most northerly airport.

ACCOMMODATION Good options in the major towns and cities, including the Jukkasjärvi Ice Hotel, rebuilt from ice every year and referred to as the world's largest igloo.

The name of the city of *Kiruna* (**2**) means "ptarmigan," the white bird that lives in northern climates.

Still waters reflect the wintry trees in northern Sweden to produce a picture postcard.

Some reindeer roam wild in Sweden, and many end up on the plate or in the pot.

–> The Midnight Sun

In the Northern Hemisphere, the phenomenon known as the Midnight Sun starts to appear as you reach the Arctic Circle. Here it happens from April to August, although this varies with the latitude. It is at this time of year when the earth's northern axis is tilted toward the sun, which therefore never dips below the horizon as the earth moves around it. At the North Pole the Midnight Sun lasts for half the year, but the farther south you go, the more this decreases until, just below the Arctic Circle, it might last for only one day of the year. Most places in northern Sweden experience it from about late May until the middle of July.

Land of Eight Seasons

In this extreme north of the country, where Sweden, Finland, and Norway meet and where the Laplanders live, they call it the Land of Eight Seasons. Here the Laplanders base their seasons around the movements and habits of their caribou, with winter stretching across six months of the year. Early winter starts in November and lasts two months, then comes winter followed by spring-winter, and it is not until April that spring proper begins. After that there is early summer and summer, early fall and fall, and before they know it, early winter comes around again.

Northern Lights

People come to places like this to see things they cannot see anywhere else. Another attraction about the lands where the Midnight Sun appears is that even stranger and more magical natural phenomenon, the Northern Lights. The Aurora Borealis, to give them their scientific name, occurs across the polar regions in both the Northern and Southern Hemispheres. *Aurora* is the Latin word for "dawn," and *boreas* the word for "north wind," which gives a clue as to what causes the Northern Lights. The full and lengthy scientific explanation, which involves atoms and molecules, protons and electrons, the earth's magnetosphere, and substances like ionic nitrogen, shows that sometimes you need to ignore the science and focus on the magic. And the Northern Lights are magical, these ghostly, swirling lights of silver and blue, red and green, and colors in between, that might or might not appear, and can give either a faint display or a full-on show as spectacular as any fireworks, seemingly as the mood takes them.

If you cannot travel to the Land of the Midnight Sun in summer and experience the endless days, you can instead go in winter when, although the sun may never rise, the Northern Lights are more likely to put on a show and have a darker backdrop to do so. You can see the Northern Lights in the summer, too, perhaps by first taking a midnight hike and then staying awake all night to watch the lights, then finishing with the dawn chorus of birdsong, even though there is no dawn. But at any time of year, there is always something magical happening here in Europe's wild north.

Kebnekaise (**3**) is the highest mountain in Sweden, and there is no higher point between it and the North Pole. Walking trails lead to the top, over the glacier that crowns its summit.

MOUNTAINOUS SNOWDONIA

The mountainous landscape of Snowdonia in North Wales includes some of the country's finest scenery, pretty villages, and everything that is good about Wales.

The lake of Llyn Idwal (1) is named after an early Prince of Wales who was said to have been murdered in its waters.

THE AREA AROUND SNOWDONIA, incorporating the Snowdonia National Park, is one of the most traditional parts of Wales, where a large percentage of the population still speaks Welsh, an estimated 65 percent in many places. It is also one of the most beautiful parts of the country, if not the most beautiful, and includes the nation's highest peak, Mount Snowdon (3,560 feet/ 1,085 m). There are several mountain ranges here, and they include all the Welsh mountains that are more than 3,000 feet (914 m) high, and Aran Fawddwy, which is the highest British peak south of Snowdon, at 2,970 feet (905 m). The mountains here do provide incomparable views, and on days when the skies are clear, it is possible to see not only much of north Wales but also as far as Ireland, Northern Ireland, the Isle of Man, England, and even Scotland some 200 miles (322 km) away across the Irish Sea.

Currently an estimated five hundred thousand people make it to the top of Snowdon every year, so it is hardly Mount Everest. The fact that you can take a train up to the top means it is not the daunting challenge it might otherwise be. Some people do choose to climb or hike to the summit, but despite the fact that it is the highest mountain in Wales, the peak of Snowdon itself is not the area's most tranquil place.

Even some of the remoter places are quieter only by comparison, as the whole area is hugely popular with climbers, hikers, mountain bikers, and other outdoor enthusiasts. As with the English Lake District, you often have to be prepared to share this stunningly beautiful corner with others.

Snowdonia National Park

There is plenty of space, though. The Snowdonia National Park, which was created in 1951 and was the first of the three national parks in Wales, covers an area of 823 square miles (2,131 sq km). People associate it with the mountains because of the name of Snowdon, but it also has 37 miles (60 km) of glorious coastline, all of which is designated a Special Area of Conservation. It makes

With Mount Snowdon in the distance (**2**), this view of an open landscape shows why the area is special.

Walking in the Snowdonia National Park (left, **3**) is a rewarding experience.

-> FACT FILE

POPULATION 26,000

CURRENCY Pound sterling

CLIMATE The climate is fairly mild, but the mountains bring lots of rain for most of the year. It can be cold in winter, especially if getting up early, and care should be taken if venturing out then. Summers are usually very pleasant, without getting too hot, though the best months for sunshine are May and June.

WHAT TO TAKE Take clothing suitable for all climates, really good walking shoes, cell phone for emergencies.

BEST TIME May and June are good months weather-wise, and midsummer too. Winter is for hardy souls only.

NEAREST AIRPORT Manchester International Airport is about 90 miles (145 km) northeast of Snowdonia.

ACCOMMODATION Lots of choices in towns in and around the National Park like Caernarfon, Barmouth, Harlech, and Dolgellau.

Seen here in winter, the poetic-sounding Cadair Idris (4) is one of the best-loved mountains in Wales, standing by the lakes of Llynnau Cregennen.

Snowdonia unusual, as it is a national park where you can go mountain climbing and windsurfing.

The park is even more varied than that, which is part of its appeal. As well as the windsurfers and mountain bikers, there are Roman forts, Stone-Age burial chambers, slate quarries, some of the world's oldest rocks, and two endangered endemic species. These are the Snowdon beetle, also known as the rainbow beetle because of its coloring, and the Snowdon lily. There are wild goats, too. Snowdonia contains no fewer than seventeen national nature reserves, more than any other national park in England and Wales.

The Hole in the Middle

Snowdonia is also special because of its people. Like all of the national parks, it is lived in, with a population of about twenty-six thousand. The people too have made their contribution to what makes Snowdonia so attractive. One unusual feature is that it is the only national park with a hole in the middle! The town of Blaenau Ffestiniog has long been a traditional area for slate mining.

The Snowdonia slate quarries, and the slate-tiled roofs of the buildings, are also part of the scenery and the story here, every bit as much as the Roman forts and the wildlife. But when the park was being established in 1951, the slate-mining industry was in serious decline and the rules of the National Park would have prevented further industrial development. So a hole was created around Blaenau Ffestiniog to allow for some light industry, to ensure that the people who lived there had jobs in the future.

A national park has to try to be all things to all people, and that especially includes those who live within its boundaries, who farm the land, and for whom it has been a home for countless generations. The Snowdonia National Park in particular is a good example of what can be done. It appeals to the rugged climbers and the mountain bikers, and to the leisure tourists who simply want a train ride to the top of Mount Snowdon. So far the park has managed this balancing act successfully for almost sixty years.

–> Land of the Eagle

The Welsh name for this area is *Eryri*, which is the Welsh word for "highlands," although it has a pleasing similarity to *eryr*, the Welsh word for "eagle."

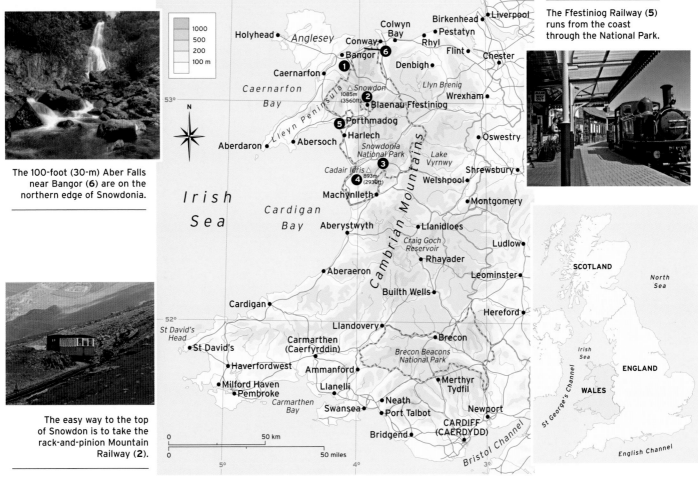

The Ffestiniog Railway (**5**) runs from the coast through the National Park.

The 100-foot (30-m) Aber Falls near Bangor (**6**) are on the northern edge of Snowdonia.

The easy way to the top of Snowdon is to take the rack-and-pinion Mountain Railway (**2**).

1000
500
200
100 m

Holyhead
Anglesey
Colwyn Bay
Birkenhead
Liverpool
Conway
6
Rhyl
Pestatyn
Bangor
Flint
Chester
Caernarfon
Denbigh
1
Caernarfon Bay
△ Snowdon 1085m (3560ft)
2
Llyn Brenig
Wrexham
Blaenau Ffestiniog
Lleyn Peninsula
5 Porthmadog
Oswestry
Harlech
Abersoch
Aberdaron
Snowdonia National Park
Lake Vyrnwy
Shrewsbury
Cadair Idris △
3
Welshpool
893m (2930ft)
4
Machynlleth
Montgomery
Cardigan Bay
Irish Sea
Aberystwyth
Llanidloes
Cambrian Mountains
Ludlow
Craig Goch Reservoir
Rhayader
Aberaeron
Leominster
Builth Wells
Cardigan
Hereford
St David's Head
Llandovery
St David's
Carmarthen (Caerfyrddin)
Brecon
Haverfordwest
Brecon Beacons National Park
Ammanford
Milford Haven
Llanelli
Merthyr Tydfil
Pembroke
Carmarthen Bay
Neath
Newport
Swansea
Port Talbot
CARDIFF (CAERDYDD)
Bridgend
Bristol Channel

53°
52°
5°
4°
3°

0   50 km
0   50 miles

SCOTLAND
North Sea
Irish Sea
ENGLAND
St George's Channel
WALES
English Channel

75

SOUTHERN EUROPE

"All journeys have secret destinations
of which the traveler is unaware."

Martin Buber, Austrian philosopher, 1878-1965

DUBROVNIK: A CITY REBORN

What humans build they can also destroy. But as Dubrovnik has shown, they can also rebuild, to retain the Pearl of the Adriatic.

NOTHING IS SACRED IN WARTIME, as the citizens of Dubrovnik—and of the world—know. The Old Town was made a UNESCO World Heritage Site in 1979, which means that it is considered a place of outstanding cultural importance, to be protected and preserved for the common benefit of all humankind. This did not stop Serbian forces from bombing the predominantly Croatian city in 1991-92, during the bloody breakdown of the former Yugoslavia. The world could only look on in horror as the distinctive red-tiled roofs were hit by bombs and the bright white walls crumbled and fell.

But what the evil in humankind can try to destroy, the goodness can try to put back together again, and the restoration of Dubrovnik in the years since 1992 has been astonishing. It has become once again what the British poet Lord Byron memorably described it, "the Pearl of the Adriatic."

Problems of Restoration

The restoration was not without its problems, of course, ironically caused in part by its having been designated a World Heritage Site. This meant that renovations had to be carried out in the original style of the buildings, but because of the passage of time since they were first constructed, many of the original materials were no longer available. All those remarkable roof tiles had in fact come from

the same local factory, which had long since closed down. It proved impossible to match the tiles exactly, and after a great deal of searching, the closest matches proved to be from France and other parts of Croatia. Even so, the slight differences in color were noticeable and so the new tiles were patchworked in with the old tiles, to make the distinctions less obvious. In time, weathering will no doubt play its part in ensuring a uniformity of color once more.

The walls of the buildings proved problematic, too. Most of them had been made from local white limestone, from a quarry that now produced only a limited amount of stone. This stone had to be used for the most visible repairs, with as close a match as possible being found for the places where the patching up would not be quite so noticeable.

City Walls

The best views of the Old Town are found by walking around Dubrovnik's remarkable city walls, which run for about 1 ¼ miles (2 km) around the city. These too were shelled in 1991-92, suffering 111 direct hits, but thankfully the damage was repairable and they have been restored to their former glory. Until the bombing started, the walls had remained unchanged since the fifteenth century, which was the last time they were fortified in order to defend the city from the forces of the Ottoman Empire.

The walls were mainly built between the thirteenth and fifteenth centuries, building on city defenses that had existed from about the ninth century onward. Originally most of the walls were about 5 feet (1 ½ m) thick, but because there was more danger from the land side than the sea side, the walls facing inland were built up over the years so that in places they are almost 6 feet (2 m) thick. The sea defenses have been added to here and there, but remain more or less at their original thickness.

Placa

Dubrovnik's main street, Placa (pronounced "Platsa"), runs all the way between the Pile and Ploce gates of the city, in the east and west walls, a distance of 984 feet (300 m). It was first laid out in the eleventh century, and this grand old street also

Walking the walls of the Old Town is an ideal starting point for any tour of Dubrovnik, and affords some fantastic views, here (1) looking out toward Lokrum Island.

The marble-paved Placa (2) is the city's main thoroughfare and splits the Old Town in two.

–> FACT FILE

POPULATION 45,000

CURRENCY Kuna

CLIMATE Dubrovnik has a pleasant Mediterranean climate with summers that are dry and hot, tempered by sea breezes, and winters that are mild and see most of the rainfall.

WHAT TO TAKE Sunscreen, but something warm, too, as temperatures can fluctuate. Be prepared for occasional Mediterranean storms.

BEST TIME Spring and fall are ideal times.

NEAREST AIRPORT Dubrovnik International Airport is about 15 miles (24 km) from the city, with taxis and buses taking passengers to the Old Town. A new terminal is being built to cope with the boom in demand.

ACCOMMODATION Most is in resort hotels along the coast, some not far from the Old Town, but staying in the Old Town is something special, and there are plenty of rooms in private homes that provide better value as well as convenience.

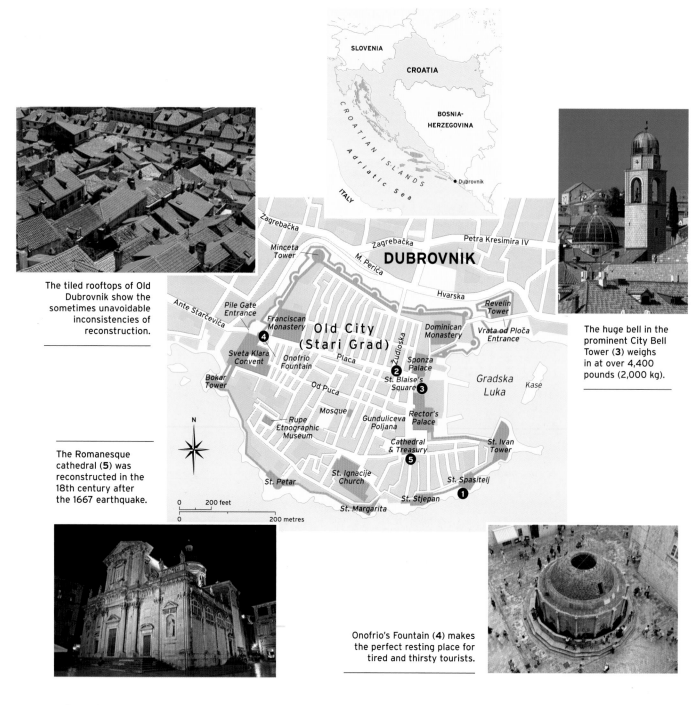

The tiled rooftops of Old Dubrovnik show the sometimes unavoidable inconsistencies of reconstruction.

The huge bell in the prominent City Bell Tower (3) weighs in at over 4,400 pounds (2,000 kg).

The Romanesque cathedral (5) was reconstructed in the 18th century after the 1667 earthquake.

Onofrio's Fountain (4) makes the perfect resting place for tired and thirsty tourists.

suffered in the months of bombing. But it, too, has been rebuilt, and is back to being the place where people go for a stroll and to shop, and where the city celebrates its feasts.

More devastating than the bombing campaign by the Serb forces was an earthquake that happened on August 6, 1667. This destroyed most of the major buildings in Dubrovnik and killed more than five thousand people. Before the earthquake struck, Dubrovnik and Placa had many fine Renaissance buildings, and one of the rare ones to have survived the earthquake is the Sponza Palace, still standing on Placa.

The Sponza Palace was built in 1516 and used as the city's Customs House, and later the Mint and the Treasury. Today it is the place where the state archives are kept, a precious collection going back almost a thousand years—as old as the Placa and even older than the city walls. It is therefore the perfect place to house the Memorial Room, which commemorates those people who lost their lives during the bombardment and siege of Dubrovnik in the 1990s—a time when the world might have lost one of its most special places.

The picturesque red-roofed buildings of the city provide a vivid contrast with the surrounding Adriatic Sea.

THE CROATIAN ISLANDS

With more than a thousand islands and islets, Croatia is blessed with a glorious part of the Adriatic Sea, with everything from chic resorts to the ultimate escape.

GREECE MAY HAVE TWICE AS MANY islands, but Croatia boasts the second-biggest group in the Mediterranean, with more of a sense of discovery. The country has boomed as a visitor destination only in the last few years, but ever since people started uncovering its natural beauty, it has been on a roller-coaster ride of mostly positive progress.

There are about 700 proper islands, and another 450 or so islets, rocks, and reefs. Of these, fewer than fifty are inhabited, but the numbers vary, as some have only temporary inhabitants, and others are still losing their populations as they decline to the point of unsustainability. At least a dozen of the islands have fewer than one hundred people living on them year-round. The island of Krk has the biggest population, with about 18,000 people, and at 157 square miles (407 sq km) it is the same size

Zlatni Rat beach on the island of Brač changes shape with the winds and the tides, but never loses its pointed form (1).

as the island of Cres, where only about 3,000 people live full-time. For those more familiar with the Greek islands, Cres and Krk together are about the same size as Zakynthos in the Greek Ionian islands.

Hvar

One of the most popular islands is Hvar, which has everything you could possibly want from a holiday island, from the tip of its mountains down to its sandy beaches and secret coves. The island's highest point is Sveti Nikola at 2,054 feet (626 m), and in summer the hills are covered with acres of green vines, hinting at the rich harvest to come. There are groves of gnarled olive trees, and bright blue lavender fields reminiscent of Provence. It is a paradise for walkers and nature lovers.

The bridge linking Krk
(2) with the mainland
is one of the longest
concrete bridges in
the world, at 4,692
feet (1,430 m).

→ FACT FILE

POPULATION 120,000

CURRENCY Kuna

CLIMATE The Croatian islands enjoy
a typical Mediterranean climate, with
hot dry summers and mild winters.

WHAT TO TAKE Beach clothes, walking
gear, a good phrase book, plenty of
cash if traveling around.

BEST TIME Summer

NEAREST AIRPORTS Rijeka for the north,
Zadar in the center, and Dubrovnik for
the southern islands.

ACCOMMODATION The larger islands have
a range, from inexpensive guesthouses
to boutique-style hotels, but on the
smaller islands you may have to settle
for simpler accommodation.

The island of Krk (above, **2**) is one of the most popular—and populous—in Croatia, renowned for its wine, cuisine, culture, and scenery.

The Hektorovic Palace on Hvar (**3**) has dominated the main town since it was built in the early years of the 16th century.

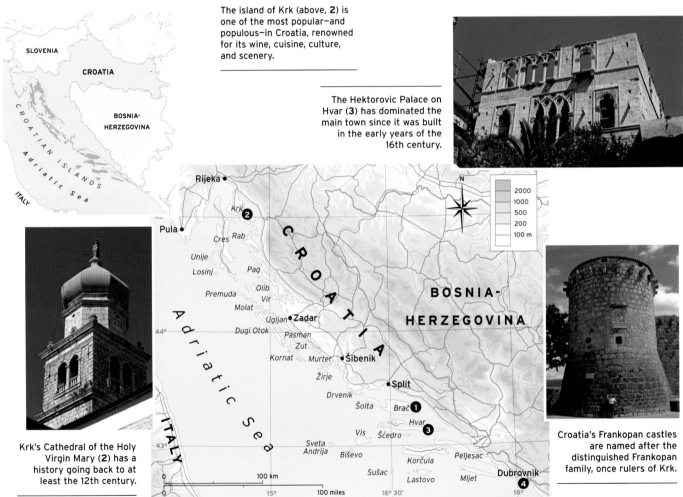

Krk's Cathedral of the Holy Virgin Mary (**2**) has a history going back to at least the 12th century.

Croatia's Frankopan castles are named after the distinguished Frankopan family, once rulers of Krk.

-> Brijuni National Park

The Brijuni Islands have been given national park status. Here you will still find the wild deer that were once found on many of the islands, and evidence that, long before even the deer, dinosaurs roamed here. The islands were once the private summer home of President Tito, from the Communist era.

Palm trees in Hvar (**3**) show the mild nature of the climate in the Adriatic Sea.

For many people a paradise island would be one endless beach and having somewhere to party at night. Hvar has these, with long stretches of sand, usually packed with young Italians and Croats in midsummer, but there are plenty of quiet coves, too, where you can feel like the hot sun and blue sea are yours and yours alone.

Brač

Brač is another large and popular place, with mountains even higher than those on Hvar. Its highest peak is Mount St. Vid, or Vidova Gora, which at 2,553 feet (778 m) is the highest point in the Adriatic. As well as grapes, olives, and lavender, lemons and oranges, figs and limes, and oleander all grow in abundance, creating a colorful landscape and tasty menus in the restaurants.

Brač also has one of the most popular resorts in the islands, the ancient town of Bol. Here you find one of the busiest and most unusual and attractive beaches in the Mediterranean, Zlatni Rat, which sounds more appealing in its English translation of Golden Cape. It is an almost perfect V-shaped beach that wraps around two sides of a wooded headland. Mostly sand, there are also lots of pebbles that move with the swirl of the strong current, giving the impression that the beach is shifting slightly. The waters here are also usually as clear as glass, so when you swim, you can gaze down at the patterns of pebbles and rocks on the seabed below.

Krk

If Brač has its Golden Cape, then Croatia's largest island, Krk, can do even better, as it has been known for centuries as the Golden Island. Its proximity to the Croatian mainland has made it popular with visitors for almost as long as it has been inhabited, and since 1980 access has been even easier with the building of a road bridge linking it with the mainland. This makes it especially busy in the summer season, as its location in the northern Adriatic tempts vacationers from Slovenia, Italy, Germany, and Eastern Europe, who can drive there, as well as those from farther afield who fly in. This gives it a very cosmopolitan feel, and a vibrant nightlife on the warm summer nights.

Krk offers plenty of history and culture, too, with churches and monasteries, some dating back to the eleventh and twelfth centuries, and there are seven ancient castles. Seven different dialects of the Croatian language are spoken here, so the number

seven has an almost magical significance to local people—the Croats are said to have arrived here and established their culture on the island from the seventh century onward.

Elaphite Islands

Part of the appeal of the Croatian islands is in the contrasts you find there. Not all are big and busy. The Elaphite Islands are a group of three small islands with fewer than a thousand people between them, and not a single car. Their unspoiled nature harks back to the time when they got their name, from the Greek word *elafos*, meaning "deer," to the days when herds of deer outnumbered the human population. Today there is still a feeling that nature is more important here than humankind, when you wander the tracks and see the abundance of limes, lemons, oranges, almonds, figs, olives, and the vines that seem to be ever present throughout the Croatian islands. It is in places like this that the Croatian islands reveal their real charms, of lush landscapes, an almost perfect climate, good food and drink, and friendly people who know they are fortunate indeed to live in such a paradise.

Lopud (4) is one of the Elaphite Islands, most of which are small and many of them uninhabited. Lopud has a population of about 200.

ATHENS: CITY FOR 2,500 YEARS

Athens is the birthplace of European democracy, of drama and philosophy, too, but the 2004 Olympics brought in a new Golden Age for the city.

THE GOLDEN AGE OF ATHENS happened in the fifth century B.C., but the twenty-first century is proving to be something of a modern Golden Age for the city. The return of the Olympic Games to Athens in 2004 was a major factor in its regeneration, and the changes are ongoing. Athens always had its history and ancient monuments to attract visitors, but even its admirers knew that its hotels, restaurants, and transport system did not—with a few notable exceptions—rival those of other European capital cities.

In the last few years, however, the city has undergone considerable transformation. There now seems to be a boutique hotel on every corner, when previously they were not so much a novelty as nonexistent. More and more restaurants are winning coveted Michelin stars, and others are providing the kind of nouvelle Greek and international cuisine that was unheard of even ten years ago. This goes alongside an enormous increase in the quality of Greek wine. Forget retsina, and think gold medals in international wine competitions.

There is also a sparkling new and sleekly efficient Metro system, which is a joy to ride on. It ensures that most visitors' first experience of arriving in Athens is a pleasant one—a brand new airport and a comfortable, cool, and quick Metro ride right into the city center, rather than the rundown old airport and an encounter with either the bus system or the notoriously dishonest taxi drivers who used to prey on new arrivals.

Sites of Ancient Athens

Despite all these changes, it is still the sites of ancient Athens that most visitors come to see. And there is something very magical about emerging from the sleek Metro system, stepping into the streets of a busy, modern city, then looking up and seeing a building that is 2,500 years old still dominating the skyline. Not just any building, either, but one of the most beautiful ever constructed: the Parthenon.

It may well have a crane hovering over it, as part of a long restoration project the Greeks are

Mount Lykavittos (1) overlooks the sprawling city of Athens, ancient and modern side by side.

-> FACT FILE

POPULATION 750,000

CURRENCY Euro

CLIMATE Mild in winter, though it does snow sometimes, usually briefly; frequent heatwaves and little rain in summer, warm and dry in spring and fall.

WHAT TO TAKE Sunscreen, earplugs (some hotels can suffer from noise problems).

BEST TIME Spring and fall, even winter, but summers are fiercely hot.

NEAREST AIRPORT Athens International Airport is 12 miles (20 km) east of the city center, and connected to it by Metro and bus links.

ACCOMMODATION Lots of new boutique hotels have opened recently, and there are plenty of cheap but clean and comfortable bargains, too.

Over the centuries the Parthenon **(2)** has been bombed and ransacked, and had parts of it taken to London by Lord Elgin, but it still stands proudly on top of the Acropolis, one of the greatest buildings in the world.

pursuing, but it is still monumentally beautiful in its simplicity. To see it illuminated at night, too, is to have it confirmed that you are in a very special city. Here was the birthplace of democracy in Europe. Here too in that Golden Age was the birth of modern European drama, and of philosophy. It was the age of Socrates and Plato, of Sophocles, Euripides, and other dramatists whose work is still performed today.

Acropolis

No one on their first visit to Athens should fail to climb up to the Acropolis (the Upper City), the rock on which the Parthenon and other monuments were built, and around which the city was born. The Parthenon was a temple to Athena, the patron goddess of the city, both a place of worship and a treasury. It is surrounded by the remains of other buildings: the Erechtheion Temple, the Temple of Athena Nike, and the Propylaia, which was the major entrance to the Acropolis.

The Acropolis also gives a good view of Athens and some of the other sites that were built during this Golden Age. Many of them still survive, and a walk around the city (most major sites are within walking distance of each other) reveals more important archaeological sites than in probably any other city in the world. Even the recent subway excavations produced new findings, some of which have been incorporated into the stations themselves. Building the New Acropolis Museum also revealed the remains of a prehistoric Athenian settlement, which is now part of the structure of the building, and around the city there are other small discoveries protected under glass to enable passersby to see them.

Ancient Agora

The Ancient Agora, below the Acropolis on the edge of the popular Plaka district, was the market and meeting place of ancient Athens, first laid out in the sixth century B.C. The main square and the foundations of some of the streets, stores, and other buildings can still be seen. It does not take much imagination to people the place with the ancient Greeks, doing their shopping here, and meeting to discuss the latest events in the city. What really makes the Agora worth visiting is its museum, not just for what it contains but for the fact that it is housed in the restored Stoa of Attalos,

The Tower of the Winds (3) used to be topped by a weather vane, which not only showed the wind direction but also indicated which of the eight wind deities was associated with it.

a graceful colonnaded building that is shown as it would have looked in the second century B.C. It is a rare opportunity to see a building not in ruins but as it would have looked to the people at the time.

The same can almost be said for the Tower of the Winds, a large and beautiful octagonal building that was constructed in the second century B.C. by Andronicus of Cyrrhus, an astronomer. On each of its sides you can still see the carvings depicting the eight main winds that were believed to exist, though lost is the bronze figure of Triton, which

stood on the top and turned around to indicate the direction the wind was blowing in—the forerunner of modern weather vanes.

These are just a few of the great treasures and temples that exist in Athens, without taking account of the modern museums, the markets, and the National Archaeological Museum, which is one of the world's great museums, in one of the world's great cities. Truly a Golden city.

The Zappeion (**4**) is a conference center and exhibition hall, and was designed to be used for an exhibition to coincide with the revival of the modern Olympic Games in Athens in 1896.

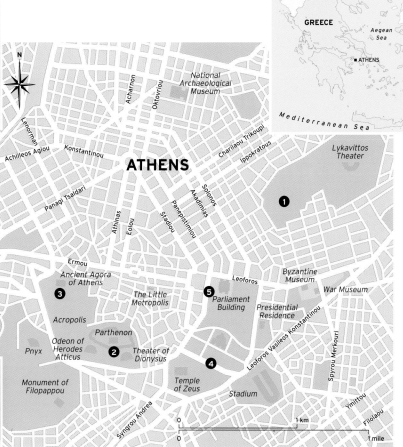

Greece's Parliament (**5**) has only one house, lacking the upper chamber that some countries' governments have.

The Stoa of Attalos (**3**) was destroyed in the 3rd century A.D. but was fully and faithfully restored to its original design in the 1950s.

SANTORINI AND THE GREEK ISLANDS

The Aegean Islands are the most beautiful in the Mediterranean, and the Cyclades is the most beautiful island group, with Santorini the jewel among them all.

THE ISLAND OF SANTORINI as we see it today, with its dramatic cliffs and large crater of a bay, was created by what was possibly the biggest volcanic eruption the world has ever known. It is thought to have happened in about 1650 B.C., when the island erupted and fell in on itself, and the sea flooded in to create the caldera that now makes for one of the most stunning sea approaches to any island anywhere in the world.

The explosion was so huge that it sent ash and perhaps a huge tsunami-like tidal wave as far as the island of Crete, about 70 miles (113 km) to the south. It is thought that this might well have been what wiped out the Minoan civilization on Crete, although there are several opinions and theories about this. The Minoan civilization did crumble and disappear about the same time, and the eruption on Santorini

would not have helped, although whether it was the sole cause for what happened on Crete is still not proven.

Akrotiri

What is known is that it certainly wiped out the town of Akrotiri on Santorini, and the suddenness of the disaster had an effect like that of Vesuvius on Pompeii, helping to preserve it for the future. Unlike Pompeii, though, no human remains were found, which suggests that the town was evacuated and the citizens knew an eruption was imminent.

Akrotiri has been one of the most popular sights on Santorini (which is also known by its Greek name of Thíra), but it is currently closed to visitors. A vast roof had been erected over the site to protect it from the elements, especially the searing summer

Aside from its history and its stunning location, Santorini (1) has beautiful beaches like many other Greek islands.

POPULATION Santorini 12,500

CURRENCY Euro

CLIMATE Mediterranean climate, with temperatures up to about 86ºF (30ºC) in midsummer, and very little rain then. Most rain falls in winter, though the temperature seldom drops to freezing. Shoulder seasons are pleasantly warm, with some chance of occasional rain.

WHAT TO TAKE Beach gear such as sunscreen, sandals, and a mat for the black sand beaches, and a Greek phrase book.

BEST TIME Early summer and early fall are beautiful, but avoid the searing midsummer heat.

NEAREST AIRPORT Santorini Island National Airport.

ACCOMMODATION Plenty of accommodation of all kinds (throughout the islands), from humble rooms in someone's house to luxury 5-star spas and boutique hotels.

The shape of Santorini (1) means its houses and churches are jumbled in together and tumble down the hillsides, making for a spectacular sight.

Red, volcanic lava provides a colorful perch on Santorini (1) for the old village of Imerovigli.

Santorini (1) is a popular cruise destination, and arriving by boat shows the island at its dramatic best.

sun, but in 2005 this collapsed and the site is not expected to reopen until at least 2010. The finds from the site are kept elsewhere, at the Museum of Prehistoric Thíra in the island's main town, so it is still possible to see these relics of almost four thousand years ago, to get a glimpse of life at that time. Santorini was also a part of that very sophisticated Minoan civilization: furniture, wall frescoes, and a rare golden ibex statuette are among the highlights.

Many visitors do find the archaeological sites fascinating, and there are plenty to see on bigger islands like Crete and Rhodes. The island of Delos, near Mykonos, also in the Cyclades, is one huge site. The incredible archaeological treasures are only one aspect of the Greek islands, and their great appeal is the sum of the many different things they have to offer. Of course, many people just want to spend their days on the beach.

Beaches and Boutique Hotels

Despite the rocky impression when you arrive, Santorini does have some good beaches—with a choice of colors! The sight of black or red sand, the result of that volcanic activity, is startling at first, and there are some stunning white sand beaches, too, as there are on many islands. One drawback of black sand is that it attracts the heat, so if you think a golden sand beach is hot underfoot in August, try stepping on black sand for a moment.

The attraction of the Greek islands for many years was their lack of sophistication. Life there was simple, with beaches to lie on, a few museums and archaeological sites to see, good walking for the energetic, and in the evening a simple meal of fresh fish caught by a local fisherman, and all the time surrounded by good weather and affable people. You will see more smiles on a Greek island than in most other places.

Although this kind of visit is still possible if you choose the quieter islands, others like Mykonos, Crete, and Santorini have smartened up considerably in the last few years, partly as a result of the 2004 Olympic Games in Athens. This so-called "Olympic effect" combined with a general change in Greek living has resulted in countless boutique hotels and fine-dining restaurants on the more popular islands. The simple life is still there if you want it, but now visitors have another choice, too.

Other Islands, Other Lives

Santorini is undoubtedly one of the most strikingly beautiful of the Greek islands, but many people are drawn to Greece because each island is different—and yet the same. Going to Greece is a little like choosing from a chocolate box. Each chocolate is tasty, but in a different way from the others. Some people choose the same flavor over and over, and others insist on something different every time. With almost two hundred inhabited islands in the Aegean and Ionian Seas, it is a chocolate box that is never empty!

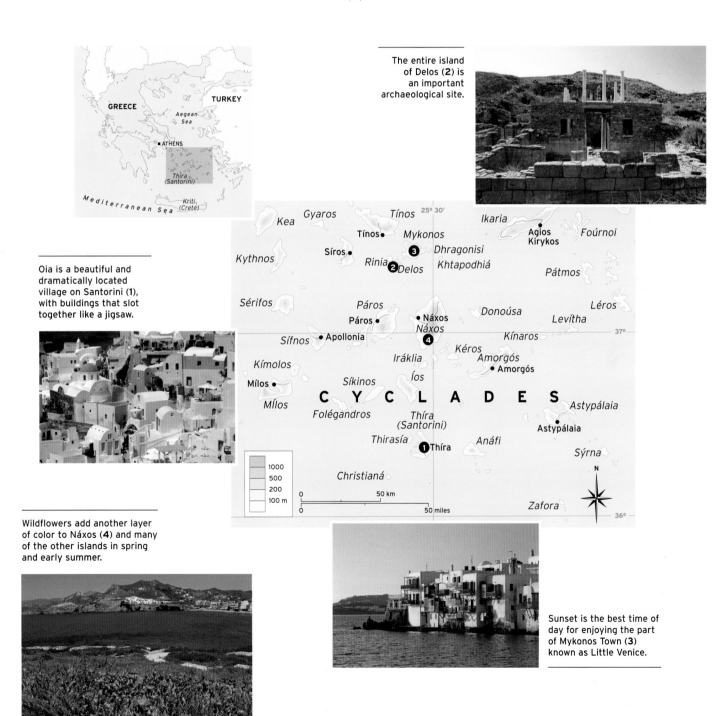

The entire island of Delos (**2**) is an important archaeological site.

Oia is a beautiful and dramatically located village on Santorini (**1**), with buildings that slot together like a jigsaw.

Wildflowers add another layer of color to Náxos (**4**) and many of the other islands in spring and early summer.

Sunset is the best time of day for enjoying the part of Mykonos Town (**3**) known as Little Venice.

DELPHI: CENTER OF THE UNIVERSE

To the ancient Greeks, Delphi was the center of the world, and today it is a World Heritage Site. Anyone visiting the ruins will immediately understand why.

AS YOU APPROACH THE ANCIENT RUINS of Delphi, you are following in footsteps that go back at least three thousand years. If you come from Athens, as many do on day trips, you are retracing the journeys of earlier pilgrims, who were coming here in the twelfth century B.C. to seek advice from the Delphic Oracle, the most famous soothsayer in the ancient world.

The Oracle was a cross between a fortune-teller and a wise woman, through whom the god Apollo spoke. Apollo was one of the most significant of all the gods, the god of truth and prophecy, and was therefore thought to be able to advise people, whether on matters of personal importance or of political significance. People would travel hundreds of miles to have an audience with the Oracle at Delphi, with the seventh day of each month being the most propitious time.

The Oracle was chosen from among the older local peasant women, and had to be someone without a stain on her character. She sat on a three-legged stool over an opening in the earth, below which the body of the dragon Python, slain by Apollo, was believed to lie rotting and releasing powerful vapors. In breathing these in, the Oracle was thought to be able to receive the voice of Apollo and know what the future held, although the answers to questions were given in riddles. In fact, it was established that natural gases did emanate from this opening, which may have helped put the Oracle into her trancelike state. Her utterings were then interpreted by the priests of the Temple of Apollo, and those consulting the Oracle would leave an offering in return.

The Athenian Treasury at Delphi (1) is just one of several built to house the offerings brought here by hopeful or grateful pilgrims.

The Treasuries

Huge numbers of people came to see the Oracle every year, from the twelfth century B.C. through to the fourth century A.D., a period of more than 1,500 years. That is a lot of offerings. Several treasuries were built to house the offerings, and also as expressions of thanks by various groups of people and towns, including Argos and the island of Corfu. The Athenian Treasury, now restored and one of the gems of the site, was built by the citizens of Athens to thank the Oracle for her advice on what to do in the impending Battle of Salamis, between the Greeks and the Persians. The Athenians followed her advice and achieved an important victory.

Another magnificent treasury was built by the island of Sifnos, which had rich deposits of silver and gold that had made the island very wealthy indeed. An elaborate and costly treasury was built in the hope that the god Apollo would smile on them in the future.

As visitors make their way up through the ancient ruins, there are plenty of opportunities to stop and gaze around and appreciate Delphi's fabulous natural setting. It is not only the presence of the Oracle that made this the center of the ancient Greek world, but its beautiful location, too.

—> Delphi Museum

Alongside the ancient site is the modern Archaeological Museum, with many finds from the site on display. The star exhibit, with a room to itself, is a fifth-century bronze known as The Charioteer. It was found in the ruins of the 2nd Temple of Apollo, which was destroyed in an earthquake in 373 B.C.

-> FACT FILE

CURRENCY Euro

CLIMATE Hot in summer, although a little cooler than Athens, thanks to the mountain elevation. Cold in winter, for the same reason.

WHAT TO TAKE Sensible shoes for scrambling around, and patience if you are there when it is busy.

BEST TIME Late spring and early fall are good times, though more important is to try to visit early or late in the day, to escape some of the crowding caused by tour groups.

NEAREST AIRPORT Athens International Airport, about 125 miles (201 km) southeast of Delphi.

ACCOMMODATION Plenty of hotels in the town of Delphi, but for a more interesting time if you have your own car, stay in the mountain village of Arachova, 7 miles (11 km) from Delphi.

The Temple of Apollo (**2**) is set high up in the site at Delphi and commands one of the best views of the surrounding scenery.

The site spreads around the foothills of the Parnassos Mountains, and you might see eagles and hawks circling in the blue skies above. Delphi stands at the head of a valley that drops away in a swirl of green olive trees down to the Gulf of Corinth far below. It is one of the largest olive groves in the whole of Greece, and a breathtaking part of the overall setting.

Temple of Apollo and Beyond

Although the temple is now in ruins, and there is no trace of any opening in the earth here, this is where the Oracle is known to have sat for her consultations. Today's ruins are of the temple that was built in the fourth century B.C., replacing one that had been destroyed in an earthquake. Before that there had been yet another temple here, built in the seventh century B.C.–and when that was built, people had already been coming to see the Oracle for more than five hundred years.

Many visitors only reach the temple and then turn back down, or have to return to their waiting bus. So beyond here the site is usually quieter, and rewards a farther small climb. There are the impressive remains of a large theater, which was built in the fourth century B.C. and could seat 5,000 people. And farther still is a stadium concealed from the view of those down below, but that has also survived well. It could seat 7,000 spectators, who came here every four years to watch the Pythian Games. These were held in honor of Apollo, and took place two years after the Olympic Games.

It is here, in the upper reaches of the Delphi complex, that you might find time to sit and reflect on this remarkable place, time to look down at the site and think about the thousands of pilgrims who made their way here, many along the Sacred Way that led from Athens to Delphi. And still they come in even bigger numbers today.

The huge theater (right, 5) at Delphi gave spectators a backdrop not just of the rest of the site but of the magnificent scenery beyond.

The Tholos is at the less famous Sanctuary of Athena on the lower slopes of Mount Parnassus, only a ten-minute walk from the museum.

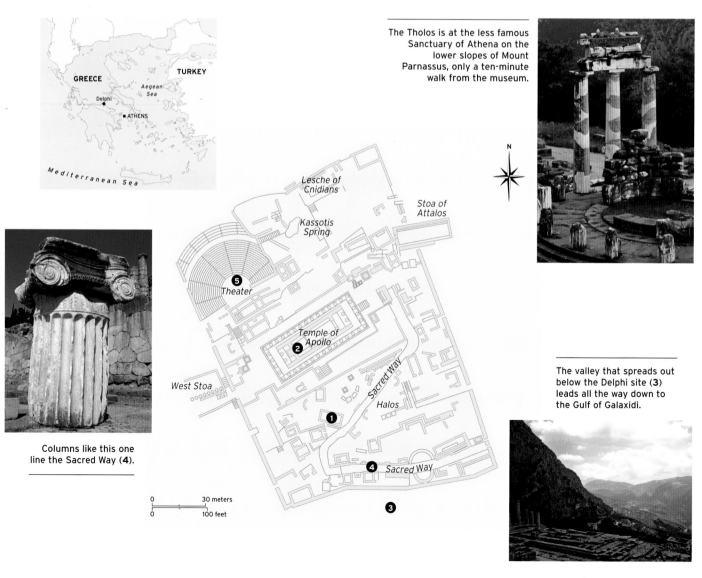

Columns like this one line the Sacred Way (4).

The valley that spreads out below the Delphi site (3) leads all the way down to the Gulf of Galaxidi.

THE MONASTERIES OF METEORA

These religious retreats hang like castles in the air from rocks jutting out of the Thessaly Plain, as if reaching for the heavens.

GREECE HAS TWO EXTRAORDINARY monastic sites. The better known is Mount Athos, the so-called Monk's Republic, an unusual autonomous region near Greece's second city, Thessaloniki. Mount Athos is the name of the mountain and also the peninsula on which it stands in the region of Halkidiki. It is renowned as the place where no woman is permitted entry, though in fact there have been occasions when women have been on Mount Athos, either with or without permission.

For most people, men and women alike, the closest you will get to Mount Athos is a boat trip around the peninsula to get a glimpse of the monasteries that have been built there. Some are in spectacular locations, perched on cliffs, and others hide inland. No one can go to them unless they acquire one of the handful of permits that is issued each day, mostly to people seeking a few days of monastic retreat.

Visiting Meteora presents the opposite problem, as it can be so busy that it is sometimes difficult to get any sense of the monastic peace that drew hermits and monks here. Despite that, there is

nowhere in the world that looks like Meteora, and the visitor's first sight of these monasteries that perch on dark rocks that jut out of the landscape is awe-inspiring. It is a surreal vision almost, a bizarre setting for which we have no reference points, but it comes as no surprise that the name *Meteora* means either "rocks in the air" or "suspended in the air."

The first man who is believed to have lived in a cave on one of these rocks was a hermit named Barnabas in about A.D. 985. Although the notion of a colony of hermits might seem like a contradiction in terms, that is what developed here as more people came to this startling place on the Thessaly Plain, and managed to eke out an existence while seeking to be closer to God.

The First Monastery

In 1336 a monk named Athanasios came to Meteora from Mount Athos to seek some solitude, and founded the first monastery at Meteora, the Megalo Meteoro. The cave in which Athanasios lived can be seen outside the entrance to the monastery, which

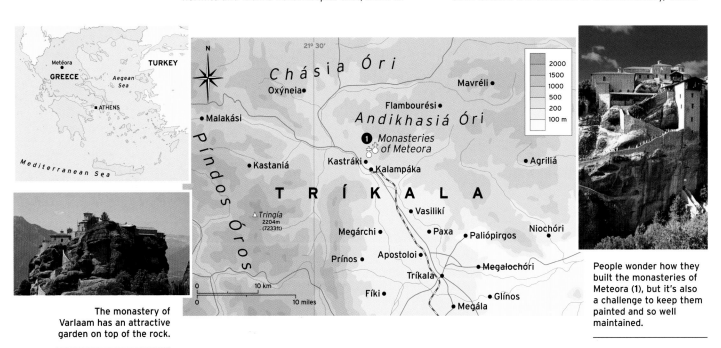

The monastery of Varlaam has an attractive garden on top of the rock.

People wonder how they built the monasteries of Meteora (1), but it's also a challenge to keep them painted and so well maintained.

-> FACT FILE

CURRENCY Euro

CLIMATE Like most of Greece, summer temperatures are very hot, and this is also the driest time of year, though being on the mainland there can be rain at any time. Winters can be cold.

WHAT TO TAKE Women should take a shawl or scarf to cover bare shoulders, and skirts should be respectable, just below the knee. Men should also dress respectfully, avoiding shorts and bare shoulders.

BEST TIME Although summers can be hot, you are almost guaranteed good weather, but late spring and early fall are also good times.

NEAREST AIRPORT Thessaloniki, Greece's second city, is about 100 miles (161 km) northeast of Meteora.

ACCOMMODATION There are hotels and other accommodation in the village of Kastráki, right by the rocks, and a great choice in the town of Kalampáka, about 1 ¼ miles (2 km) away.

VISITING It is possible to visit several monasteries in one day by foot, though it would be a long and tiring day. Having transport is better. A daily bus takes visitors from Kalampáka and Kastráki to Meteora in the morning, and returns in the afternoon. Hiring a taxi is another alternative. You will need to ask locally for current visiting hours, as there is no good tourist information office nearby.

The Agia Triada monastery was featured in the James Bond movie *For Your Eyes Only* and still has the old winch system that once hoisted supplies and visitors up to it.

still exists. It stands on one of the rocky pinnacles, some 1,752 feet (534 m) high, and is one of the thirteen monasteries that remain here at Meteora. At one time there were twenty-four. Six of the remaining thirteen are open to the public, but not all at the same time so that the remaining monks and nuns can still find peace.

The Building of the Monasteries

The question that everyone wonders is, of course, how the monasteries were built. And the answer is that no one knows for sure, though there are several theories. They begin with the belief that St. Athanasios, as he became, was carried up there by an eagle. Later arrivals had to be more pragmatic, not to mention inventive, to haul themselves and building materials up the sheer rock faces.

One possibility is that kites were used to float light ropes over the tops of the rocks. These light ropes were attached to heavier ropes, which could then be pulled up and over, allowing for rope ladders to be built. Another suggestion is that wooden ladders were roped together to provide a long and nerve-racking climb up. Once up there, pulleys were put in place so that people and goods could be brought up. When asked how often the ropes were replaced, the monks' usual response was, "Every time they break."

Rocks of Meteora

The rocks on which the monasteries are built are probably about sixty million years old, having been formed in the Tertiary Period—the time between the dying out of the dinosaurs and the beginning of the last great Ice Age.

Back then the Thessaly Plain was a huge lake or vast inland sea, filled by the waters of rivers and streams that flowed down from the Pindos Mountains. The waterways brought with them rocks and other sediment, which washed into the lake and built up over thousands of years. Some cataclysmic event caused the land around the lake to collapse, and the waters flooded away toward the Aegean, leaving behind the sedimental deposits. Wind, rain, and earthquakes gradually wore away the softer sandstone rocks, leaving behind the harder rocks in the form of the columns that we see today. There is also speculation that the rock towers were forced up out of the earth's surface by movements in the earth's tectonic plates.

However they were formed, and however the monasteries were built, the result is a unique and unforgettable part of the world.

This huge rock on the Thessaly Plain (1) shows the inspiration and the challenge that faced the first hermits and monks who arrived here.

THE CANALS OF VENICE

The Most Serene Republic of Venice is one of the most attractive cities in the world, with nowhere to rival its canals and bridges, its history and mystery.

WHERE MOST CITIES GROW OUT OF SETTLERS and water sources, Venice grew out of swamps and fugitives. The historians do not know for sure, but it is thought that the first people to call this marshy lagoon home were a Celtic tribe, the Veneti, who came here from the east in about 1500 B.C. These damp islands, subject to flooding and away from the mainland, did not exactly lure people to come and live in them, and it was only out of desperation that Venice was born. From about the second century A.D. onward, people fled various Roman cities nearby to escape successive waves of invading forces, such as the Germans, the Visigoths, and the armies of Attila the Hun. Some of them came to hide out in small settlements in the

Venetian lagoon, hoping to turn their disadvantages to advantage, and make a peaceful life.

What they found, and founded, was La Serenissima Repubblica, the Most Serene Republic. Those swampy settlements built by refugees fleeing invading empires would themselves become a great empire, trading with the rest of the world and ruled for more than a thousand years by the powerful doges.

Creating the Canals

The creation of the canals of Venice was a necessity. They originated in streams that flowed through lagoons, but that were subject to silting up from the sediments washed down the rivers.

The high central arch of the Rialto Bridge (1) allowed for the passage of galleys when the bridge was opened in 1591. For over 250 years it was the only bridge across the Canale Grande.

POPULATION 270,000

CURRENCY Euro

CLIMATE People visit Venice despite its climate, not because of it. Midsummer is usually hot and humid, winter cold and damp, though it can–and does–rain all year-round. Spring and fall are pleasant, but the city is prone to flooding at these times.

WHAT TO TAKE Waterproof clothing, even boots if going when there might be flooding.

BEST TIME Avoid the Carnival, the Film Festival, and the middle of summer, with many people preferring winter travel despite the cold and threat of rain.

NEAREST AIRPORT Venice Marco Polo Airport is on the Italian mainland, a few miles north of the city, with bus and water transport connections into Venice.

ACCOMMODATION Venice's popularity ensures that it has countless hotels, of all standards, from cheap and basic to top-end luxury. Prices are surprisingly reasonable, except at very busy times of year.

The Historical Regatta takes place on the Canale Grande (2) on the first Sunday in September, and is a chance to see gondoliers and other boatmen in their finest costumes.

The Santa Maria della Salute church (**3**) was built in 1682 and rests on 1,156,627 wooden pilings.

Monks prepared the way for The Church of San Giorgio Maggiore (**4**) when they drained the marshland back in the 9th century. It is seen here from the Campanile of St. Mark's Square (**5**).

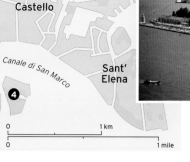

The Bridge of Sighs (**6**) was built in 1600, but its name was a 19th-century creation, popularized by Lord Byron.

St. Mark's Square (**5**) has been called the drawing room of Europe, though it's a drawing room prone to occasional flooding.

–> Bellini Cocktail

The Bellini cocktail is a Venetian creation, combining fresh juice from white peaches with the distinctive sparkling local wine, prosecco. There are variations on the recipe involving peach schnapps or peach purée when fresh peaches are not in season, but it is a drink that should be made only when the white peaches are ripe. It was invented in Harry's Bar by the head bartender, Giuseppe Cipriani, and he gave it its name because the peachy-pink hue reminded him of a particular color in a painting by Bellini.

To keep the waters flowing, the Venetians turned the natural streams into canals that they could control. That is why so many of the 150 or so canals in Venice curve gently: they are following what were originally natural water courses.

Anyone visiting Venice for the first time should try to arrive by boat. The grandest entrance is from the airport, where there are public ferries and private water taxis, bringing visitors skimming over the waters of the lagoon and then snaking into the city through its canals. From here the magic of the city is revealed, with its palaces and piazzas, and markets and bridges, all seen from the unusual angle of the water. It is a unique city.

Canale Grande

Part of the uniqueness is that whereas other cities have main streets for which they are known–the Champs-Élysées, Fifth Avenue, Oxford Street–Venice has the Canale Grande. And at some point in everyone's visit, they should "walk" the canal. Take boat number 1, which follows the curving shape of the Canale Grande from outside the train station to where the canal emerges into the lagoon near St. Mark's Square.

So many of Venice's treasures are visible from the Canale Grande that you start to understand what Truman Capote said about the city: "Venice is like eating an entire box of chocolate liqueurs in one go." The Canale Grande's tasty treats include the famous fish and produce market, the Rialto Bridge, several palaces, the Accademia Bridge and Museum, the Peggy Guggenheim Collection, the Gritti Palace Hotel, the imposing seventeenth-century La Salute church, and finally, as the Canale Grande widens into the lagoon, the edge of St. Mark's Square and the Doge's Palace. That trip alone takes you past so many landmarks, so many stages in the city's history, and so many aspects of its makeup: markets, museums, palaces, churches, bridges.

The Canale Grande takes you back to the origins of the city, as it was the River Brenta rather than a stream that cut out the reverse S-shape of what is now the canal, as it pushed its way through the lagoon toward the Adriatic Sea. There are about four hundred bridges in the city, because canals beget bridges to get people to and fro. However, only four go over the Canale Grande, which is 300 feet (91 m) wide in places. Of these, the first, the most striking, the most memorable, is the Rialto Bridge.

Rialto Bridge

The first bridge in the Rialto district was put up in about 1180, being no more than a wooden platform. The Rialto was one of the earliest settlements in Venice, and gets its name from the term *riva alto* or "high bank of the river." It was consequently one of the first to grow, and the city's main market developed here, which remains to this day. The market brought lots of foot passengers back and forth, and more and bigger boats wanting to get by. So in about 1250, a wooden bridge was built, with a raisable central section to allow tall ships through.

However, the wooden bridge was prone to collapse, and did so on one notable occasion through the sheer numbers of people standing on it to watch a boat parade go by. Finally, in 1591, the present stone bridge was built. It was similar to the previous wooden bridge in several ways, with stores built into the sides of it, and a high central arch for the convenience of boats, but there is one important difference—this one has survived for more than 400 years. The Rialto Bridge is now as much a symbol of the city as its canals. There is no bridge quite like it anywhere in the world, and certainly no city like Venice.

The Doge's Palace (**4**) dates back to the early 14th century but has been much changed and added to over the years.

THE CINQUE TERRE

The Cinque Terre towns of Italy's Ligurian coast have been made a UNESCO World Heritage Site as "a landscape of exceptional scenic quality."

THE FIVE LIGURIAN TOWNS that make up what is called the Cinque Terre, or Five Lands, are a very special part of Italy. They sit in dramatic coastal locations to the south of Genoa, where inlets in the cliff-face coast allowed people to settle and find a little space for a few houses. Small harbors were built to shelter the fishing boats, and the worst of the land was terraced to enable the cultivation of two of life's essentials—olives and grapes.

Unspoiled Italy

The irresistible charm of the Cinque Terre is that this is still pretty much the way that life is, despite the influx of visitors that any beautiful part of the world draws to itself. Even though the towns are now linked by train, as well as by boat and by that most basic transport link, the footpath, the income from tourism is still dwarfed by the wine, the olives, and the fishing. After all, tourists may come and go, but the land and the sea have provided over the centuries.

It is the very nature of the terrain here that prevents the places, which are somewhere between small towns and large villages, from becoming

The stony beach at Monterosso is a popular place to enjoy the sun and sea of the Mediterranean (1).

The grape harvest at Riomaggiore (right, **2**) requires some ingenious solutions to the problems set by the landscape.

POPULATION 6,000

CURRENCY Euro

CLIMATE The Mediterranean climate brings hot summers, though never totally dry, and mild winters. Rain can fall at any time, with storms and showers in spring and fall. These can even wipe out the footpaths, so always check the weather ahead.

WHAT TO TAKE A good walking map or guide, in case you need to go off the main trail; an Italian phrase book or dictionary.

BEST TIME September sees the wine harvest and November the olive harvest, and walking then brings more direct contact with land and people.

NEAREST AIRPORT Genoa Airport is about 50 miles (80 km) northwest of Monterosso.

ACCOMMODATION Each of the villages has places to stay, but you need to book ahead. If traveling out of the main season, you may find somewhere if you just turn up and ask. The two largest places are at either end, Riomaggiore and Monterosso, and most people base themselves there.

The houses of Riomaggiore (2) cluster together and cling to the precarious slopes in the rugged Ligurian landscape.

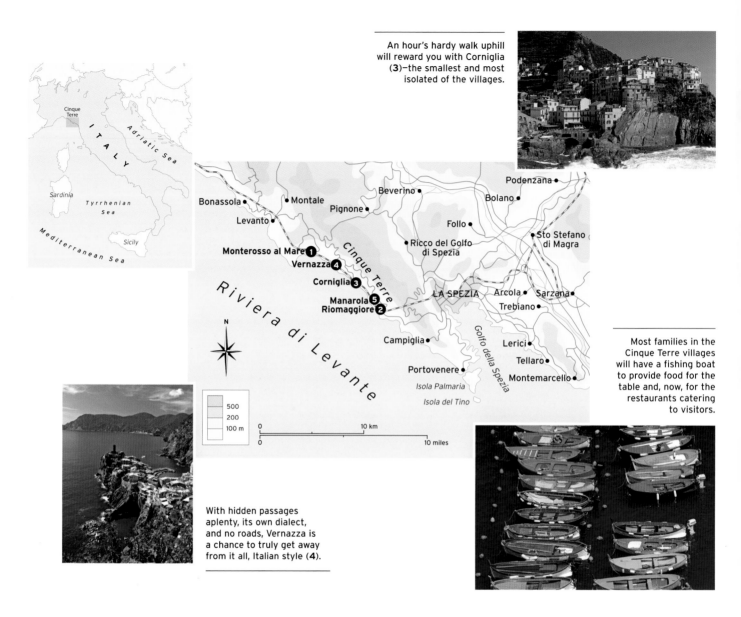

An hour's hardy walk uphill will reward you with Corniglia (**3**)—the smallest and most isolated of the villages.

Most families in the Cinque Terre villages will have a fishing boat to provide food for the table and, now, for the restaurants catering to visitors.

With hidden passages aplenty, its own dialect, and no roads, Vernazza is a chance to truly get away from it all, Italian style (**4**).

overdeveloped, although obviously tourism has had its impact. But space is limited, and the settlements are squeezed in between the rocky cliffs, making expansion difficult. There are a limited number of places to stay, and most people come for a few hours during the day, on the regular trains from Genoa to the west and La Spezia to the east. Evening is the time to be in the Cinque Terre.

The Five Towns

The towns, from west to east, are Monterosso al Mare, Vernazza, Corniglia, Manarola, and Riomaggiore. Each is different, and as well as the UNESCO designation, the whole area along this coast and stretching inland is a national park. The best way to see it all is on foot, and the towns are linked by ancient paths—some with a little modern help—that climb up and down, take you along the tops of cliffs, inland through the lemon groves and fields to skirt around natural barriers, and eventually down into the heart of the next settlement.

The most striking of these is Riomaggiore, whose pastel-colored houses tumble down the steep slopes that lead to the water, looking like a pile of building blocks that have been dropped haphazardly into a narrow box. The town was founded in the eighth century by Greek fugitives, although some of the other places are even older. Corniglia goes back to Roman times, and its name comes from the Cornelia family who owned the land then.

Manarola also has Roman origins, the name coming from *manium arula*, the Latin phrase for an altar in someone's house that is dedicated to the Mani, or the god of the house. Vernazza is said to date from about the year 1000, and was allegedly settled by freed slaves, and Monterosso was settled as a village in 1217, although there was already a castle here in 1201. It is the history as well as the landscape and the people that combine and explain why UNESCO regard this as such a special place—as does everyone who visits it.

Getting Around

It is only about 7 miles (11 km) from one end to the other, and it can easily be walked in about five hours. It is slow going because there are several steep ascents and descents along the way, and you also need to allow for the fact that parts of the coastal route are sometimes closed and you will need to divert inland along other paths on occasion. For that reason, it is wise to buy a walking guide to the area before setting out.

But this is a walk for taking slowly anyway. The point is not to get from A to B in the shortest time possible, but to linger along the way. Take a picnic, take a book—especially a phrase book, as you will need some Italian to speak to some of the people you meet, particularly if you travel in September when the grapes are picked, or in November when the olives are harvested. You might even get called in to help.

The short walk between Riomaggiore and Manarola is also one of the busiest, and is called the Via Dell'Amore, or the Lovers' Way. It is only a fifteen-minute stroll from one town to the next, mostly flat, and for that reason it is also one of the most crowded sections. It does not even have very special views, and part of the way has been concreted to prevent rock falls, whereas another stretch is through a passageway where lovers have scrawled graffiti on the walls. It does have a kind of folk-art charm, in a gritty, urban kind of a way, but it is so at odds with the rest of the area that the Lovers' Way is the one part of the whole walk that does not live up to expectations.

There is a regular train service between Genoa in the west and La Spezia in the east, which stops at each of the five places along the Cinque Terre. There are usually about two trains an hour during the day, so traveling back and forth, and walking part of the way or indeed the whole way, is quite easy if you need to get back to base the same night. There are also ferries from La Spezia that go along the coast and give impressive views from the sea, but naturally they take a lot longer and are less regular than the trains.

Manarola (5) is a place where you have to be happy about living close to your neighbors.

ROME: THE ETERNAL CITY

Rome wasn't built in a day, nor can it be seen in a day. Even a month would not do justice to the Capital of the World.

THEY CALL ROME THE ETERNAL CITY, and it does feel eternal, particularly when you are sitting in its traffic for what seems like hours at a time. It has been said that there is more to see in Rome than in any other city anywhere in the world, and another name for it is the Capital of the World. It is also the City of the Seven Hills, and contained within those seven hills is the result of nearly three thousand years of habitation, civilization, and of being the capital of what was the greatest empire in the world at the time—the mighty Roman Empire.

Legend has it that Rome was founded by the twins Romulus and Remus in 753 B.C. Archaeologists at least agree that the date is probably about right for the change of what were rural settlements in the hills into the recognizable beginnings of a city. Traditionally, Romulus was said to be the first king of Rome; then legend transforms into history. For about three hundred years Rome was the capital of the Roman Kingdom, then of the Roman Republic for another five hundred years or so, followed by the Roman Empire. All this emanating from one

city, because what we now think of as Italy is, by Roman standards, a fairly modern creation.

Not only this, but Rome also became the seat of one of the world's great religions, with the head of the Roman Catholic Church based in a city within this city. It really is one of the most remarkable cities, not just in Europe but in the world.

Colosseum

Even today on a map of the city, the sites of ancient Rome stand out. The enormous Colosseum was the largest ever built in the Roman Empire, taking ten years to construct, finally being finished in A.D. 80. Naturally there were later changes and improvements, as with any modern stadium, although it is doubtful that anything built today will be in operation for a full five hundred years as the Roman Colosseum was. And almost two thousand years after it was built, most of it is still standing; any damage has been has been caused mostly by earthquakes and thieves making off with the stones. The Romans built things to last.

Rome's Colosseum (1) was used for entertainment and executions, and was even capable of staging mock sea battles.

-> FACT FILE

POPULATION 2,700,000

CURRENCY Euro

CLIMATE Rome's Mediterranean climate makes it pleasant for much of the year, although it can get very cold for a spell in winter, and in August unbearably hot. Rain can fall all year, though the driest months are May–August.

WHAT TO TAKE Comfortable walking shoes, as there is a lot to see.

BEST TIME April–June and September–October are normally very pleasant times to visit.

NEAREST AIRPORT Leonardo da Vinci Fiumicino Airport is 16 miles (26 km) southwest of the city, with train and bus links into the center, as well as taxis.

ACCOMMODATION There is no shortage of hotels of all kinds in Rome, but if you want to stay right in the center, be prepared to pay extra for the privilege. You will often get better value for money by being prepared to stay a little farther out.

Today a pantheon is a place where the notable dead are buried, but Rome's original Pantheon (2) was where the gods were honored.

The Foro Romano (3) was not merely the center of life in the city, where its citizens met, but also the center of the whole Roman Empire.

The Colosseum could hold fifty thousand spectators, and the noise must have been tremendous when the gladiators were in combat. The arena was used for many more things than just gladiators and animal fights, though. There were re-enactments of various battles put on here—even sea battles—so the people in Rome would know what had been happening in the fight to keep and extend their empire. There were conventional and large-scale dramas, and there were public executions, too. It has also been used as a church, a castle, a cemetery, and home to a religious order, and as a backdrop to concerts by the likes of Paul McCartney and Elton John. In 2007 it was rightly included in a list of the New Seven Wonders of the World alongside places like the Taj Mahal and Petra in Jordan. The story of the Colosseum has not reached its ending yet. It is an eternal building in the Eternal City.

Foro Romano

The story of Rome begins in the adjacent Forum, which was at the center of the city that grew out from here. Because it is next to the Colosseum, and it is where Rome first started, most visitors to the city will go to see the Forum, although it has certainly not survived as well as the Colosseum. Much more imagination is needed to reconstruct the life that went on here, but the scale of the place and the sheer number of buildings is a vivid reminder of just how important Rome was, and that in the days of the Roman Empire at least, the title of Capital of the World was one it had earned.

Pantheon

Northwest from the Forum is the only other building in Rome that can rival the Colosseum for its importance, grandeur, and certainly its state of preservation—the Pantheon. It has survived even better than the Colosseum, and dates from roughly

The Piazza del Popolo (**7**) was one of the main entrances to ancient Rome.

The Trevi Fountain (**4**) is one of the most celebrated sites in Rome.

The Monumento Nazionale a Vittorio Emanuele II (**6**) honors the first king of the Italy we know today.

The Emperor Hadrian built the Castel Sant'Angelo (**5**) as a mausoleum for his family, and today it's a museum.

the same period, having been finished by the Emperor Hadrian in about A.D. 125. It is widely regarded as the best-preserved building of its age in the world.

Although it is impressive enough from the outside, it is the interior of the Pantheon that is really stunning. The top of the central dome is 142 feet (43 m) high, which is also the diameter of the area beneath it. In the center of the dome is an open circle that is 29 1/2 feet (9 m) across, through which the outside light pours in and moves around the building, which would otherwise be quite dark. There are also no visible supports or arches holding up the dome—they are there, but are concealed within the walls of the building, offering invisible support to the structure.

The inside of the Pantheon has to be seen to be appreciated, and that is true of the whole city of Rome. When faced with the Capital of the World, the Eternal City, only seeing is believing.

No visit to the Eternal City is complete without a visit to the Holy City: the Vatican (**8**), the smallest independent state in the world.

RENAISSANCE ITALY

The European Renaissance, when art and architecture flourished, began in Tuscany, and in particular in the cities of Siena and Florence.

The warm light of dawn over Florence and The Duomo (1) creates a picture of its rooftops any artist would be proud to emulate.

TUSCANY IS ITALY'S BEST-KNOWN REGION, and with some justification. Tuscany's landscape is everything we think of when we conjure up rural Mediterranean scenes—walled towns rise behind vine-covered hills as the hot sun burns down and the cicadas sing on a still afternoon. And it was this landscape, and the vibrant light and color found there, that inspired artists such as Donatello and Michelangelo, along with architects, writers, scientists, sculptors, musicians, and thinkers, all thriving at the same time to produce great works that transformed first Italian and then European life, and had a profound impact on the world.

It was during this period that the Tuscan dialect became the language of the whole of Italy, so important was the region's influence. The

Renaissance lasted only about two hundred years, from the late fourteenth century until the first few years of the seventeenth century, but it was a period when culture generally took great steps forward, and life followed it. As well as Michelangelo and Donatello, it was also the period when Botticelli and Leonardo da Vinci (the ultimate Renaissance Man) were working. In the literary world it was the era of Petrarch, Boccaccio, and—another Renaissance Man—Machiavelli.

Florence

In architecture, it was when Florence Cathedral was built, as well as St. Peter's Basilica in Rome, as the Renaissance movement spread throughout the land. Florence has often been called the most beautiful city

-> FACT FILE

POPULATION Tuscany 3,600,000

CURRENCY Euro

CLIMATE Conditions vary between the hills and valleys, but generally the climate is mild, although there is plenty of rain. July and August are the hottest months with an average temperature of about 86ºF (30ºC), and in the winter it can drop below freezing in the mountains, but will be milder lower down.

WHAT TO TAKE Rain gear and sunscreen, the biography *Leonardo da Vinci* by Charles Nicholl.

BEST TIME April-June and September-October are probably the best times to hope for good weather combined with fewer crowds. Midsummer is unbelievably busy.

NEAREST AIRPORTS Some flights use the small Amerigo Vespucci Airport in Florence, but most major airlines use the Aeroporto Galileo Galilei in Pisa, about 50 miles (80 km) west of Florence.

ACCOMMODATION Plenty of accommodation of all kinds in Florence and Siena, but they can get busy in midsummer, when advance planning is recommended.

in Italy, and its cathedral, the Basilica di Santa Maria del Fiore, is its crowning glory. It is also known just as The Duomo, after its imposing and beautiful brick dome, which still dominates the city skyline today, almost six hundred years after it was completed.

That was in 1436, and the dome contains more than four million bricks, a spectacular challenge that the architect Filippo Brunelleschi took upon himself. Brunelleschi's buildings are everywhere in Florence and are part of the fabric of the city, but The Duomo was not something he designed. It was conceived by the architect and sculptor Arnolfo di Cambio, in response to a request for the largest dome ever built, to outdo the cities of Pisa and Siena. Di Cambio dutifully designed the dome, but had no idea how to build it; nor did anyone else.

Brunelleschi stepped in and said that he could, but even he did not quite know how he would do it. But build it he did, and The Duomo today, and the whole city of Florence, is a visual statement of just what the Renaissance meant.

Siena

Florence's great rival, Siena, is the other Tuscan city that best embodies the spirit of the Italian Renaissance. It is a rival and yet very different. It is a walled hilltown, smaller in scale than the grandiose Florence, and its center has been declared a UNESCO World Heritage Site. The façade of its own cathedral was finished in 1380, when the sturdy Romanesque and dour Gothic styles of architecture were about to give way to the lighter

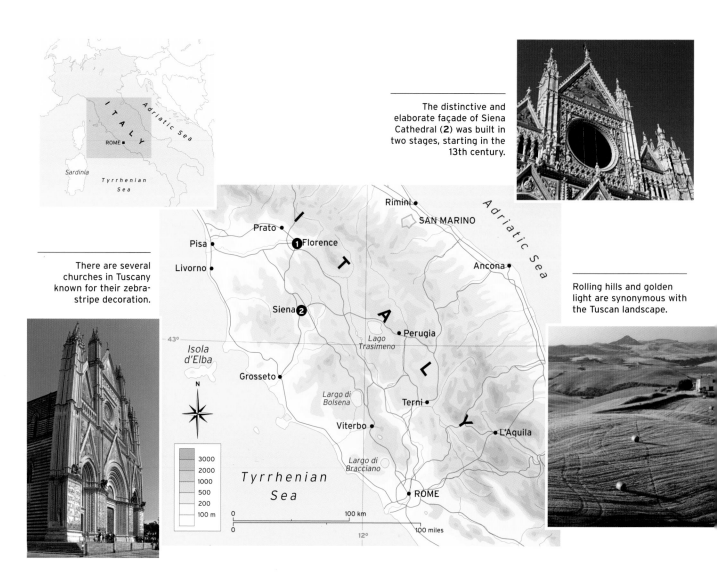

The distinctive and elaborate façade of Siena Cathedral (**2**) was built in two stages, starting in the 13th century.

There are several churches in Tuscany known for their zebra-stripe decoration.

Rolling hills and golden light are synonymous with the Tuscan landscape.

Statues abound in Florence (**1**), especially depicting David, who became a symbol of the Italian Renaissance.

and brighter Renaissance style. At this time Siena was one of the most important cities in Europe, almost as big and as important as Paris, much to the envy of Florence, less than 40 miles (64 km) to the north.

Although the cathedral's structure and façade were completed before the Renaissance really took hold, the interior of the building does show some of the flair of the period that was just beginning. Statues and paintings by several Renaissance artists can be seen in some of the chapels and on the altars. One fine Renaissance building in the city is the Palazzo Spannochi in the Piazza Salimberi, which now houses the city's post office.

Leonardo da Vinci

An hour north of Siena and to the west of Florence, the little town of Vinci would probably be virtually unknown if not for the baby that was born on April 15, 1452, in a farmhouse just outside the town. His name was Leonardo di ser Piero da Vinci, Leonardo the son of Piero from Vinci, later just Leonardo da Vinci.

Da Vinci was an extraordinary man, the Renaissance made flesh. He was a writer, a painter,

Siena's Palazzo Pubblico, or Town Hall (**2**), dates back to 1297, and work on its bell tower, the Torre del Mangia, began in 1325.

The Torre del Mangia (see above) provides an impressive view over the Piazza del Campo (right, **2**) and the Siena rooftops.

a scientist, an inventor, a musician, an engineer, a sculptor, and many other things. He will be remembered forever as the man who painted the *Mona Lisa*, but that was just a tiny part of his talent, one of the many achievements packed into the sixty-seven years of his life. He had a restless and fertile mind, and came up with ideas for things that were way ahead of their time—the helicopter, the parachute, gliders, bridges, tanks, hydraulic pumps, musical instruments, shoes that could walk on water, and even a primitive motor car.

This astonishing man studied anatomy and the way that birds fly. He kept detailed journals, with notes and drawings of his ideas—some of them practical, some of them whimsical. It was this kind of inquiring mind that was at the heart of Renaissance thinking. To learn what that remarkable period in history was all about you must visit not only the cathedrals and palaces of Florence and Siena, and the other Tuscan towns, but go also to little Vinci, to the Leonardo Museum, and even to the humble farmhouse where the great man was born, the illegitimate son of a wealthy lawyer and a poor local peasant girl.

ISTANBUL: ON THE EDGE OF EUROPE

One of the fascinations of travel is to journey through lands and see the cultures slowly transform. Around the fringes of Europe, there is no city as fascinating as Istanbul.

The Süleymaniye Mosque (1) overlooks the Bosporus and is one of the most distinctive buildings in Istanbul.

WALK DOWN ANY STREET in this vast and historic city, and you would have no doubt that you were in Asia or the Middle East. Istanbul does not look or feel European, at first glance. The noise, bustle, smells, heat, traffic, bazaars, faces, colors, and the general feel of chaos—all this is decidedly un-European, emphatically Oriental. But at the same time Istanbul looks toward Europe.

Istanbul has always looked toward Europe, though not necessarily in the friendly manner that it does today, as it seeks to enter the European Union. One of the problems to be resolved before that can happen is the question of Turkey's invasion of northern Cyprus. For the Greek people especially, this is too close a reminder of the hundreds of years when Greece was ruled from Constantinople—

as Istanbul was known until 1930. The two neighbors have never had an easy relationship, feuding a little like brothers who share some genes but are still very different.

It is this edge that adds another layer to the already multilayered city that is Istanbul. It is the largest city in Turkey but no longer the capital, which was moved to Ankara in 1923 when the modern Republic of Turkey came into existence. The city's name is less than a hundred years old, but it was founded way back in the seventh century B.C. It was ruled from Rome as the eastern capital of the great Roman Empire, before itself becoming the center of the mighty Ottoman Empire, which at one time spanned three continents. How could such a city not be fascinating?

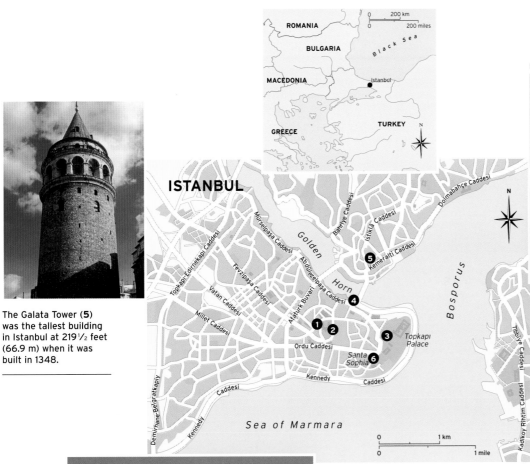

The Galata Tower (**5**) was the tallest building in Istanbul at 219½ feet (66.9 m) when it was built in 1348.

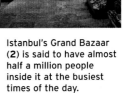

Istanbul's Grand Bazaar (**2**) is said to have almost half a million people inside it at the busiest times of the day.

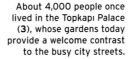

The Bosporus Bridge (**4**) is one of the longest suspension bridges in the world, opened in 1973 to link Europe with Asia.

About 4,000 people once lived in the Topkapı Palace (**3**), whose gardens today provide a welcome contrast to the busy city streets.

Grand Bazaar

In some ways being in Istanbul is like being in one big bazaar, and the city's Grand Bazaar is one of its major attractions. Enter this city within a city armed with a guide or a good map, or you may emerge baffled and blinking in the sunlight, in a part of Istanbul you've never seen before. There are several ways in and out of this maze, this covered labyrinth, where thousands of stores line hundreds of streets, and where it sometimes seems as if all the goods in the world are for sale—if the price is right. Here are spices and sandals, carpets and coffeepots; here are moneylenders, too, and a mosque, even a police station and a post office, serving the needs of the visiting shoppers and also

the sellers, who spend more time at their stalls than they do in their homes.

The Grand Bazaar has its own venerable history, having been founded by Sultan Mehmet II in the 1450s. It was part of a regeneration initiative for the city, showing that there is nothing new in that idea! In the next two hundred years, two more of Istanbul's most compelling buildings began to grace the skyline—the Süleymaniye Mosque and the Blue Mosque (or Sultan Ahmet Mosque).

The Mosques

The Süleymaniye Mosque takes its name from the man who commissioned it, Süleyman the Magnificent. It took seven years to build, being finally finished in 1557, and it is quite overwhelming in its beauty and grandeur, though at the same time the feeling is one of simplicity and humility. The Mosque is part of a large complex, which included a kitchen, hospital, schools, and a *caravanserai*, or lodging house, for passing travelers and pilgrims. It was where the poor of the city could come for medical treatment and for food, if they were hungry.

Fifty years later, the Blue Mosque was built, although its official name comes from its founder, the Sultan Ahmet. It is called the Blue Mosque because of the blue tiles used to decorate the domes and minarets on the outside, and also the blue Iznik tiles in the interior. Like the Süleymaniye Mosque, it is grand in scale and stunning in its beauty, and gives off a peaceful, serene feeling.

Topkapı Palace

If there is one other building in Istanbul that must be seen to appreciate the city's splendors fully, it is the Topkapı Palace. This was also built by Sultan Mehmet II, not long after he built the Grand Bazaar. It was to be his home, and then the homes of subsequent Ottoman sultans, for almost four hundred years. It was later opened as a museum, and a spectacular one at that, in 1924. The Topkapı Palace overlooks the Bosporus, the stretch of water that divides European Istanbul from Asian Istanbul. It is quite literally on the very edge of Europe.

-> The Proof of the Pudding

Turkey is renowned for its milk puddings. Although they are desserts, they are also eaten as snacks all day long and come with a variety of fillings—even meat. Look for a *muhallebici*, or pudding shop.

POPULATION 11,400,000

CURRENCY New Turkish Lira (Yeni Türk Lirasi)

CLIMATE A Mediterranean climate with hot summers, though winters can be cold and wet, even snowy.

WHAT TO TAKE Sunscreen, respectable clothing for visiting mosques, a phrase book.

BEST TIME Summer can on occasions be too hot, and winters are best avoided, leaving late spring and early fall the best times for visiting Istanbul.

NEAREST AIRPORTS Atatürk International Airport serves the European side of Istanbul, but the Sabiha Gökçen International Airport, which is on the Asian side of the Bosporus, is being expanded to cope with the increasing air traffic to the city. The Atatürk Airport is 9 miles (14 km) southwest of the city, with buses and a light-rail connection into Istanbul.

ACCOMMODATION Istanbul is a major conference destination as well as a tourist one, and has a lot of accommodation available. Finding a suitable room is rarely a problem.

More than 200 stained-glass windows let light flood into the Blue Mosque (**6**).

ROMAN EPHESUS

Ephesus in Turkey is a time machine that takes visitors back two thousand years to see what it was like to live in a Roman city, the best preserved in the Mediterranean.

TURKEY IS NOT AS WELL KNOWN for its Roman remains as Greece, Tunisia, Sicily, and, of course, Rome itself are, but in this one site of Ephesus it outshines them all. It is a vast area, but is so well preserved and in places sympathetically restored that it is in some ways like wandering around a city that has been only recently deserted. The scale and beauty of the main buildings really does take the breath away, and it is all the more astonishing because only about 15 percent of the whole place has yet been excavated. It has been called one of the greatest outdoor museums in the world.

The story of Ephesus is a long and complicated one, as it has been occupied by different peoples and in different places in the same general area. There were Bronze Age settlements here dated back to about 6000 B.C., but the name Ephesus derives from the town of Apasas, which is known to

have been here in the thirteenth and twelfth centuries B.C. It grew into an important town and was conquered by various people, including the Persians and, in 334 B.C., by Alexander the Great, who was welcomed as he liberated Ephesus from the Persians.

In those days Ephesus flourished as a Mediterranean power alongside such places as Athens and Sparta, and it was already a city of some significance before the Romans ever set foot here. In fact, it had existed for about a thousand years before St. Paul arrived here in A.D. 52. But when the Emperor Augustus made Ephesus the capital of the Roman province of Asia, it prospered like never before. Money was lavished on the buildings here in what was the third most important Roman city after Alexandria and Rome itself. But it was a comparatively short-lived prosperity, as

The Castle of St. John is the highest point around Ephesus (1).

The 1,970-foot (600-m) Arcadian Way leads from the Great Theater at Ephesus (1) down toward the harbor.

-> FACT FILE

CURRENCY New Turkish Lira (Yeni Türk Lirasi)

CLIMATE Mediterranean climate with hot dry summers and mild winters.

WHAT TO TAKE Sunscreen, comfortable shoes, a good guidebook.

BEST TIME Spring and fall to avoid the midsummer heat.

NEAREST AIRPORT Adnan Menderes International Airport at Izmir, about 20 miles (32 km) north of Selçuk.

ACCOMMODATION Plenty of small hotels and simple but comfortable guesthouses in the nearest town, Selçuk, 2 miles (3 km) away.

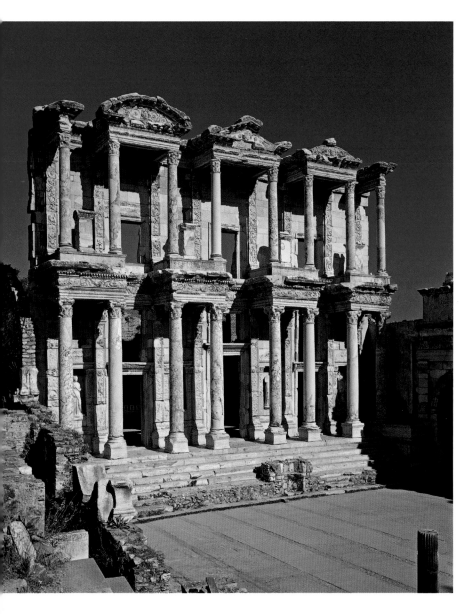

The impressive façade of the Library of Celsus (1) has been reconstructed from the material of the original building.

–> Pheidias

Pheidias lived in the fifth century B.C., the Golden Age of Greece, and was regarded as the greatest sculptor of the age. He created a huge bronze statue of the goddess Athena that stood on the Acropolis and was apparently visible way out at sea, and he was also responsible for the Athena statue that dominated the inside of the Parthenon. He produced statues at Delphi and Olympia, the latter apparently one of the biggest and most admired statues of the time. Sadly it is lost, like most of the work of this remarkable artist.

Ephesus was sacked by the Goths in A.D. 262, and although it continued to exist as a Turkish city, it never regained its former glory and was eventually abandoned completely in the fifteenth century.

Books and Brothels

Part of the appeal of Ephesus is that it shows a real and lived-in city, not merely a collection of ruins. In this way the inhabitants come to life, and the kind of lives they led is made very real. One of the grandest buildings is the Library of Celsus, which was finished in A.D. 135 and contained up to fourteen thousand scrolls. This was quite a small number by Roman standards, but the façade was built large to emphasize the building's importance. It had double walls, which helped keep out the damp and also moderate the extremes of temperature in this part of the Mediterranean. It was very much an active library, and was built facing east to get the best of the sunlight in the morning to enable the scholars to work.

What some of the scholars might have done when they finished studying is shown by the proximity of the brothel. An advertisement for the house of pleasure is carved into one of the paving stones near the Library, making sure that everyone passing by knew what was on offer. The façade of the Library is all that remains, as the interior was destroyed by the Goths, and the brothel, too, is now in ruins, as is the gentlemen's toilet nearby–although it is still easy to make out exactly what the building was.

The Great Theater

The Great Theater at Ephesus is thought to have been the largest outdoor theater in the ancient world, and could hold about twenty-four thousand spectators. Today it is still a wonderfully impressive sight, a vast auditorium that was part stage theater and part sporting arena. Sit for a while and it is very easy to imagine watching a play performed here, and even easier to imagine the bloodthirsty battles between men and animals, or between men and men, who often fought to the death for the entertainment of a raucous crowd.

Lost Wonder

One reason Ephesus is so wonderful is that visiting it is an emotional and not just an intellectual pleasure. It is as much about people as history, about brothels as well as temples and theaters. There is sadness, too, at knowing that only one column remains of the Temple of Artemis, which was not only one of the Seven Wonders of the Ancient World but was described by one historian of the time as outshining all the others in its splendor. How marvelous it would be if that still survived here at Ephesus and we could see it today, or at least get some feeling of that splendor. It took 120 years to build, and was on the edge of what is now Selçuk, again indicating the vastness that was Ephesus. The temple was said by Pliny to have been three times the size of the Parthenon in Athens, made almost entirely of marble, and containing within it sculptures by some of the finest artisans of the day, including the Greek Pheidias (see panel), the acknowledged genius of that period.

So much was lost and yet enough still remains to make Ephesus one of the greatest archaeological sites in the world. It is a place where you are rewarded not just by using your eyes but by using your imagination.

-> **The Best Way to Visit**

Although you can do day trips to Ephesus from Istanbul and from many of the vacation resorts in the region, by far the best way to see the site is to stay in the nearby town of Selçuk. Rise early in the morning and walk the 2 miles (3 km) to the site in time for its opening, before the heat of the day builds up and the tour buses start to arrive. You will never have the place to yourself, but you can escape the worst of the crowds and wander around in relative peace and quiet. Allow at least two to three hours to visit.

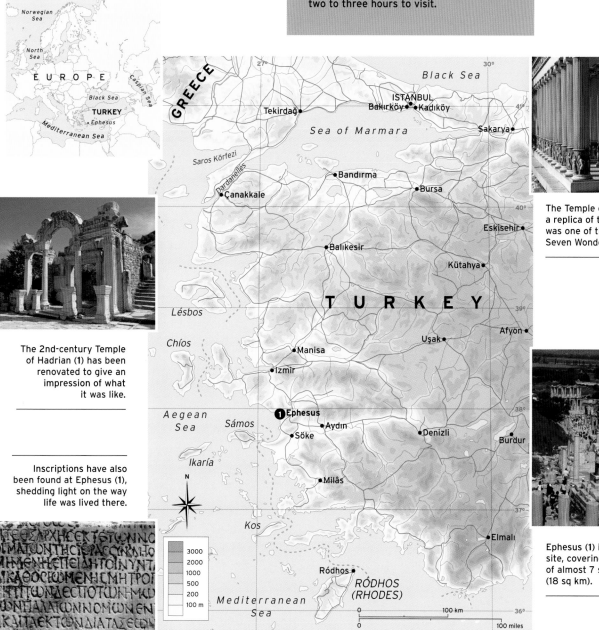

The Temple of Artemis (1) is a replica of the building that was one of the original Seven Wonders of the World.

The 2nd-century Temple of Hadrian (1) has been renovated to give an impression of what it was like.

Inscriptions have also been found at Ephesus (1), shedding light on the way life was lived there.

Ephesus (1) is a vast site, covering an area of almost 7 square miles (18 sq km).

125

WESTERN EUROPE

"I met a lot of people in Europe. I even encountered myself."

James Baldwin, American writer and civil rights activist, 1924-87

THE PYRENEES: A NATURAL BORDER

The Pyrenees mountains that separate France from Spain, with tiny Andorra squashed in between, may not be as high as the Alps, but they still boast beauty and drama.

THE HIGHEST POINT IN THE PYRENEES is Aneto, Spain's third-highest mountain. At 11,168 feet (3,404 m) it is a few thousand feet shorter than the highest mountains in the Alps, but size is not always everything. For many visitors the Pyrenees have more character, forming a natural barrier between France and Spain, and running for more than 280 miles (451 km) from the Atlantic to the Mediterranean. If the Alps are cool and Swiss, then the Pyrenees are fiery and Basque.

One distinctive feature of the Pyrenees is that they have no mountain lakes, but instead have many waterfalls and their own characteristic gushing torrents known as *gaves*. These are small—and sometimes not so small—but powerful rivers that race high through the peaks and produce the impressive waterfalls as they plunge over cliffs. One of these, the Gavarnie Falls, has the longest drop of any waterfall in France, plunging for an astonishing 1,385 feet (422 m) down a rocky face into the Cirque de Gavarnie. These *cirques* are another unusual Pyrenees feature that help distinguish them from many other mountain ranges—they are rounded valleys, hence the French word *cirque* or "circus" to describe them.

Andorra

Because of its unusual location, high in the mountains and surrounded by France and Spain, many people think of Andorra when they think of the Pyrenees. This tiny principality, slightly smaller than the Isle of Man or Guam and with a population of fewer than seventy-five thousand, is nevertheless one of the wealthiest and healthiest countries on earth. The wealth comes from curious tourists and those taking advantage of its tax haven status, and the health perhaps comes from its location high in the mountains, where people get lots of exercise, clean air, and a good diet, though no doubt the prosperity helps, too.

In a way Andorra is like a little Shangri-La, its main town, Andorra la Vella, resting gently on a plateau surrounded by the high Pyrenean peaks. It is an odd little place, its modern aspect represented by tourism and tax-free shopping, but it has an ancient side, too. Despite its remote location high in these mountains between two powerful nations, it has been inhabited since the

–> FACT FILE

CURRENCY Euro

CLIMATE The climate in these mountains varies enormously, and not just with the height. Generally speaking it is temperate, and the Spanish side, facing south, is warmer than the French side. The west, nearer the Atlantic, also gets more rain and snow than the east. Figures also vary with the height, but in midsummer you may get average temperatures of about 77–79°F (25–26°C), and in the coldest month, January, the average is nearer 41°F (5°C).

WHAT TO TAKE Clothing for all weathers and for outdoor activities, something warm for the evenings (even in summer).

BEST TIME Spring and fall are favorite times, as the summer can be intensely hot with the risk of evening thunderstorms. In spring the plants will be at their best, and fall is often warm and dry.

NEAREST AIRPORTS On the French side the Pau-Pyrénées Airport is about 40 miles (64 km) north of the border, as is the Tarbes-Lourdes-Pyrénées Airport; the airports at Biarritz, Toulouse, and Carcassonne can also be used. There are fewer on the Spanish side, with Barcelona being the main choice, about 80 miles (128 km) from Andorra, and Girona about 120 miles (192 km) from Andorra.

ACCOMMODATION Plenty of options at all price ranges.

The Cirque de Lescun (1) is one of the most famous of the cirques in the Pyrenees, in one of the passes between France and Spain.

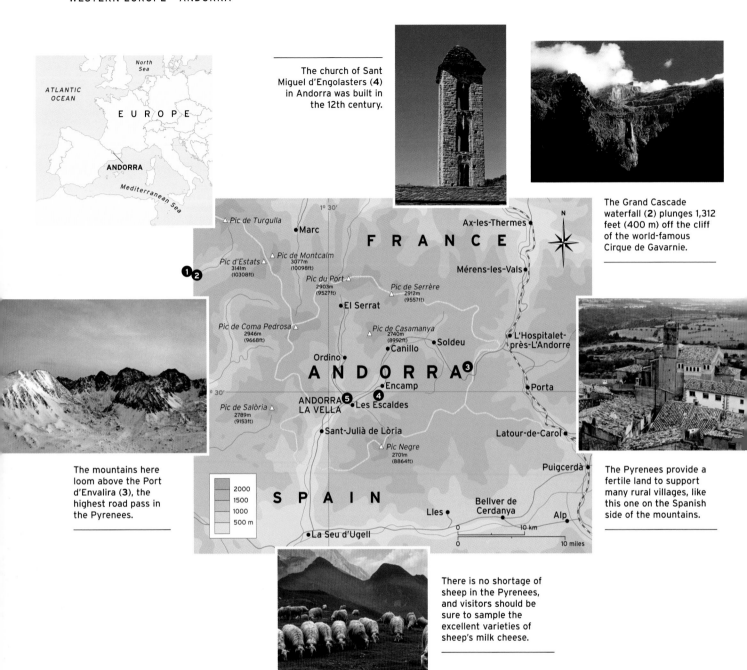

The church of Sant Miguel d'Engolasters (4) in Andorra was built in the 12th century.

The Grand Cascade waterfall (2) plunges 1,312 feet (400 m) off the cliff of the world-famous Cirque de Gavarnie.

The mountains here loom above the Port d'Envalira (3), the highest road pass in the Pyrenees.

The Pyrenees provide a fertile land to support many rural villages, like this one on the Spanish side of the mountains.

There is no shortage of sheep in the Pyrenees, and visitors should be sure to sample the excellent varieties of sheep's milk cheese.

late Neolithic era (about 3000-2000 B.C.). Some of its streets and buildings date back to 1278, when Andorra gained its principality status thanks to a treaty between the powers in France and Spain.

There is much more to the Pyrenees than Andorra. In the east they reach into Spanish Catalonia, that nation within a nation, and the western feet of the Pyrenees are in the volatile Basque region. They also spread into such characterful and distinctive regions like Aragon in Spain, which was once the proud Kingdom of Aragon, and the French district of Aude, heartland of the Cathars.

Brown Bears and Other Animals
The Pyrenees have their own endemic species of wildlife, of which the most notable is the

Pyrenean brown bear, though you are unlikely to see one. They are the smallest of all the brown bear species, and smallest in numbers, too. They have always been widespread in the upper slopes of the Pyrenees, till the twentieth century, when numbers dwindled to a dangerous degree, and by the early 1990s there was only a handful left. Then a few Slovenian brown bears (very similar to the Pyrenean species) were introduced and slowly started to breed with the native bears, although they are still hovering on the verge of extinction, not helped by the local farmers, who see them as a threat to their herds of sheep.

The Pyrenean ibex has already died out, and only recently, with the last known wild ibex killed by a falling tree in January 2000. In some ways it is a miracle the species had lasted so long;

Andorra la Vella is the capital of Andorra (**5**), the sixth-smallest country in Europe but one of the most prosperous.

although these striking creatures were widespread a few hundred years ago, they were down to fewer than one hundred in the wild at the start of the twentieth century. By the start of the twenty-first century, they were gone.

The Pyrenean desman is a peculiar creature—peculiar to the Pyrenees and northwest Spain, and peculiar in appearance, too. It is like a cross between a mole and a mouse, but it swims in the water, catching crustaceans and insects, and has a long snout and webbed feet. It grows up to about 12 $\frac{1}{2}$ inches (32 cm) in length, half of which is its tail. This strange and endearing creature, which lives only here in northern Spain and southern France, is classed as vulnerable, meaning it is on the way to becoming endangered unless its circumstances improve.

It would be a tragedy if the Pyrenean desman and the brown bear went the way of the Pyrenean ibex, as they are part of the very nature of the Pyrenees, which helps set them apart from other mountain ranges. The mountains will survive, but some of the blood will have drained away.

Walking Routes

If you want to see the best of the Pyrenees, and you're fit enough, then the GR10 is a way-marked long-distance walking path that runs for about 500 miles (800 km) from Hendaye on the Atlantic coast to Banyuls-sur-Mer on the Mediterranean. The walk is designed to be done in about fifty days, 10 miles (16 km) a day. That may not sound like much, but it involves a lot of up-and-down hiking even though it sticks mainly to the lower slopes. There is a similar GR11 path, also on the lower slopes, and the even tougher HRP (Haute Randonnée Pyrénéenne), which takes hardy hikers along the top of the mountain range.

–> The Cathars

The Cathars, also called the Albigensians, were a Christian religious sect that grew in Languedoc and southern France in the eleventh century, and were at their height in the twelfth century. They were condemned as heretics for some of their beliefs by the Roman Catholic Church, and it was to root out the Cathars that the Inquisition was founded in 1229.

PARIS AND THE RIVER SEINE

Paris began as a tiny fishing and trading settlement by the River Seine, where it grew to become one of the most beautiful and romantic cities in the world.

MOST CITIES OWE THEIR EXISTENCE to a river, and Paris is no exception. It owes its name to a Celtic tribe called the Parisii, who settled by the Seine about 2,300 years ago. They chose a spot on the Île de la Cité that was well used by travelers. It was a convenient place to cross the river, with the island in the center narrowing the waters, and so not surprisingly, a little village of fishermen and traders grew up.

Later, before Paris became the city of romance, it was the city of the Romans. They were the first ones who called the place Paris in about A.D. 300. A few Roman ruins remain, in among the famous cafés and jazz bars of the *rive gauche*, the left bank, but it is the nineteenth- and early-twentieth-century architecture that makes Paris what it is. It is a place, like Prague or London, where the pleasure comes from walking and looking just as much as doing. And a lot of what has happened in Paris has happened by the river.

When it was built, the glass pyramid outside the Louvre (1) was highly controversial, but now it is one of the most photographed buildings in Paris.

Pont Neuf

Stand on the Pont Neuf, the New Bridge, which was built in 1607 and is now the oldest surviving bridge across the Seine, and wipe the modern city from your mind. Picture that original simple village of fishermen and a few traders, and imagine the City of Light growing and spreading around it over the centuries—the huge edifice of Notre Dame looming over the river, and later the Royal Palace rising on the right bank, now housing the Musée du Louvre.

The river and its bridges may no longer be the lifeblood of the city, as they were for centuries past, but they are still a magical part of Paris life. Find time to walk the banks of the river, and cross from side to side over the old and the newer bridges. They all have stories to tell, pieces of the mosaic that make up the picture of Paris. The Pont Neuf was opened by King Henri IV racing across it on his horse, and it was the first pedestrian bridge

Like the Louvre pyramid opposite, the Eiffel Tower (**2**) was derided at first, yet today it is one of the most recognized buildings in the world.

–> FACT FILE

POPULATION 2,200,000

CURRENCY Euro

CLIMATE Temperate, with rare instances of extremes, although recent years have started to see more of both. It can rain at any time, and rainfall is spread fairly evenly throughout the year.

WHAT TO TAKE A healthy appetite and someone you love.

BEST TIME Perfect any time of year.

NEAREST AIRPORTS The Charles de Gaulle International Airport is about 14 miles (23 km) northeast of the city center, with a free airport shuttle bus linking with the RER rail network. The airport at Orly in the south is closer, at 9 miles (14 km), but less used by international traffic.

ACCOMMODATION Paris has everything you could want, from some of the most luxurious hotels in the world to cheap and comfortable little guesthouses, with many in fine historic buildings.

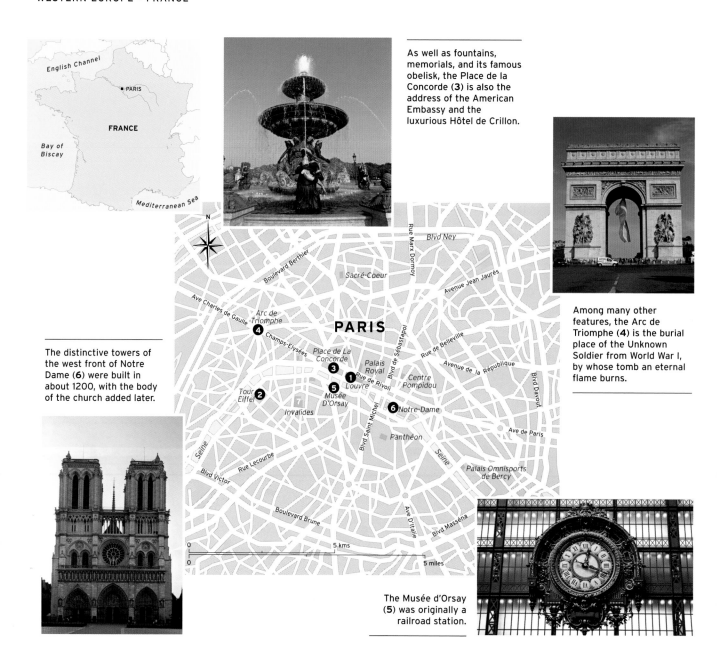

As well as fountains, memorials, and its famous obelisk, the Place de la Concorde (3) is also the address of the American Embassy and the luxurious Hôtel de Crillon.

Among many other features, the Arc de Triomphe (4) is the burial place of the Unknown Soldier from World War I, by whose tomb an eternal flame burns.

The distinctive towers of the west front of Notre Dame (6) were built in about 1200, with the body of the church added later.

The Musée d'Orsay (5) was originally a railroad station.

-> River Cruises

The Parisian Batobus cruises the river from April till December, taking a relaxing thirty minutes or so to visit the eight stops from the Port de la Bourdonnais, near the Eiffel Tower, to the Jardin des Plantes, to the east of Notre Dame at the Pont de Sully. Note that they travel in a counterclockwise circle, calling at places on the left bank first and then the right bank. Then there are the Bateaux Mouches, the huge boats that take visitors on river cruises. There are regular daytime trips and special lunch and dinner cruises, too. Bateaux Mouches is the name of only one of the companies doing this kind of cruise; there are several others, so look around.

to be built in the city without any houses on it. In summer the banks of the river along from here are turned into Paris Plage, a typically French bit of fun, creating a beach in the center of the city.

Louvre

Downstream from the Pont Neuf stands the former Royal Palace of the Louvre, showing that royalty, too, enjoyed being close to the river. It is now, of course, one of the greatest museums in the world, though Paris is so rich in art that almost opposite the Louvre you find the equally impressive Musée d'Orsay. This holds the state collections of art covering just the period of 1848–1914, but it is a period that was so rich, which included the hugely popular impressionists and postimpressionists, that the museum is just as big a draw as the Louvre.

A little farther down the river, the Pont Alexandre III was built for the Paris Exposition of 1900 to make it easier to cross from the left bank to the newly built Grand Palais and Petit Palais on the right bank. Cross from the right bank toward the left and you get the best view of the Hôtel des Invalides and the Dome Church, under which is Napoleon's tomb.

Les Invalides

The complex in which Napoleon now lies is a stunning example of Parisian architecture, built in the late seventeenth century by King Louis XIV, not a man for doing things on a modest scale. It was erected as a hospital for the soldiers of his army, at a time when he was having difficulty recruiting enough men. He thought the hospital would show them that they would be cared for if injured. Today much of it is given over to the Musée de l'Armée, an impressive museum about warfare, and behind it in the church is the imposing last resting place of the Emperor Napoleon.

Other bridges, other views: Cross the Pont de la Concorde toward the Place de la Concorde with the Egyptian obelisk at its center; cross from the Trocadéro over the Pont d'Iéna during the day and you will get the second-best view of the Eiffel Tower you will ever have. The best view is to be had by crossing the same bridge at night, when the tower is lit up. It is a view that is quintessentially Paris, and being by the river seems to provide an additional romantic glow to the tower's own lights. The Parisii and the Romans may have come and gone, but as Bogart said in *Casablanca*: "We'll always have Paris."

Directly beneath this dome in the church at Les Invalides (7) lies the body of Napoleon Bonaparte. Around him are several members of his family and some of France's most noted military leaders.

THE VINEYARDS OF BORDEAUX

The vines and grapes that grow around Bordeaux make up one of the world's largest vineyards. It's also one of the most stunning, with stately châteaux by the thousand.

The popular Merlot grape is grown in Bordeaux.

A view of Place de la Bourse (1) from the river shows why it is known as Bordeaux's most beautiful 18th-century square.

BORDEAUX CLAIMS TO BE the largest vineyard in the world for producing fine wines. Certainly it seems that you can head out from the city center in any random direction and soon find yourself passing seemingly endless rows of vines, at their best when ripe and luscious-looking under the late summer sun. With an estimated annual production of 800 million bottles of wine—including such famous names as Château Margaux, Pomerol, Saint-Émilion, and Château Petrus—Bordeaux has every right to think of itself as being at the heart of the world's wine industry.

There are many reasons why Bordeaux grew into one of the world's great wine regions. Julius Caesar called the area *Aquitaine*, meaning the "country of the waters," as here two important French rivers, the Garonne and the Dordogne, converge to create the Gironde Estuary. The Gironde is Europe's largest estuary, starting just downriver from Bordeaux and flowing into the Atlantic Ocean in the Bay of Biscay. The wide and long estuary meant that Bordeaux became a popular trading port for the export of its wines. In winter there is no snow or frost, and the Gulf Stream brings warmth and humidity, both of which are good for the growing grapes.

World Heritage Site

The significance of the wine trade becomes obvious as you walk around Bordeaux, a city with a prosperous feel and handsome buildings. In 2007 Bordeaux was made a UNESCO World Heritage Site, making it one of the most historically important places in France, alongside the medieval walled city of Carcassonne and Chartres Cathedral.

The city's most beautiful square is the Place de la Bourse, a square that is in fact a half circle gazing out across the Garonne. Lining the Place de la Bourse are several early-eighteenth-century buildings that would look quite at home on the banks of the Seine in Paris. In the center of the large open space is a fountain that is topped by a statue of the Three Graces. Traffic restrictions make it a perfect place for pedestrians, especially when it is bathed in the early morning light, and it is equally impressive when seen from across the river at night.

The prized vineyard of Château Pichon Longueville (2), Médoc, grows a wide range of grapes, including Cabernet Sauvignon, Merlot, and Petit Verdot.

–> FACT FILE

POPULATION 230,000 in the city, 650,000 in the greater area.

CURRENCY Euro

CLIMATE Bordeaux has a temperate climate with short mild winters and long, warm summers. November to January are the wettest months, but there can be rain at any time of year. In July and August the average temperature is 68ºF (20ºC), but of course many days are much hotter than this, with average maximums in the upper 70sºF (about 25ºC).

WHAT TO TAKE Some comfortable shoes if visiting vineyards, where there are often both indoor and outdoor tours and tastings done while standing.

BEST TIME In the late summer or early fall when the grapes are full on the vine. At harvesttime there is a sense of occasion but also less time for showing people around.

NEAREST AIRPORT Bordeaux-Mérignac Airport is about 6¼ miles (10 km) west of the city center.

WHAT TO BUY Wine bought at the cellar door is often at a good price, and by touring vineyards you may be able to pick up some rarer vintages held back from trade distribution.

ACCOMMODATION Bordeaux has a range of hotels from cheap to boutique, but there are lots of trade shows and events, so it is usually worth booking ahead.

Château La Lagune (**4**), Médoc, is one of nearly 9,000 vineyards in the Bordeaux region.

Some of the finest wines in the world are made in Bordeaux.

The skyline of Bordeaux, with the Cathedral St.-André (**3**) in the foreground.

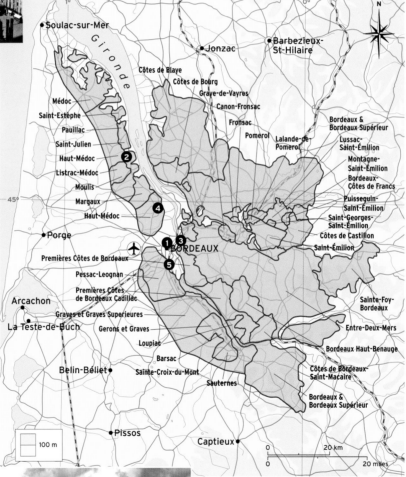

The famous vineyard of Château Smith-Haut-Lafitte (**5**) (left), and one of its vast cellars (right).

Chartrons District

North of here is the Chartrons district, historic home of the wine trade, a trade that paid for much of Bordeaux's lovely old city center, including the area known as the Golden Triangle. But it was in the Chartrons district that the wine merchants had their mansions often built with cellars to store the wine before shipping it out from the nearby *quais*. Today the winemakers tend to live on their vineyards, in equally handsome houses, and some of their former homes have been turned into boutique hotels, antiques stores, or into homes for the well heeled of today, like lawyers and bankers, no doubt with their own fine cellars.

The easiest way to visit the vineyards is to take an organized tour from the city's tourist office at 12 cours du XXX Juillet in the city center. There are plenty to choose from, and advantages include the fact that no one has to have the sober duty of driving. You also get to see some vineyards that open only for large groups and not for individuals. Usually a generous and impressive lunch is provided, with tastings of special wines that are held in reserve, and a chance to buy them, too.

It helps to study a map of the different wine-growing areas around Bordeaux, to decide if you want to visit the Médoc region, Entre-Deux-Mers, Graves, or the wine region closest to Bordeaux, the lesser-known Pessac-Léognan. Wine tours also often choose a variety of different vineyards, from ancient to modern, and from large commercial operations to small, friendly, family-run wineries.

Entre-Deux-Mers

One wine region of Bordeaux well worth seeing is the *Entre-Deux-Mers* region, which means "between two seas." It is actually between two rivers, the Garonne and the Dordogne, and is almost one solid mass of vines from one river to the next. The waters of the Garonne are a brownish color because of the large amount of clay in the subsoil, which is good for the vines, as it helps retain water. The rivers also ensure a high level of humidity—also good for the growing grapes.

There are some ten thousand châteaux in the Bordeaux region, but here the word does not mean a castle but rather a wine estate with its own cellars. There are plenty to choose from, and part of the fascination of vineyard visits is to see contrasting styles, and learn not just about the wine but the history of the area that is tied up with it.

The famous vineyard of Château Smith-Haut-Lafitte near Saucats was established back in 1365, and now produces some of the most exclusive of Bordeaux's wines. It is currently owned by the former French Olympic skiing champion Daniel Cathiard and his wife Florence. This is a château on a grand scale, with stone staircases, wooden roof beams, and dark cellars, like the Red Cellar, one of the biggest underground cellars in Bordeaux, where barrels disappear into the distance as far as the eye can see.

In contrast is the small family business of Château Montlau in Moulon, though this too is packed with history. The name *Montlau* means "hill of laurels" and refers to the time when there was once a Roman villa here, on this small hill overlooking the Dordogne. In 830 a wooden tower was built here to help control the area, and in 1150 a stone tower was built. The wine making here goes back to 1472, and the present owner, Armand Schuster de Ballwil, says that instead of modernizing he is trying to return the winery to the way it was in the nineteenth century. "Stainless steel doesn't make wine," he says. "Grapes make wine."

–> Wine-Tasting Etiquette

Wine-tour guides are naturally knowledgeable, and the wine novice or even the keen amateur is sure to learn something from them. Tastings are an inevitable part of every visit, and if you are at all uncertain, the guides will give you a quick lesson in what you are supposed to be doing and looking for.

Professional tasters always spit out their wine, as the appreciation comes in several ways and swallowing is not necessary—when tasting hundreds of wines a day it is also simply not possible. Even on a tour where you may visit only three or four vineyards, you may want to be cautious, although no one will notice if you do drain your glass. Be sure to drink water and/or nibble bread in between sips, both to cleanse the palate and to help soak up the alcohol. You will also learn how to tell a good wine from its color and bouquet, as well as its taste.

THE CHÂTEAUX OF THE LOIRE

France's Loire Valley is a land of vineyards and castles,
a fast-flowing river, fine food, and medieval towns that
are charged with history.

Peacocks add an exotic touch to the splendid Château de Valençay (1), whose 16th-century dome (to the right) is one of its most notable features.

LESS THAN TWO HOURS FROM PARIS, making it appealing to the wealthy and aristocratic in days gone by, the Loire Valley still attracts people looking to find a château of their own in a landscape almost too beautiful to be true. The valley brings visitors, too, keen to tour the gorgeous châteaux with their stunning settings and vast gardens. They also come to drink the wine, taste the food, and get that sense of well-being that seems to be magnified tenfold when you are doing these things in France.

There are over three hundred châteaux lining the banks of the Loire, and in the landscape around that has been called the Garden of France. The castles range from smaller buildings that might still be private homes for families (though some operate as hotels and guesthouses) up to the huge and grand mansions such as the Château de Valençay

and the Château de Villandry. The history, architecture, and opulence of these châteaux fill you not with a sense of envy, but a sense of admiration that humans could conceive, construct, and, today, conserve such magnificent buildings.

Château de Villandry

With so many châteaux to choose from it is hard to single individuals out, but there is no doubt that the extensive gardens at Villandry, which are works of art in themselves, make this one of the classic châteaux in the Loire. The house was finished in about 1536, and an indication of its grandeur is that during the French Revolution Villandry was seized and Napoleon Bonaparte acquired it as a home for his brother Joseph.

The gardens at Villandry are even more extraordinary than the superb house, and they owe

The gardens at the Château de Villandry (**2**) include these ornamental gardens, known collectively as the Love Garden.

-> FACT FILE

CURRENCY Euro

CLIMATE The climate in the towns along the Loire is pleasant, if a little wet. Average summer temperatures are about 67-68ºF (19-20ºC), and it seldom falls to freezing in winter, with snow a rare occurrence. Rain falls throughout the year, with an average of seven rainy days per month even in the summer.

WHAT TO TAKE A cooler bag, for food and drink you might buy at markets, and plenty of memory cards for your camera.

BEST TIME Summer for blue skies, but spring and fall are also good times.

NEAREST AIRPORTS Nantes in the west or Tours in the east of the region.

ACCOMMODATION A wide variety, from farmhouses and guesthouses to sumptuous châteaux.

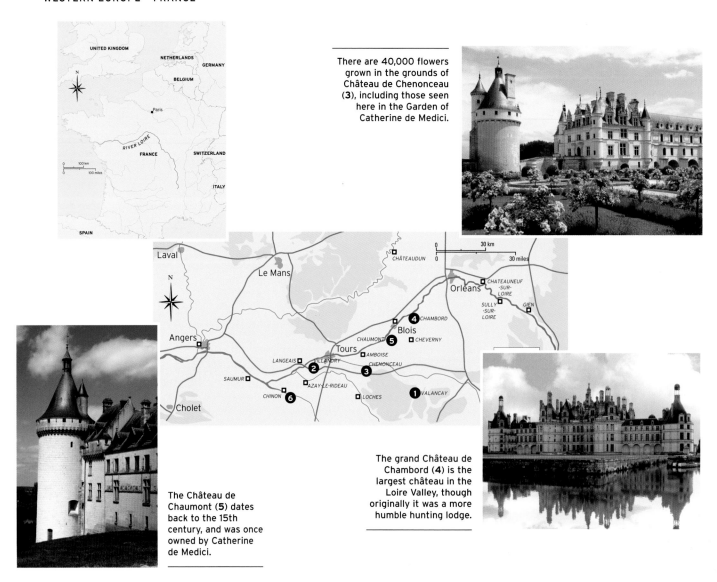

There are 40,000 flowers grown in the grounds of Château de Chenonceau (3), including those seen here in the Garden of Catherine de Medici.

The Château de Chaumont (5) dates back to the 15th century, and was once owned by Catherine de Medici.

The grand Château de Chambord (4) is the largest château in the Loire Valley, though originally it was a more humble hunting lodge.

their existence to Dr. Joachim Carvallo, who bought the Château in 1906 with his American wife Ann. Dr. Carvallo came to Paris from his native Spain to study medicine, and when they saw Villandry, they determined to buy it and restore the rather sad-looking house to its original glory. This they did, and it took them many years of devotion and hard work, but it was the gardens that took over, and they are regarded today as among the finest gardens in the world. They are so big you will need a map to make sure you do not miss anything, and their patterned shapes are best seen from the château tower, although there are viewing areas around the gardens, too. Villandry is part of the central stretch of the Loire Valley that has been declared a World Heritage Site by UNESCO.

Château de Valençay

As work on Villandry was completed in 1536, the construction of the Château de Valençay started in 1540, about 60 miles (97 km) upstream. Like Villandry, this is a masterpiece of Renaissance-style architecture, and another of the châteaux that was acquired by Napoleon. In this case he commanded his foreign minister, Talleyrand, to buy it so that he could receive visiting dignitaries in impressive style. Talleyrand obeyed his emperor, and the Château remained in his family, handed directly down the male line, until 1952. During that long period it was not only maintained but expanded to become one of the grandest of the Loire châteaux, and it remains so today.

–> Charles Perrault

French author Charles Perrault penned many of the most popular stories known today, including *Little Red Riding Hood* and *Sleeping Beauty*. He turned them into familiar favorites all over the world. Born in Paris in 1628, he pursued an active career in the arts and working for the state—for thirty-two years he was secretary of the Academy of Inscriptions and Belles-Lettres. He also wrote, but he was almost seventy when his book *Tales of Mother Goose* was published, which contained many of the stories that would make him famous and create a new genre of writing—the fairy tale.

Château d'Ussé

If many of the Loire châteaux speak of wealth and power, the Château d'Ussé reminds us that these castles also have a fairy-tale and romantic appeal. It is set on the edge of the Chinon forest and inspired the French author of fairy tales Charles Perrault. Perrault is famous for writing such classic stories as *Puss in Boots*, *Cinderella*, and *Little Red Riding Hood*, but he used the Château d'Ussé as the setting for one of his most famous tales of all–*Sleeping Beauty*. One look at the soaring towers and you will see that the inspiration passed on, influencing Walt Disney and his own vision of Sleeping Beauty's castle. Naturally a tour of the Château reveals a model of Sleeping Beauty in her tower, awaiting the arrival of her handsome prince–though while she waits, she does have stunning views of the surrounding countryside.

Other Châteaux

Each and every château in the Loire has some kind of story to tell, and there are many others worth seeking out. The château at Azay-le-Rideau appeals for its more intimate nature, and its pretty setting with its buildings reflected in a moat. The Château de Blois dates back to the thirteenth century and was once the home of King Louis XII, as well as being where Joan of Arc was blessed

by the Archbishop of Reims before fighting the English at Orléans. Chambord and Chenonceau are two more of the great châteaux, but seeing one after another can be overwhelming. Allow time for touring the medieval towns, walking in the countryside, visiting food markets, and sampling the fine local wine, all of which make this part of France so very special.

The Château de Chenonceau (**3**) has stood reflected in the River Cher for 500 years.

The Château d'Ussé (**6**) is open to the public, though it is privately owned.

THE PAINTING OF PROVENCE

The landscapes of Provence inspired artists Renoir, Cezanne, Van Gogh, and Matisse, and they still inspire visitors today, with many of the scenes the artists painted little changed.

IN MANY WAYS OUR IMAGE of Provence and the Côte d'Azur comes from the artists who lived here, including Renoir's impressionistic portrayal of subjects like the gnarled olive trees in his garden at Cagnes-sur-Mer, and Van Gogh's dazzling and sometimes disturbing canvases of sunflowers and haystacks, the café at Arles, and of swirling starry nights.

It is an inspiring landscape that rouses all the senses: the smell of lavender, the sound of cicadas on a hot afternoon, the sight of a field of huge sunflowers towering high, the touch of medieval stone walls, and, above all, the taste of the food and wine from this fertile part of southern France.

Van Gogh in Arles

A main attraction in the small Provençal town of Arles are its Roman remains, which were made a UNESCO World Heritage Site in 1981. Its arena and Roman theater date back to the first century B.C., and other remains, such as the baths of Constantine and the necropolis of Alyscamps, go back to the fourth century A.D. But it is not the Roman remains, the Romanesque church, or the excellent Musée de l'Arles et de la Provence

Antiques that cause groups of tourists to stand in the little place du Forum and take pictures of a seemingly ordinary French café. The snapshots are because of one man, and a rather eccentric one at that, who would probably have the visitors moving nervously away if he approached them in the street—Vincent Van Gogh.

Van Gogh painted the Café de la Nuit along with more than three hundred other paintings and drawings during his short time in the town. He arrived in February 1888 and planned an artists' colony here with his colleague Paul Gauguin. However, his increasingly disturbed behavior first drove away Gauguin and then upset his neighbors so much that they signed a petition to have him evicted from his rooms. He was often drunk, frequented the town's brothels, and smelled badly, as he never washed. It was on December 23, 1888, only ten months after he arrived, that Van Gogh pursued Gauguin with a razor and then cut off part of his own ear, which he then gave to a prostitute he knew. Gauguin fled, Van Gogh was hospitalized, and he later moved voluntarily to a mental institution at nearby Saint-Rémy-de-Provence. In May 1890 he moved to see a doctor in Auvers-sur-Oise near Paris, and by July he was dead.

Renoir in Cagnes-sur-Mer

Pierre-Auguste Renoir had a much happier time in Provence, and spent the last twelve years of his life here. He came in 1907 and bought La Ferme de Collette (the Farm on the Little Hill), partly to help save some olive trees on the land that were threatened. The trees were planted in 1538, and the olive groves are another typical sight in this Mediterranean countryside. Renoir did save them, both in reality and in his paintings, the trees as twisted and gnarled as his hands became through rheumatoid arthritis by the end of his life in 1919. However, he carried on painting by having his family tie his brushes to his hands. Renoir's home is now a museum, where you can still see his studio, his easel, some of his works—and his olive trees.

Hilltop Towns

Medieval hilltop towns are another feature of the Provence landscape. Renoir's house was well below the hilltop old town of Cagnes-sur-Mer, and a few

The medieval town of Haut-de-Cagnes (1) sits above the house where Renoir lived and worked, and features in some of his paintings.

The sunflowers of a French summer are mainly associated with Provence, and with the work of Vincent Van Gogh.

-> FACT FILE

POPULATION 4,500,000

CURRENCY Euro

CLIMATE The Mediterranean climate is hot in the summer, with little rain, but it does get down to freezing in winter, especially when the mistral wind starts to blow. June and July are the driest months, although some rain falls every month of the year, with September–December being the wettest.

WHAT TO TAKE Sunscreen, a healthy appetite, biographies of the artists who lived in Provence.

BEST TIME May, June, and September are good months, though there is no particularly bad time to go.

NEAREST AIRPORTS There are major airports in Nice and Marseille, and smaller ones at Cannes, Toulon, and Aix-en-Provence.

ACCOMMODATION Plentiful, everywhere, for all budgets, though cities such as Nice and Cannes get busy at popular times of year, so plan ahead.

Dozens of artists still live or have studios in and around the hilltop town of St.-Paul (**2**), and enjoy the café society there.

The vast lavender fields are a colorful scene strongly associated with Provence, scenting the air from June to mid-July.

miles inland is one of the most appealing walled towns of them all—St.-Paul. Often called St.-Paul-de-Vence to distinguish it from other towns of the same name, this one stands proudly and dramatically behind its thick walls on top of a small hill that juts out from the land around.

St.-Paul has attracted artists of all kinds, including the actors Yves Montand and Simone Signoret, and the American writer James Baldwin, who died here in 1987. The artist Marc Chagall also lived in St.-Paul, and is buried in the town's little cemetery. The medieval feel of the narrow and cobbled streets, where cars are prohibited, still appeals to artists today. Several live here, and there are art galleries galore—along with a fabulous private art collection at the famous Colombe d'Or restaurant, where artists including Picasso, Chagall, Braque, Léger, and Matisse all paid for their meals by providing paintings and drawings to the owner.

Artists in the Landscape

Several of the artists inspired by the Provence landscape have now, in their turn, left their mark permanently by having some of their greatest works on show here. Some of Chagall's stunning huge canvases are on show at the museum in Nice devoted to his work, and close by is the Matisse Museum. Matisse's finest legacy, though, is the Chapelle du Saint-Marie du Rosaire (Chapel of Our Lady of the Rosary) in Vence. It is often called the Matisse Chapel, as the artist designed every single aspect of it, at the request of one of the nuns who tended him when he was ill. In Villefranche Jean Cocteau also decorated a chapel, a fisherman's chapel, and along the coast in Menton people now get married in a chapel in the town hall that was also decorated by Cocteau. It is a striking room, and a fitting symbol of the union between these famous artists and this part of southern France that moved them so much.

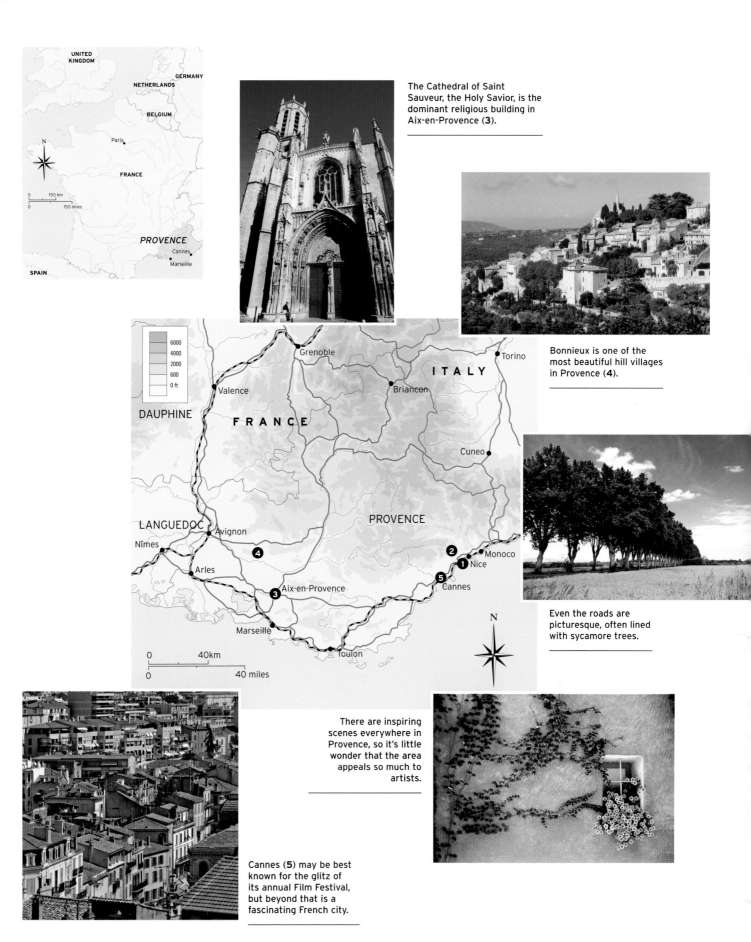

The Cathedral of Saint Sauveur, the Holy Savior, is the dominant religious building in Aix-en-Provence (**3**).

Bonnieux is one of the most beautiful hill villages in Provence (**4**).

Even the roads are picturesque, often lined with sycamore trees.

There are inspiring scenes everywhere in Provence, so it's little wonder that the area appeals so much to artists.

Cannes (**5**) may be best known for the glitz of its annual Film Festival, but beyond that is a fascinating French city.

147

PORT HOUSES OF THE RIVER DOURO

The River Douro rises in Spain and flows on into Portugal, through the beautiful port wine-producing area in the north of the country and its historic port houses.

ALTHOUGH THE SOURCE of the River Douro is in Spain, probably the best-known and most scenic stretch of its 557-mile (896-km) length is the region it flows through in eastern Portugal, home of the country's port wine houses. When you see the grapes in the fields and climbing up terraced hillsides in the sun, you just know the result is going to taste good.

There is more to the Douro than just port, though. It does not simply flow from Spain into Portugal, as for 70 miles (113 km) of its length it actually forms the border between the two countries. Here it runs through a series of steep-sided dramatic canyons, forming natural frontiers for two nations that in the past have had plenty of reason to want to keep a watchful eye on each other. Today the area is protected not for political reasons but to conserve it, as the International Douro Natural Park.

The Old Town of Porto (1) rises up from the River Douro, which brings the port down to the coast for maturation.

Once the River Douro turns west into Portugal and takes the shortest route to the Atlantic Ocean, it becomes not a barrier but a uniter. It brings together the port houses and vineyards on either side of the river, as it flows another 62 miles (100 km) through the port wine region of Portugal.

Port

Port wine has to come from the Douro Valley to be allowed to call itself that. The appellation was established and protected in 1756, which means it is the second-oldest wine appellation in the world—the first was in Hungary in 1730. Port did not exist until the previous century, as until then the Douro Valley was just another wine-producing region. But when British merchants arrived in Portugal in the seventeenth century, they wanted to take Portuguese wine back to Britain. To help preserve it for the journey there on ships, they experimented

The colorful and graceful barges, the *barcos rabelos*, with their port barrels, line the river in front of Porto's port warehouses (1).

POPULATION Porto 240,000

CURRENCY Euro

CLIMATE Porto has warm dry summers, and mild but damp winters. Summer heat can reach 104ºF (40ºC). The Douro Valley has half the amount of rain that Porto gets, but the summers can be even hotter, and winters much colder, often falling below zero.

WHAT TO TAKE A good dictionary/phrase book for the Douro Valley. Despite the long English connection, most visitors who go here are Portuguese, and other languages are not widely spoken.

BEST TIME Late September is the usual harvesttime, and in the weeks leading up to that the vineyards are at their finest.

NEAREST AIRPORT Porto International Airport is about 60 miles (97 km) west of the Douro Valley.

ACCOMMODATION There are plenty of towns and villages with accommodation in the Douro Valley, and Porto has all you would expect from a big city.

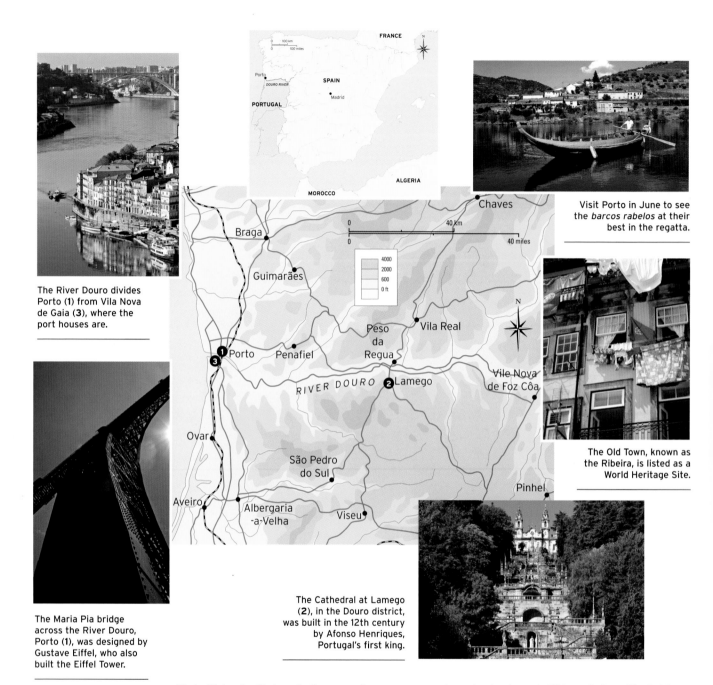

The River Douro divides Porto (1) from Vila Nova de Gaia (3), where the port houses are.

Visit Porto in June to see the *barcos rabelos* at their best in the regatta.

The Old Town, known as the Ribeira, is listed as a World Heritage Site.

The Maria Pia bridge across the River Douro, Porto (1), was designed by Gustave Eiffel, who also built the Eiffel Tower.

The Cathedral at Lamego (2), in the Douro district, was built in the 12th century by Afonso Henriques, Portugal's first king.

with fortifying it with brandy. Some results were better than others, and it was found that the stronger sweeter wines combined best with brandy, to produce an appealing and distinctive drink. Further experimentation was carried out—as it still is—to improve the quality and vary the taste of this unique style of wine. Port benefited from the fact that it started to grow in popularity just as the English were at war with the French. With no French wine being imported, the new drink, port, filled the gap very nicely, and an English-Portuguese love affair was born.

Vineyards

In Portugal the wine estates are called *quintas*, and many of them in the Douro Valley can be visited. Some of the vineyards climb in terraces up the steep riverbanks and still have to be cultivated by hand. To be there in harvesttime, late September onward, shows how backbreaking the work is, although some of the terraces have been widened to allow tractors to pass through and collect the grapes mechanically.

Many of the big names in port, as in the sherry from Jerez (see pages 164-167), are English and Scottish—names such as Croft, Graham, Cockburn, Osborne, Taylor, and Sandeman. They have a presence not only in the Douro Valley, but also in Oporto, or Porto, the city at the river's mouth.

Barcos Rabelos

The vineyards and wine estates are all up in the Douro Valley, and here the wine is made and stored. But after some maturation in the *quintas*, the port barrels have to be taken to the main trading port, Porto. Until the mid-1950s the port was taken down the river in a kind of boat that is as distinctive as the wine itself, known as a *barco rabelo*. These flat boats with a full sail were in use as long ago as the thirteenth century. They were specially made quite flat to enable them to take the weight of the wine barrels without sitting too low in the water, as there are places where the Douro is very shallow. In its upper reaches in Spain it is unnavigable in parts. Rather unromantically, the port is now transported in trucks.

Porto

The name of port, and of the country Portugal, derives from Porto, its second city after Lisbon. The Roman name for it was Portus Cale, or Warm

Port, and it was from here that the port was shipped to Britain. It is a city with a very attractive Old Town, and down on the river are the port lodges. They are still working concerns, but many now also benefit from visitors, who enjoy a tour of the lodge and a sample of port. There are no cellars or vineyards here, but the port lodges themselves are fascinating, with the British names rubbing shoulders with the Portuguese port houses, such as Ferreira, Barros, and Borges.

Anyone lucky enough to be able to follow the same journey the port wine makes, from the vineyards in the Douro Valley and down the river to emerge at Porto, will have had one of the best experiences Portugal has to offer.

Vines line the slopes of the Douro Valley (**2**), with the angled terrain allowing more sunlight to reach more of the grapes.

THE LEVADAS OF MADEIRA

The largest laurel forest in the world is on the Portuguese island of Madeira, and people visit by the thousands every year to experience the forest and walk the unique irrigation paths known as *levadas*.

The Pico do Arieiro (1) is the third-highest peak on Madeira, reaching up through the clouds from the valleys below.

THEY SAY THAT THERE ARE only two flat parts of Madeira—the seafront in the capital, Funchal, and the airport landing strip. And even the airport landing strip is supported on 180 huge columns, to cope with the island's undulating landscape. It is a lush island, stuck 580 miles (933 km) out in the Atlantic from its home country, Portugal.

About 80 percent of the rain that provides the lushness and the rich crops of fruit and vegetables falls in the north of the island, but about 80 percent of the people live in the more hospitable and slightly flatter south. The solution to this problem was found by the Portuguese settlers, after Portugal discovered first the neighboring

island of Porto Santo in 1419. In the sixteenth century engineers began to build *levadas*, which are water channels like miniature canals that carry the rainwater from where it falls high in the mountains down imperceptibly sloping paths to where it can feed the crops far below. The word *levada* comes from the Portuguese verb *levar*, meaning "to carry."

The *levadas* were—and still are—tended by the *levadeiros*, who walked the narrow paths built alongside the water to help keep the channels clear. Today the paths may still carry a few *levadeiros*, but they carry far more walkers, who enjoy the mountain scenery and the dramatic routes the *levadas* sometimes take.

POPULATION 245,000

CURRENCY Euro

CLIMATE Madeira enjoys hot dry summers, with mild but wet winters. Most rain falls from about October to March, but from June to August there will be very little, if any. Summer temperatures average in the upper 70sºF (about 25ºC), with January averaging about 59ºF (15ºC). But this is a mountainous island, and in the mountains it will be much cooler and wetter.

WHAT TO TAKE Warm and waterproof walking gear, and sunscreen for hot days. Sometimes you need both on the same day.

BEST TIME July and August are almost perfect, but it is a good year-round destination, and in January there is an annual walking festival.

NEAREST AIRPORT Madeira Airport is also called Funchal Airport and is 10 miles (16 km) east of the capital, Funchal.

ACCOMMODATION Some lovely old *quintas* or restored manor houses enhance the range of options, from 5-star luxury to charming little guesthouses.

Levada walking feels fairly safe when there's a protective rope to hand, though it's nerve-racking when there isn't!

Agricultural terraces make full use of the water the *levadas* bring.

Madeira's damp climate brings an abundance of flowers to the fields and hills, especially in spring.

Building the *Levadas*

There are said to be about 1,350 miles (2,173 km) of *levada* paths snaking around the mountains, and occasionally through tunnels, which can be a problem if you forget to pack your flashlight. In places the paths can be less than 18 inches (46 cm) wide, and with a sheer drop of a few hundred feet alongside them. Many *levadas* now have safety wires strung next to them, but not all do, and that can make for a nerve-racking walking experience.

The engineers and laborers who built the *levadas* had no need of such safety features. They used a very simple theodolite system to get the line of the *levadas*, enabling the water to flow gently downward without gushing too fast. Recently some engineering experiments were done to see if the lines of the *levadas* could be improved by using modern methods, but it was found that the lines were near perfect.

Then the *levadas* actually had to be built. The workers were often suspended on ropes from trees and from cliff faces as they hacked out the route, then built the *levadas* (at first of wood and later concrete) and also the paths that ran alongside them. Many lives were lost, but the result was this unique irrigation system that still works perfectly to this day—and now provides a recreational use, too.

The Laurel Forest

One of the most popular walks is along a stretch of the Levada do Furado, which was begun in 1911 but took sixty years to complete its full length of 34 miles (55 km), every bit of it done by hand. It goes through parts of the unique *laurisilva*, or laurel forest, which was made a UNESCO World Heritage Site in 1999. At one time these forests were common across Europe, but now they can be found only in the Atlantic islands of the Azores, the Canaries, and here on Madeira, which has the largest and finest example.

The laurel forest is a refuge for rare plants and some endemic species like the Madeiran long-toed pigeon, or Trocaz pigeon. This bird finds all it needs in the laurel forests and is dependent on them for

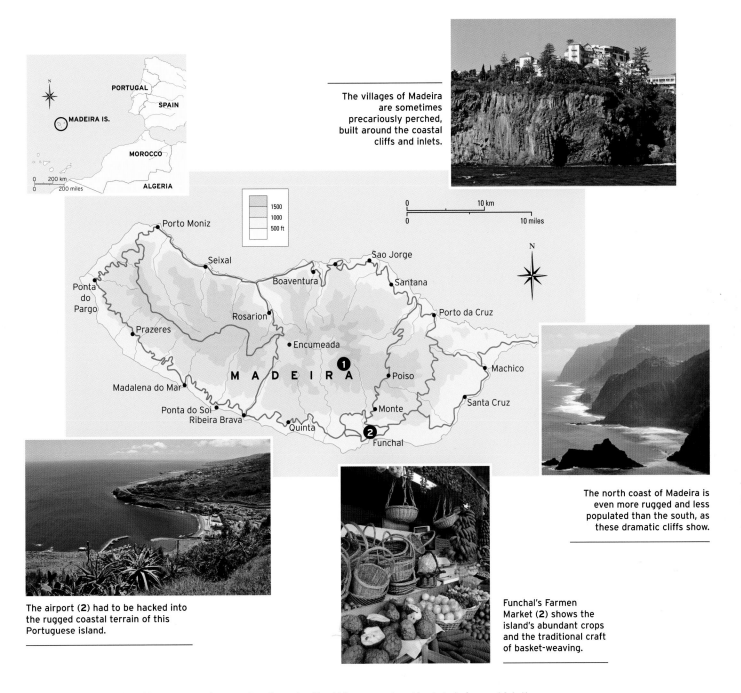

The villages of Madeira are sometimes precariously perched, built around the coastal cliffs and inlets.

The north coast of Madeira is even more rugged and less populated than the south, as these dramatic cliffs show.

The airport (2) had to be hacked into the rugged coastal terrain of this Portuguese island.

Funchal's Farmen Market (2) shows the island's abundant crops and the traditional craft of basket-weaving.

its survival. At one time they were endangered and down to about twenty breeding pairs, but now that the forests themselves are protected, the pigeon has recovered and the five thousand or so that now exist can be commonly seen, and heard, while walking in the *laurisilva*.

Curandeiras

In some mountain villages where the *levadas* begin, or course their way through, there are still found a few of the old wise women known as *curandeiras*. They are like medicine women, always over sixty years of age and always dressed in black. They have knowledge of the plants that grow in and around the laurel forest, and to what use they can be put. These include plants like liverwort, for cleansing the liver; kidneywort

for the kidneys; and maiden's hair fern, which they say can help diabetes.

Ideally you won't need the help of the medicine women on this green and pleasant island, where the only stress comes from walking along a *levada* and having the safety rail suddenly disappear–as they occasionally do. Those brief and nervous moments of edging along the path are exhilarating, though you might be ready for one of the island's other special features–a *puncha*–when you reach the other end safely. It's a fiery cocktail made from lemon and sugarcane, very popular at the end of a *levada* walk.

MOORISH SPAIN

Take the dramatic beauty of sultry southern Spain and add to it the Arabic legacy and you have a region of Europe like no other, with some of its finest buildings.

The bell tower of Seville's cathedral (1) is known as La Giralda. The bottom part was formerly a minaret and was the tallest tower in the world when it was built in 1184.

THE MOST SIGNIFICANT EVENT of 1492 was not the one everyone remembers, of Christopher Columbus reaching the Americas, but something that happened in the Spain he left behind. That was the year the Moors left the country after a presence there spanning 781 years, never to return permanently to European soil. The Arabs left behind them a proud legacy, though, especially in the major cities like Seville, Córdoba, and Granada. Indeed, the Alhambra Palace in Granada is considered the finest example of Arabic architecture outside of Arabia.

The Alhambra Palace

The Alhambra Palace was built in the fourteenth century, and its grandeur and beauty indicate that its builders had no idea they had little more than a

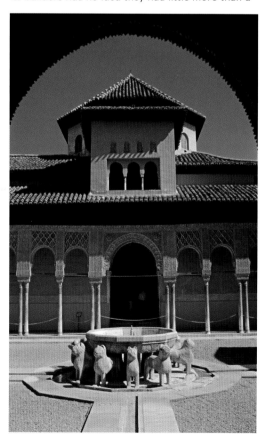

The Alhambra's Patio of the Lions (*Patio de los Leones*) (2) is named for the twelve stone lions that guard the fountain and spurt out jets of water.

century left of their rule in southern Spain. Why would they? They had arrived in Spain in A.D. 711 and within the short space of seven years had conquered most of the Iberian Peninsula as far as the Pyrenees.

The word *alhambra* means "red castle," the name derived from the distinctive local red clay used in its construction. There were buildings on this prominent spot overlooking the city long before the Moors arrived, but it was they who transformed it first into a defensive spot and then into its full palatial splendor. The castle came first, in the ninth century, not long after the Moors arrived. They saw what a powerful defensive location it was, from where they could watch the entire city, although the castle they built was not very strong, apparently, and began to crumble. It was rebuilt in the eleventh century, and then the transformation began in 1238, when plans were drawn up to build no fewer than six palaces in the citadel, along with towers, bathhouses, and a complex watering system for the gardens that remain one of the Alhambra's delights to this day.

So large is the palace and the rest of the Alhambra complex that you need a good plan (in both the physical and mental senses of the word) before setting off. And so popular is it that you need to book ahead, as the number of tickets each day is limited, currently to 8,100. It is worth it, though. The graceful arches, the rusty-red stone, the cool pools, and the greenery in places like the Courtyard of the Myrtles all combine to produce the soothing feeling that the best Islamic architecture provides.

Seville: The Alcázar

Seville is one of the other great Spanish cities where the Moors had a strong presence. It is a vibrant and pulsating Spanish city at any time, especially during its Christian Easter celebrations (see pages 168-171), but the Moors left their mark here. It was one of the first cities they conquered, in A.D. 712, and consequently became a significant site in their empire. The most impressive Moorish building was actually built after the Moors were vanquished from Seville—the Royal Palace of the Alcázar—with its mosaics and tiles, arches and courtyards, tinkling water and soaring interiors. It is a remarkable reminder of how sophisticated

The sun's rays highlight the splendor of the Alhambra Palace (2), with the Sierra Nevada mountains as a backdrop.

–> FACT FILE

POPULATION Seville 700,000, Córdoba 325,000, Granada 240,000.

CURRENCY Euro

CLIMATE Seville is one of the warmest cities in Europe; even in winter the temperature seldom drops below about 40°F (4°C), though there might be a few days of frost. In July and August the thermometer often reaches 90°F (32°C) and beyond.

There is very little rain then, and it rains on average only fifty days a year, with December being the wettest month.

WHAT TO TAKE In summer take a sunhat; you'll need sunscreen at almost any time of the year. *Andalus: Unlocking the Secrets of Moorish Spain* by Jason Webster is an entertaining account of travel in the area, as is Washington Irving's *Tales of the Alhambra*.

BEST TIME May–June and September–October.

NEAREST AIRPORTS There are airports in Córdoba, Granada, and Seville.

ACCOMMODATION All kinds, all prices.

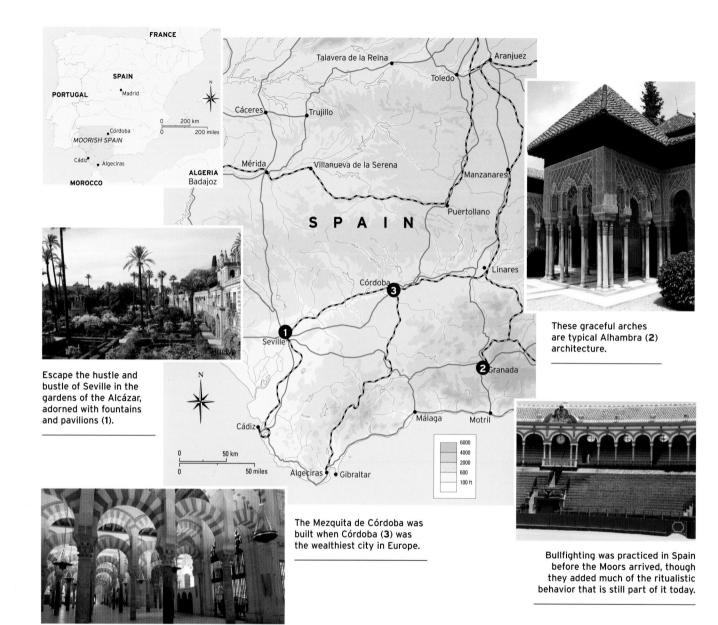

Escape the hustle and bustle of Seville in the gardens of the Alcázar, adorned with fountains and pavilions (1).

These graceful arches are typical Alhambra (2) architecture.

The Mezquita de Córdoba was built when Córdoba (3) was the wealthiest city in Europe.

Bullfighting was practiced in Spain before the Moors arrived, though they added much of the ritualistic behavior that is still part of it today.

and imaginative the Moorish designers and builders were. Work on the Palace of Pedro I began in 1364 during the reign of King Pedro of Castille, after the Moors had left the city, but the design continues the Moorish tradition, and Moorish workmen, still living in the city, carried out the construction.

–> Al-Andalus

The name Andalucia comes from the Arabic name for the areas of the Iberian Peninsula that they conquered: Al-Andalus. It referred to a much wider area, almost to the border with France, and is not the same as the present-day area of Andalucia in southern Spain. No one knows where the name originally came from, but there are several different theories about its derivation, including that it came from the Germanic tribe the Vandals, and that it was an Arabic version of the Lost City of Atlantis, the Island of Al-Andalus.

Opposite the Alcazár, Seville's grand cathedral was built on the site of the mosque, using some of its columns and converting its minaret into a tower. Nevertheless, the imposing Gothic style of the building was totally at odds with the graceful designs used by the Moors, showing what a cultural and aesthetic divide existed at the time between the two cultures. Also in Seville is the Torre del Oro, the Gold Tower, built as a watchtower by the powerful and feared Almohad Dynasty in the early thirteenth century. As well as watching for enemy approaches up the river, it was also used to stop them getting any farther as a chain was lowered from the tower and stretched across the river under the water to the other side, preventing ships from progressing. The fact that it is still standing, about eight hundred years after it was built, is a testimony to not only the style of its design but also the sturdiness of its structure.

Seville's Torre del Oro (right, **1**) may have been covered in gold, or gold tiles, but might also have got its name because it was a storehouse for gold brought up the river.

Córdoba

The other major Spanish city to be seen in order to get a feeling for Moorish Spain is Córdoba. The Moors arrived here in A.D. 716 and made it their capital. By the tenth century it is estimated to have had a population of five hundred thousand, which would have made it one of the biggest cities in the world. There were said to be twenty-seven schools and fifty hospitals here. Its most notable surviving building is the mosque, the Mezquita de Córdoba. This was originally a church built in about A.D. 600, but converted into the grandest of the city's one thousand mosques in A.D. 784. It was at one time the second-biggest mosque in the whole Arab world, and today its columns (more than one thousand of them), its arches, and its sense of space are as breathtaking as they ever were.

To see Al-Andalus, the palaces and the pools, the gardens and the graceful mosques, is to see an absolutely unique and beautiful part of Europe.

Córdoba's cathedral towers over the city's Puente Romano (**3**), which harks back to the city's Roman foundation.

GAUDÍ'S BARCELONA

The stylish and surreal buildings of the Catalan architect Gaudí are perfectly at home in this classy Spanish city by the sea.

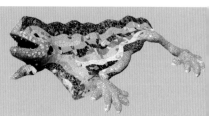

ANTONI PLÀCID GUILLEM GAUDÍ I CORNET–better known just as Gaudí–was a Catalan genius of an architect, a man who was to building what Dalí was to painting, and there is nowhere better to see his work than in the Catalan capital, Barcelona. Gaudí was born in Catalonia in 1852, and most of his most famous work was done in Barcelona, where he died in 1926.

Barcelona has one of the world's great streets–Las Ramblas. A river once flowed into the sea here, before it dried up (and the name comes from the Arabic word for a riverbed, *raml*), but today it is a constant flow of people, under the shade of the avenue of plane trees. On the way they pass flower vendors, buskers, cafés, newsstands, churches, and not a few pickpockets, so visitors need to take care.

Market of the Butchers

About halfway along Las Ramblas is Barcelona's main market, the Mercat de la Boqueria, the Market of the Butchers, though its official name is the Mercat de Sant Josep. It is housed in a glass and iron structure reminiscent of Parisian architecture,

with some modernist flourishes at the entrance. Inside, though, it is strictly traditional–fishmongers, cheese stalls, vegetable vendors, wine sellers, and the butchers who give it its name.

Palau Güell

Farther on down Las Ramblas is one of Gaudí's most distinctive buildings–the Palau Güell. This is the town house, or palace, that Gaudí created for the wealthy Catalan industrialist Eusebi Güell in the late 1880s. In the last few years the palace was closed for renovations, but it is now partially open again for visitors. From the outside you can see the distinctive Gaudí style–distinctive, yet as hard to describe as a Dalí painting. It starts with a grand Gothic design, but this is softened by Gaudí's own liking for swirls and flourishes, and the use of forms and patterns influenced by nature.

Even from the outside you can see how Gaudí was suited to this project. Two huge entrance doors are big enough to enable horses and carriages to pass into the building, and out again by the other door. If the visitors were staying, the horses would be led down a ramp to the stables, on the level where the servants lived, while the distinguished guests would be escorted upstairs into the mansion. In the receiving room the guests were seen through secret windows by the owners, who could check out their dress and improve their own outfits, if necessary. Even the roof is spectacular, with turrets and chimneys decorated in colorful ceramic tiles, and with stunning views.

House of Bones

Not far from the top of Las Ramblas on Passeig de Gracia are two more major Gaudí buildings. The Casa Batlló looks like no other building you have ever seen anywhere. It is also called the Casa dels Ossos, or House of Bones, as it does look rather like a building made up of bones taken from an ossuary. The balconies below some of the windows also look like masks. It is not just that there does not seem to be a straight line in the entire façade, but that the curves are so extravagant they make you giddy just looking up at them.

The other Gaudí house on the same street is La Pedrera, which is not quite as extravagant, although when talking about Gaudí, it is all relative.

Gaudí designed these distinctive mosaic works for the Park Güell (1).

La Pedrera, a private apartment block, has been called more of a sculpture than a building, and it is possible to visit both this and the Casa Batlló.

In 1900 Gaudí was able to express his creativity outdoors, too, by creating the Park Güell, now a municipal garden on the hill of El Carmel. It took him fourteen years to finish, and as well as the spectacular entrance to the park, which looks like a Greek temple crossed with a wedding cake, the gardens also contain Gaudí's own house, La Torre Rosa, which can be visited.

Sagrada Família

There are several other Gaudí buildings around Barcelona, and part of the fun of strolling in the city is spotting the outside of an apartment building and recognizing Gaudí's distinctive style from a distance. But there is one building that towers above all others as Gaudí's crowning achievement– or it will when it is finished–the Sagrada Família, the Roman Catholic Church of the Holy Family.

In 1883 Gaudí began work on this immensely grand and ambitious project, a Gaudí-Gothic

-> FACT FILE

POPULATION 1,600,000

CURRENCY Euro

CLIMATE Barcelona has a Mediterranean climate, with mild winters and hot summers, tempered by its location on the water. Rainfall is low and winter snow an unusual occurrence.

WHAT TO TAKE Beachwear as well as city stuff, and some smart outfits, as Barcelona is a stylish city.

BEST TIME Late summer if you want to swim, but any time is good for city sightseeing.

NEAREST AIRPORT Barcelona International Airport is about 6 miles (10 km) southwest of the city center, a short bus, train, or taxi ride away.

ACCOMMODATION This stylish and growing city has new hotels opening every year.

The Sagrada Família (**2**) is the architect's major achievement in Barcelona, and is still not finished.

cathedral that was to take over his life. Indeed, he worked on it for a total of forty-three years, including the last fifteen years of his life, which he devoted exclusively to this one project. He was working on it when he was killed in a tram accident in 1926. It is now hoped that the cathedral might be finished in 2026, a hundred years after Gaudí's death, and 143 years since his work on it began.

Words cannot do justice to this bizarre and unique structure, though many people have had something to say about it. The writer Jean Cocteau called it an "ideascraper" not a skyscraper, and George Orwell thought it was one of the ugliest buildings he had ever seen. Salvador Dalí loved it and thought it sensual, and Gaudí himself, when asked why the project was taking so long, said simply, "My client is not in a hurry."

These sentinel chimneys are found on the top of La Pedrera (3).

No explanation is needed for how the House of Bones (right) (4) got its name.

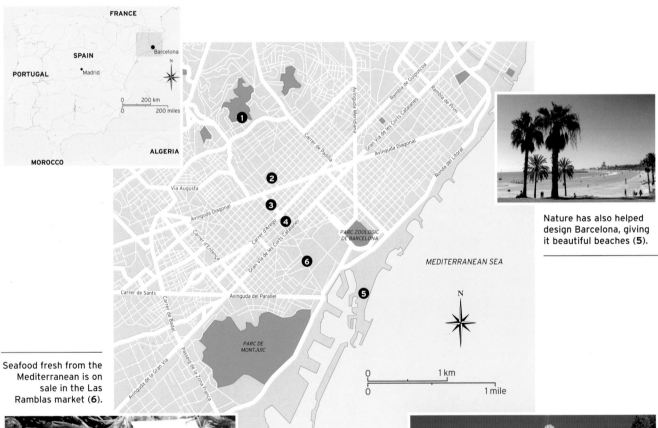

Nature has also helped design Barcelona, giving it beautiful beaches (5).

Seafood fresh from the Mediterranean is on sale in the Las Ramblas market (6).

La Pedrera (3), or The Quarry, was so dubbed as an insult, as the family it was built for and the public mostly disapproved.

JEREZ AND ITS SHERRY BODEGAS

Jerez is known for its sherry and it is also a city of gypsies, flamenco, and horseback-riding—but its historic sherry cellars are not to be missed.

TRAVEL IS ABOUT MUCH MORE than simply lying on beaches, or visiting cathedrals and museums. It is about discovering a local culture, a way of life different from your own. It is about meeting people, trying the local food and drink, learning something of the language and history of a place.

All these aspects of a destination are usually tied up together, the one affecting the other. By learning about the best-known local product from Jerez de la Frontera—sherry—you learn also about the landscape, language, climate, trade and history, humankind's inventiveness, and nature's remarkable ways.

Name of Jerez

For a start, there's the language and history of the town. Its name, Jerez, comes from the Arabic name for the town, Xerez or Xeres, reminding us that the Moors were here in Andalucia and ruled much of Spain for eight hundred years. That name itself was a corruption of the Arabic word *Sherish*, so from that we get the name of the drink of the region—sherry. It is also ironic that those notable nondrinkers, the Arabs, not only gave us the word *sherry* but the very word *alcohol* itself. It is thought to derive from the Arabic *al-ghol*, which was a genie or spirit who could take your mind away.

Jerez and Sherry

Sherry is made in only a small part of the world, a so-called Golden Triangle, whose three points are the neighboring towns of Sanlúcar de Barrameda, El Puerto de Santa María, and Jerez de la Frontera. In fact, the name Golden Triangle is misleading, as it suggests there are other triangles, and this is merely where the best sherry is produced. It is in this part of Spain that the *only* sherry is made, as nowhere else can call its wine by this name. Travel to other parts of Spain and you may not even be able to buy or drink sherry at all, as each region produces and supports its local wines. These days you are more likely to find a good range of sherries on menus in New York or London than in Madrid.

The bodegas at the sherry house of Domecq are among the many fine old buildings in Jerez (1).

Jerez is also known for its Gypsy culture, in particular the art of flamenco dancing.

POPULATION 200,000

CURRENCY Euro

CLIMATE Grapes are fussy about where they grow, and like moderate climates and not too much rain. Jerez has warm, mostly dry summers, and mild winters, almost an ideal climate.

WHAT TO TAKE A bottle opener and a phrase book for the local menus, which are mostly in Spanish only.

BEST TIME If also visiting the vineyards, late summer sees them at their prettiest, but Jerez is an attractive proposition any time of year.

NEAREST AIRPORT Jerez Airport is about 6 miles (10 km) north of the city, with buses and taxis into the center.

ACCOMMODATION There are numerous hotels in the center and farther out, many of them characterful old buildings, and inexpensive by European standards.

WHAT TO EAT Do try the tapas menus; local seafood is superb.

WHAT TO DRINK Be a local and drink sherry before, during, and after a meal, using your newfound knowledge to help you choose.

At the Royal School of Equestrian Art (1) there are dramatic horse-riding displays every week.

It took more than 500 years to complete the Gothic church of Santa Maria (1).

The Cathedral at Jerez de la Frontera (1) was begun in 1695 and as well as a mix of architectural styles has five different naves.

There is a great deal more to Jerez than just its sherry bodegas (cellars). It is a center for horseback-riding, bullfighting, flamenco music, and Gypsy culture. But there is no doubt that its name is known throughout the world for producing this one type of fortified wine–sherry. Although it is only one type of wine, it is capable, like other wines, of almost infinite variety–from crisp and bone-dry whites, to the luscious dark taste of Pedro Ximinex sherry. The varieties come from the various different microclimates in the area, and each town produces a range of tastes, but Jerez is the capital of sherry, and a tour of its many well-known bodegas is an entertainment and an education.

The Oldest Bodega

Domecq is the oldest bodega in Jerez, dating back to 1730. Next door at Gonzalez Byass they make the best-selling sherry in the world, Tio Pepe. The name simply means "Uncle Joe" in Spanish, and Joe was the uncle of one of the founders. The man could not afford to pay Joe for his work in the early days, so Joe cannily asked for the key to the cellar, to take his wages in kind. He used to invite his friends, too, so there was a popular saying, "Let's go around for a drop of Uncle Joe's Sherry." It remained as an unofficial name for the sherry, and when registered trademarks were introduced in Spain, the name was registered officially: Tio Pepe.

One of the storage rooms at Gonzalez Byass was designed by Gustav Eiffel, of Eiffel Tower fame, and elsewhere they have sherry barrels signed by the many personalities who have visited the bodega, including Margaret Thatcher, Orson Welles, Pablo Picasso, Cole Porter, and Martin Luther King, Jr.

Other sherry bodegas that can be visited include well-known names like Harveys, Lustau, Sandemans, Williams & Humbert, and Osbournes. Many of them bear English names because they were founded by English people, in some cases Catholic refugees from the Protestant-dominated England of the sixteenth century. Later they built up successful businesses here, and started the strong English connection with the sherry trade, a connection that has remained to this day.

Sherry Production

You learn not only history when visiting the bodegas, but also about the fascinating production process of sherry. Some of the old cellars are filled with cobwebs, but they have a part to play in the production of sherry. Spots of black fungus on the walls aid in the maturation process. The production of good sherry is labor-intensive, and a complicated process. Sherries from different years and different barrels are blended to produce a more consistent taste, which is why you do not have vintage years for sherry. The wine is also blended with brandy, to fortify it. One reason it was popular in the early days of sea travel was that this fortification meant it would survive a long sea voyage better than other wines.

So there is more than just sherry in a barrel of sherry—there is history, language, and climate, too. A whole world, in fact.

The annual Feria del Caballo (above) dates back to 1284 and brings thousands of visitors into Jerez (1) to see displays of horsemanship and flamboyant costumes.

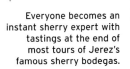
Everyone becomes an instant sherry expert with tastings at the end of most tours of Jerez's famous sherry bodegas.

SEVILLE AT EASTER: SEMANA SANTA

The celebration of Holy Week in Seville is one of the most dramatic religious celebrations in the Christian world, a powerful experience no matter what your beliefs.

JUST AS YOU DO NOT NEED TO BE AN ACTOR to watch a drama, you do not need to be religious to attend the celebrations of Holy Week, or Semana Santa, in Seville. The comparison with the theater is apt, because the events in the week leading up to Easter Sunday are as dramatic as anything you will see on stage or screen. In fact, they are more so, because you are part of the action, and the emotions expressed are real, not pretend.

Seville is the capital of Andalucia and the fourth-largest city in the country after Madrid, Barcelona, and Valencia. It is number one, however, for its Holy Week celebrations, the biggest event in the city's calendar and one of the biggest religious celebrations in Spain. Seventy-five percent of the Spanish people are Roman Catholic and many of them practice their faith fervently.

The Brotherhoods parade through the streets of Seville day and night, in their distinctive colored costumes.

Death in the Afternoon

The Spanish also have a love of drama and spectacle, with bullfights being one notable example of this. Love it or hate it, you have to admit it is dramatic. What could be more dramatic than, as Hemingway called it, "death in the afternoon"?

Well, there is one thing more dramatic than the possible death of a bull, or a bullfighter, and that is the story of the death of Christ, followed by his resurrection. Not even the Greek tragedians could have written a story like that. The Greeks also celebrate Easter in a big way, but nowhere in the world comes close to the way it is commemorated every year in Seville. If you wish to see it, you should book your accommodation a long way ahead, as the city fills to bursting point.

-> FACT FILE

POPULATION 700,000

CURRENCY Euro

CLIMATE Seville is one of the warmest cities in Europe, often too warm in August, when the temperature can soar to uncomfortable heights. In winter, though, it seldom falls below freezing. The period June–August sees very little rain, with December and March being the wettest months of the year.

WHAT TO TAKE Sunscreen, even at Easter, earplugs if you plan to sleep at night, and lots of energy if you do not.

BEST TIME May–June and September are the months with the least rain and most sun, without being unbearably hot.

NEAREST AIRPORT Seville's San Pablo Airport is about 6 miles (10 km) northeast of the city, with buses and taxis into the center.

ACCOMMODATION There is no shortage of rooms at most times of the year, but you should book ahead if you want a city center room during Easter week.

The cross bearing Christ is here carried in front of Seville's cathedral (1), the biggest Gothic cathedral in the world.

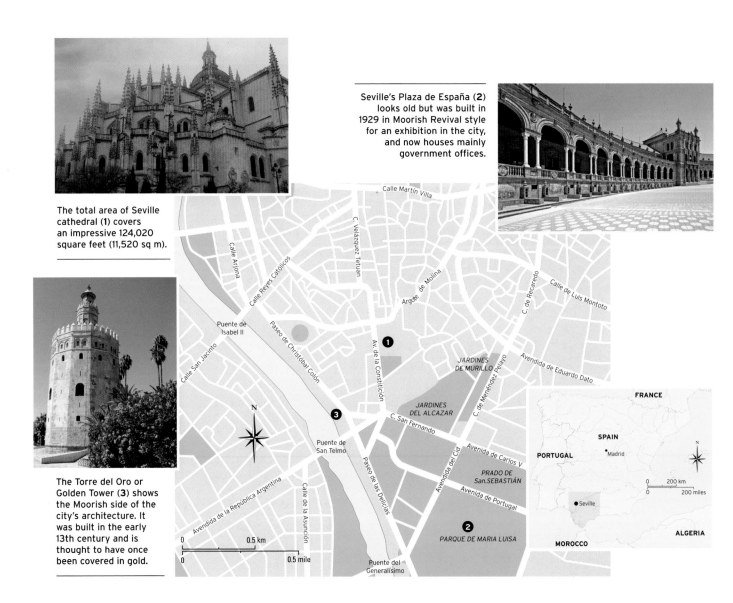

The total area of Seville cathedral (1) covers an impressive 124,020 square feet (11,520 sq m).

Seville's Plaza de España (2) looks old but was built in 1929 in Moorish Revival style for an exhibition in the city, and now houses mainly government offices.

The Torre del Oro or Golden Tower (3) shows the Moorish side of the city's architecture. It was built in the early 13th century and is thought to have once been covered in gold.

The Brotherhoods

The events begin one week before Easter Sunday, on Palm Sunday, when the first of the Brotherhoods start their processions. The Brotherhoods are groups of Catholic laypeople, sometimes affiliated with a particular church or neighborhood, but not always. Some have their own chapels, and membership is often handed down from father to son, as they have traditionally been all-male affairs. They perform religious and charitable acts all through the year, but at Easter they organize processions through the streets.

These are no ordinary processions, though. Some can last for up to twenty-four hours as each Brotherhood makes its way from its own chapel or church, through the streets of the city to the cathedral, and then back again. The men wear robes, and many of them are hooded, making them look rather sinister. They also carry huge wooden floats that can weigh more than a ton, needing as

many as sixty-four men underneath to take them through the streets. The floats have skirts around them, making the men invisible, so it is as if the floats really are floating down the streets. Beneath them, though, these dozens of men will be straining and sweating, just as Christ strained and sweated as he carried the heavy cross on which he was to be killed.

Music and Silence

More drama is provided by the music, with some Brotherhoods having rousing brass bands, others singing and chanting unaccompanied, and others traditionally processing in silence, which can be even more powerful than the music. The oldest of the Brotherhoods is called El Silencio, The Silence, and was formed in the mid-fourteenth century. Many other Brotherhoods go back to the fifteenth and sixteenth centuries, and there are almost sixty Brotherhoods in all. It is hard to give a definite number, as there has been a revival of interest in them, and new ones are still being formed today.

You will need some stamina and have to be prepared for lack of sleep if you are to experience the most intense moments of the Semana Santa. Shortly after midnight on Good Friday morning about half a dozen of the Brotherhoods begin their procession to the cathedral, including Los Gitanos, The Gypsies.

There is a strict order for each procession, beginning with the Cruz de Guía, or Guiding Cross, which leads the way for the followers. Then the *nazarenos*, the penitents, follow in silence, in their robes and sometimes barefoot, and in the center of the parade is the float, carrying the Brotherhood's statue of Christ or the Virgin Mary. If the Brotherhood has music, the musicians will follow, then more penitents carrying wooden crosses, like Christ himself did.

The scale of the processions is hard to imagine, and some of the larger Brotherhoods might have up to 2,500 people marching. It can take more than an hour for the entire procession to leave their church, and the bearers of the float have to make frequent stops to rest, such is the burden they carry. It is indeed a powerful and potent spectacle, especially at night when the smell of candles adds to the noise of the chants and the music, and the eerie look of the hooded penitents. Semana Santa in Seville is unique.

A good vantage point is essential for the most important Easter processions, as the streets down below can get unbelievably crowded.

Seville's cathedral (1) has the longest nave of any church in Spain, a fitting setting for the Easter services held here.

CENTRAL AND EASTERN EUROPE

"Let us satisfy our eyes with the memorials and the things of fame that do renown this city."

William Shakespeare, English playwright, 1564-1616

VIENNA: CAPITAL OF EMPIRES

Vienna has a grandeur that few other cities can equal.
Its architecture impresses at every turn, and it claims
to have the best chocolate dessert in the world!

IN A RECENT "QUALITY OF LIVING" SURVEY of
the world's major cities, Vienna came joint third
alongside Vancouver, narrowly behind Geneva and
the winner, Zürich. If the survey had taken account
of stunning architecture as well, no doubt Vienna
would have jumped into first place. It is undoubtedly
one of the most visually striking and distinctive
cities in Europe.

Vienna is the city of Strauss and Freud, which
hints at its mix of intellectuality and a kind of
formal fun. It is also renowned as the city of Wiener
Schnitzel and of Sachertorte, and any city that can
invent a dessert that combines chocolate cake with
apricot jam and whipped cream has to be one
that enjoys its pleasures. It has been known for
centuries as a center for fine cuisine, and for music
and other arts, which is not surprising, as it was
first the capital of the wealthy Hapsburg Empire,
then the Holy Roman Empire, and then the Austrian
Empire. Today it is the capital of and largest city in

Austria, and this rich legacy of history, wealth, and
power has made it one of the most impressive
and imposing cities to visit.

Many of its buildings are so grand that the
human passerby can feel quite insignificant. There's
also an air of mystery, perfectly captured in the
1949 film *The Third Man*, which was shot on
location in Vienna and starred Orson Welles as
Harry Lime. The film brilliantly evokes the feel
of a postwar Vienna, badly damaged, slightly
nightmarish, and yet with its magnificent past all
around. The film reminds us that Vienna is a city
of sewers as well as cathedrals and palaces.

Hofburg Imperial Palace

The greatest palace of all is the Hofburg Imperial
Palace, which has been the seat of power in Vienna
for whichever dynasty or empire has been in charge
since 1279. Today it is the official residence of the
president of Austria, and parts of it date back all

...e breathtakingly vast
...hönbrunn Palace (left)
...has equally impressive
...rdens large enough to
...ntain a zoo, a maze,
...eenhouses, French
...rdens, English gardens,
...orangerie, a palm
...use, a botanical garden,
...d many more features.

POPULATION 1,700,000

CURRENCY Euro

CLIMATE Vienna has a temperate climate, with warm (if sometimes wet) summers, but cold winters when the temperature can drop to freezing. It can rain at any time of year, with June being the wettest month.

WHAT TO TAKE Umbrella and plenty of money, as Vienna is an expensive city.

BEST TIME Go for the warmth and blue skies of summer, despite the increased chance of rain.

NEAREST AIRPORT Vienna International Airport is 11 miles (18 km) southeast of the city, with several train and bus connections, and taxis.

ACCOMMODATION Vienna has lots of hotels at all prices, but can get busy with both business and leisure travelers at some times of year. July and August will need booking ahead, as well as Christmas and when any trade fairs are on.

WHAT TO EAT Sachertorte is essential, at least once.

The Hofburg Imperial Palace (**2**) is home today to the Austrian president and was also the birthplace of Marie Antoinette in 1755, as well as having been home to various Austrian rulers and royals, most notably the Hapsburgs.

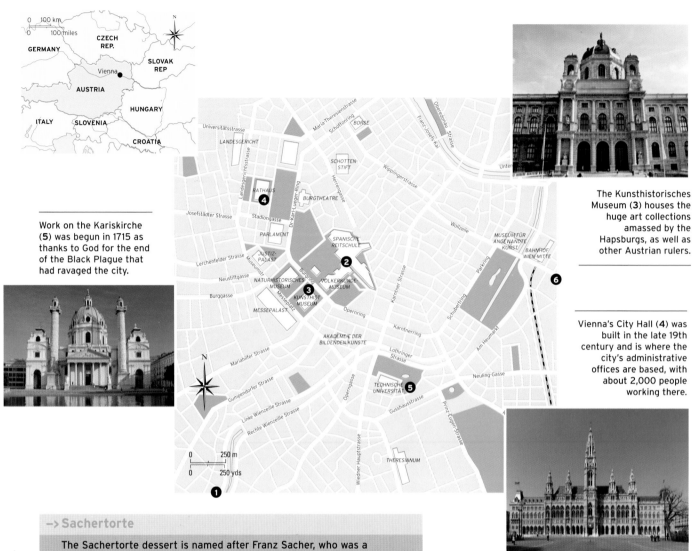

The Kunsthistorisches Museum (3) houses the huge art collections amassed by the Hapsburgs, as well as other Austrian rulers.

Work on the Kariskirche (5) was begun in 1715 as thanks to God for the end of the Black Plague that had ravaged the city.

Vienna's City Hall (4) was built in the late 19th century and is where the city's administrative offices are based, with about 2,000 people working there.

→ Sachertorte

The Sachertorte dessert is named after Franz Sacher, who was a sixteen-year-old trainee confectioner when, because of a chef's illness, he had to quickly create a dessert for a banquet for the Austrian minister for foreign affairs. The resulting combination of chocolate sponge cake, chocolate frosting, apricot jam, whipped cream, and chocolate shavings was a hit, and Sacher's name has gone down in history. The exact recipe is still a secret guarded by his descendants.

the way to the thirteenth century. It has been enlarged over the years so that the complex now also houses the famous Spanish Riding School, the National Theater, the Treasury, the Natural History Museum, and the Museum of Fine Arts, as well as the various former royal apartments and the Royal Chapel, where the Vienna Boys' Choir performs.

Museum Quarter

To show that Vienna does not solely live off its past, there is the Museum of Modern Art (MUMOK) in the recently created MuseumsQuartier (Museum Quarter), although even this manages to look rather dour in its own modernist way. Here too is the Leopold Museum, which actually has a larger collection of modern art than the MUMOK, some 5,500 pieces, but here again the grandeur of the past seems to influence the design, holding it back. Vienna is not a city where you would expect to see, for example, the frivolity of Paris's Pompidou Center or Bilbao's Guggenheim Museum with a giant metal spider on one side of it and a dog made of flowers near the entrance.

Hundertwasser House

There are surprises, though, like the colorful and surreal Hundertwasser House that was built in the 1980s. The reds, yellows, blues, and whites of its façade conceal an apartment and office block that has trees growing in some of the rooms and out through the windows, a roof that is covered in earth and grass, undulating floors inside, and an onion dome on top. It was designed by the Austrian artist and architect Friedensreich Hundertwasser, but this cheerful and unreal-looking building is the exception rather than the rule in Vienna.

Schönbrunn Palace

Vienna is about sumptuous palaces, not modern art. If the Hofburg Imperial Palace is not enough to impress you, take a trip out to the Hapsburg Summer Palace, the Schönbrunn Palace, a UNESCO World Heritage Site. This has been compared to Versailles, and is one of the most impressive—and most visited—tourist attractions in Austria. In fact, the first plans for the palace, drawn up in the seventeenth century for Emperor Leopold I, were

for it to be even bigger and more impressive than Versailles, but the plans were scaled down and the palace on which work began in 1696 did not quite top its French rival.

Still, the Schönbrunn Palace is not exactly a modest construction, with 1,441 rooms, give or take a closet here and there, and containing within its grounds such extra features as an orangery, a palm house, and the *tiergarten*—the oldest zoo in the world. There's also an unusual feature called a *gloriette*, which is a French term for a building put up in a garden in an elevated position, on top of a mound or a hill. The *gloriette* at the Schönbrunn Palace is one of the finest and biggest examples in the world, and gives a stunning view back to the palace and to the city of Vienna beyond. It is a good reminder of the past and the power of this great city.

Vienna is not all baroque and Gothic architecture—the playful modern Hundertwasser House (6) adds some color to the city streets.

177

PRAGUE'S OLD TOWN

Prague has rightly become one of the most popular city destinations in Europe, and after years under the gloom of Communist rule has emerged, sparkling and bright.

A CURTAIN FELL IN EUROPE IN 1991, an Iron Curtain, and if there is one city that has been affected more than any other by this change, it is Prague. From 1948 until 1989, a long forty-one years, the city of Prague was then capital of Czechoslovakia, a Communist state along with other Eastern Bloc countries. There was a brief spell of hope and hints of democracy in the Prague Spring of 1968, but this was ruthlessly quashed. Anyone old enough will never forget the TV news showing tanks in Wenceslas Square, and brutality on the streets, against the backdrop of Prague's beautiful old buildings.

Velvet Revolution

In 1989 came the Velvet Revolution, though, when several countries that were on the fringes of the Russian Empire rebelled against their Communist leaders and overthrew them, returning the countries to democracy. The result for Prague was a change like the people could never have imagined. When the Iron Curtain was pulled back, the West discovered a fabulously beautiful city, a Paris of Eastern Europe, and visitors began to go there in the millions.

Prague's economy was transformed. For most it was a blessing, for some a curse, as the once quiet, cobbled streets were soon packed shoulder to shoulder with visitors. But who could blame people for wanting to see this wonderful city that had once been, if not quite forbidden, at least forbidding?

The New Town, The Old Town

The city remains as busy and popular as ever. And, of course, just as beautiful. Prague Castle—the largest ancient castle in the world—attracts many visitors, as does the New Town area, in particular those who want to see that grandest of European squares, Wenceslas Square, but there is no doubt that it is the Old Town that is the most picturesque and historic part of this very special city.

The Astronomical Clock (1) on the Old Town Hall is more than 500 years old, and is still in good working order.

–> FACT FILE

POPULATION 1,200,000

CURRENCY Czech koruna

CLIMATE Prague has a comparatively mild climate, but the warm summers can be wet and in midwinter the temperature can plunge to freezing, though it doesn't snow too often.

WHAT TO TAKE Your camera, all-weather clothing, and plenty of patience to cope with crowds.

BEST TIME March–April and September–October have a good combination of drier days and warmer temperatures.

NEAREST AIRPORT The Ruzyne International Airport that serves Prague is 12 miles (20 km) northwest of the city. Transport connections include an airport bus taking passengers to the nearest Metro station, a night bus service after the Metro is closed, and taxis.

ACCOMMODATION The tourist boom has brought an increase in luxury hotels, and prices in the city center are quite expensive, with a lack of good-quality budget accommodation.

Across the Vltava River from the Old Town stands Prague Castle (**2**), incorporating St. Vitus Cathedral, whose spires provide its crowning glory.

However, in a city as old as this, terms like *new* and *old* are relative. The New Town or Nové Město was built in the fourteenth century during the reign of King Charles IV, after whom the Charles Bridge is named. This bridge was built to connect the New Town to the area of Malá Strana, on the other side of the Vltava River. The Malá Strana, or Little Quarter, had itself been built below Prague Castle in 1257.

Old Town Square

Any journey around the Old Town, the Staré Město district, begins and will probably end at the Old Town Square, one of the most impressive squares in the whole of Europe. It dates back to at least the eleventh century, when a market was known to be held here. Part of its charm, and of the Old Town generally, is that it has grown up in a natural rather than a planned manner. Streets go off at angles, making sudden bends and twists, and most of the area today is pedestrianized—which is just as well, as so many people stroll around gazing up in awe at the splendor of the buildings, rather than watching where they are walking.

One building people are certainly staring up at, on the hour, is the Old Town Hall, whose Astronomical Clock is one of the city's most famous features. The first clock on the Town Hall was built in 1410, and part of the workings still remain in the present clock, which mostly dates from 1490, though it has been added to and rebuilt over the centuries. This incredible feat of engineering includes a calendar at the bottom, with a rotating clock above it that indicates three different kinds of time. And above that, carved wooden apostles and other figures (including a skeleton) come out and process just before the clock strikes the hour.

All around the Old Town Square, buildings compete for your attention, demanding to be photographed. Seeming to peer over a pretty parade of houses are the Gothic towers of the Týn Church, or to give it its full title, the Church of Our Lady in front of Týn. Work on this, the main church in the Old Town, began in 1365, but the roof was not completed until the 1450s, and the southern tower not finished until 1511.

On the south side of the Old Town Square is a building that is easy to miss: At the Stone Ram. The practice of giving buildings—including the bars—names like this comes from a time when most people were illiterate, and instead of a written

The Vltava River is the longest river in the Czech Republic and passes through Prague beneath many beautiful and historic bridges.

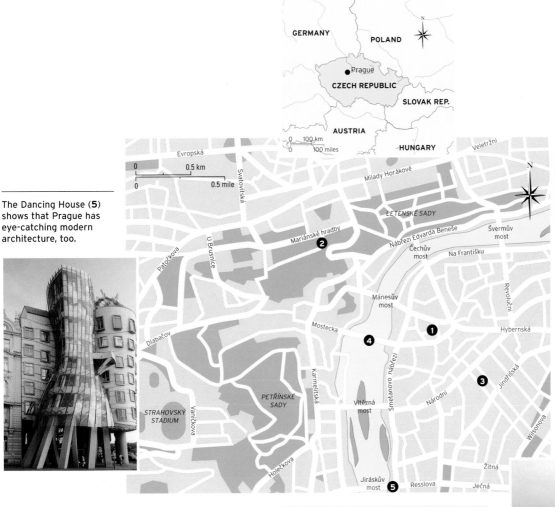

The Wenceslas Monument (**3**) looks down over Wenceslas Square, scene of many meetings and political protests over the years.

The Dancing House (**5**) shows that Prague has eye-catching modern architecture, too.

The Church of Our Lady in Front of Týn (**1**) stands proudly on the Old Town Square.

The Jiráskův (Charles) Bridge (**4**) is the most famous in Prague and dates back to the 14th century.

name, a painting or carving would be used to differentiate each address. Here where you see a rather elongated stone ram, there used to live a lady named Berta Fanta. She held literary salons that attracted Prague writers and intellectuals, and one regular attendee was Franz Kafka, probably Prague's most famous writer—though not until well after he died.

These few buildings are just a small glimpse of the treasures to be found, sometimes hiding, in the streets and squares of Prague's Old Town. It is one of the most handsome quarters in one of Europe's finest cities.

-> Franz Kafka

Franz Kafka (1883-1924) was born in Prague and is now regarded as one of the greatest European writers, though he had very little success in his lifetime. His novels such as *The Trial* and *The Castle* describe nightmarish, bureaucratic worlds, and in some ways were foretastes of the Communistic oppressions to come. His best-known work is probably the strange story "Metamorphosis," in which the main character wakes up one morning to find he has turned into a giant insect.

THE CASTLES OF BOHEMIA

The Czech countryside of Bohemia harbors hundreds of castles, which are among the most historic and beautiful in Europe.

WHETHER YOU DRIVE, cycle, walk, or travel through Bohemia on public transport, it seems there are castles wherever you look. This wonderfully scenic part of Central Europe, which makes up about two-thirds of the Czech Republic, is filled with wooded hills and rolling farmland, and with towns and villages that seem to have stepped out of a medieval fairy tale. So, too, do the castles that adorn the landscape. There are many hundreds of castles in Bohemia that range from the grand and Gothic to more humble family homes.

Landštejn Castle might look sturdy, but it's a deceptive view, as much of it is in ruins (1).

The Velvet Revolution

What makes this area all the more interesting is that its story is as much in the recent past as in the distant past. It is only in the last twenty years, since the Velvet Revolution of 1989 in the former Czechoslovakia, that some of these castles have been returned to their rightful historic owners. In 1938 the part of western Bohemia known as the Sudetenland was annexed to Nazi Germany. Then from 1939 to 1945 the rest of Bohemia, along with Moravia, became a German protectorate. After the war, right through until that Velvet Revolution, the whole of Czechoslovakia was, to a greater or lesser degree, under the control of the Soviet Union. So between 1938 and 1989, many people either abandoned their homes to flee to a safe refuge or a more democratic way of life, or had their homes confiscated by the state.

In the years since 1989, people have been returning and trying to reclaim the land and houses they once owned. And since tourism started to boom, first in Prague and then in the rest of the Czech Republic, there has been a greater incentive to open castles to the public, to help raise funds for what in some cases is much-needed restoration work.

Český Krumlov

One of the most famous and beautiful castles in southern Bohemia is that at Český Krumlov. The whole Old Town that grew around the castle in this attractive riverside town has been declared a UNESCO World Heritage Site, one of no fewer than a dozen within the Czech Republic, putting Český Krumlov on a par with the Old Town of Prague.

Like Prague, Český Krumlov stands on a bend in the Vltava River, the longest river in the country, and lies between Prague and the Austrian border. In the late twelfth century the river here could be easily forded, so it became an important point on the Vltava, and by the turn of the thirteenth century the grand castle was already an imposing site, elegantly curving above one of the river bends. It became one of the largest castles in Central Europe, and has five different courtyards inside it.

Although the castle has been added to and altered over the centuries, many of its original features survive. The most striking of these is its

POPULATION 6,250,000

CURRENCY Czech koruna

CLIMATE Bohemia has a continental climate, with hot summers (though they can also be wet) and cold winters, when snow is common. Summer temperatures can reach the high 80s°F (low 30s°C).

WHAT TO TAKE Outdoor clothing for hiking, a good phrase book.

BEST TIME Summer

NEAREST AIRPORT Prague

ACCOMMODATION From smart spa resorts to country lodges and simpler rural inns.

At 197 feet (60 m) high, the Great Tower dominates Karlštejn Castle (**2**) and contains within it the 14th-century Chapel of the Holy Cross.

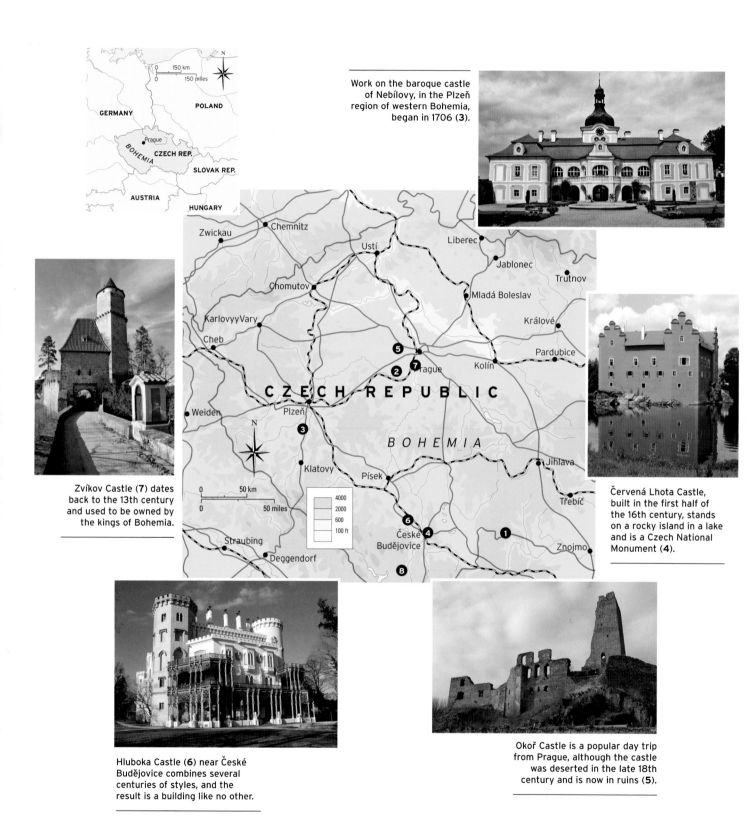

Work on the baroque castle of Nebílovy, in the Plzeň region of western Bohemia, began in 1706 (**3**).

Zvíkov Castle (**7**) dates back to the 13th century and used to be owned by the kings of Bohemia.

Červená Lhota Castle, built in the first half of the 16th century, stands on a rocky island in a lake and is a Czech National Monument (**4**).

Hluboka Castle (**6**) near České Budějovice combines several centuries of styles, and the result is a building like no other.

Okoř Castle is a popular day trip from Prague, although the castle was deserted in the late 18th century and is now in ruins (**5**).

eighteenth-century baroque theater. It was built by the Schwarzenberg family, who owned the castle from 1719 until 1945. This huge and grand theater has survived intact, complete with its scenery, props, and all the stage machinery. The theater is so precious and rare that it is now used only three times a year, to help preserve it.

Landštejn Castle

Even older than Český Krumlov, Landštejn Castle was built at the start of the twelfth century. It has survived remarkably well, and is one of the biggest and best-preserved castles from that era in the whole of Europe. One of its surviving towers is six floors high, and can still be seen just as it was, although the height of its towers led to the castle's destruction, as one was hit by lightning in 1771 and the castle burned to the ground, leaving only the stone walls that we see today.

Karlštejn Castle

Karlštejn Castle is a few miles southwest of Prague, which was one day on horseback when it was built by King Charles IV in 1348 as a retreat from the capital. It is easily visited on a day trip from Prague, and is one of the most remarkable of the country's many castles. At the time, Charles IV was also the Holy Roman Emperor, and the castle was used to house the empire's crown jewels, the Czech royal treasures, and the holy relics owned by the king, including a piece of the true cross. This was housed in the Chapel of the Holy Cross, which was consecrated in 1357 and can still be visited today—though you need to book in advance. The chapel still has its original fourteenth-century wall paintings, done by the most talented Prague painter of that era, Master Theodoric. It is just one of the many astonishing features of this huge and hugely impressive building, whose towers echo the architecture of Prague's Old Town, although they are from a neo-Gothic reconstruction in the late nineteenth century.

These are just three of the most striking Bohemian castles. There are more than two thousand castles in the whole Czech Republic, more per square mile than in any other country in the world.

The Round Tower is one of the most distinguishing features of the castle at Český Krumlov (**8**), and before it stands the green tip of the five-story tower of the former Church of St. Jošt.

THE NEW BERLIN

Berlin has gone through many incarnations, and today the city is reinventing itself yet again with grand building projects but without losing its sense of allure.

The Potsdamer Platz (1) symbolizes Berlin's changes in recent years, being transformed from a home for notorious cabaret clubs into a display of striking modern architecture.

THERE ARE MANY BERLINS. There have been many Berlins throughout history, as the city has changed with–or been changed by–the times. There is a Berlin of the imagination, which for most people is probably the decadent Berlin of the 1930s, most notably depicted in the book *Goodbye to Berlin* and the movie *Cabaret*. There is the political Berlin, the city that U.S. President John F. Kennedy addressed on June 26, 1963, when he made one of those political statements all the more resounding for being kept simple, *"Ich bin ein Berliner"* ("I am a Berliner"). That was a response to the divided Berlin, the Berlin of the Berlin Wall, but even though the city is now united

again, and is the largest in Germany, there are still many Berlins.

Whereas many cities have a center that is popular with visitors, and that can easily be walked around, Berlin has several districts, each with a different feel to it. It is as if several cities, with different pasts and architectural styles, have merged, and you flow from one to the other.

Potsdamer Platz

If there is one place that reflects the new Berlin that is growing from the old Berlin, it is Potsdamer Platz. It was here around this square that many of the city's notorious prewar cabarets existed.

The Fernsehturm or Television Tower (**2**) was built in the late 1960s and was an indication of the changes to come.

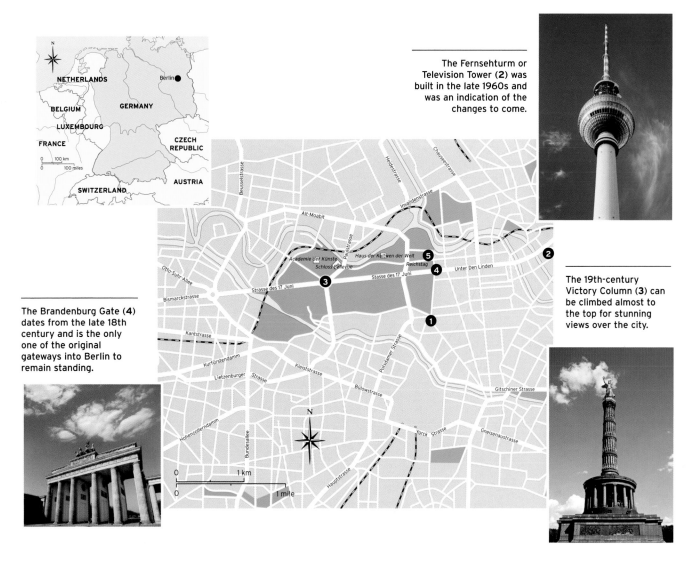

The Brandenburg Gate (**4**) dates from the late 18th century and is the only one of the original gateways into Berlin to remain standing.

The 19th-century Victory Column (**3**) can be climbed almost to the top for stunning views over the city.

They did not know it at the time, but it was a swan song they were singing. During World War II (1939–45), the Potsdamer Platz was bombed almost out of existence. It lay ignored and virtually derelict, and then during the Cold War it lingered, unwanted and unloved, in the no-man's-land that divided East and West Berlin during the period that the Berlin Wall stood nearby. The Potsdamer Platz in those years was lit not by the brash lights of cabaret clubs but by the lamps of the Berlin Wall itself, a discouragement to any East Berliners wanting to escape to the West.

Although the Wall first came down in 1989, it was another ten years before the last remnants were removed from Potsdamer Platz. In the years since Potsdamer Platz was officially reopened in 1998, a remarkable transformation has taken place here, the creation of a whole new Potsdamer Platz, the result of over $5 billion of investment. Where there were cabarets there are now cinemas, a piazza, 5-star hotels, a huge modern shopping mall, businesses—a whole new life for the new Berlin, and the new Germany.

The Berlin Wall went up in 1961 and was torn down in 1989 with great delight by the people, who were happy to see their city united once more.

Daimler City

To design the new city the architects Renzo Piano and Richard Rogers were brought in, the team that built the remarkable Pompidou Center in Paris. In Berlin they had nineteen buildings to play with, and Daimler City, the DaimlerChryser headquarters, is an echo of the "inside out" Pompidou Center architecture: A green-tipped ventilation shaft for the Tiergarten Tunnel rises into the sky, visible all over the city.

The audacious Daimler City was followed by the even more startling sight of the Sony Center. This vast construction of steel and glass reminds us that the future is happening now, with its remarkable and colorful tentlike roof, and six floors of apartments suspended between the two main legs of an office block. Inside the Sony Center is the Filmmuseum, and since the year 2000 this is where the prestigious Berlin Film Festival has been held, bringing the eyes of the world onto this spectacular part of the new Berlin.

Reichstag

Elsewhere, one of the iconic buildings of Berlin, the Reichstag, has also been brought into the twenty-first century. It was built in 1894 and was the seat of Parliament of what was then a united Germany, at a time when east and west were just geographical locations. It remained the home of Parliament until a fire in 1933 destroyed the main chamber, and there have been suspicions ever since about how the fire was started—some blaming the Nazi Government itself, with several possible motives, including that it was a means of ushering in its repressive laws.

It was not until 1999 that the German Parliament, now called the Bundestag, returned to the Reichstag building. The renovation was designed by the acclaimed British architect Sir Norman Foster, whose other projects include the new Hong Kong International Airport, Stansted Airport near London, and London's new Wembley Stadium.

Foster added a large glass dome to the building, 75 feet (23 m) high, to which the public has access by walking around a tower containing 360 mirrors, which are both visually striking and also practical, as they reflect sunlight into the chamber below. From the dome there is a 360-degree view of Berlin, as well as a view down into the government chamber below. It is an apt arrangement for the changing city.

POPULATION 3,400,000

CURRENCY Euro

CLIMATE Berlin has a temperate climate, and even in summer it rarely gets unbearably hot. Rain can fall all year-round, and in winter it can fall below freezing for quite long periods.

WHAT TO TAKE A copy of Christopher Isherwood's *The Berlin Stories*, for a flavor of the city's past.

BEST TIME Summer is the best time to enjoy warm weather, although it is also the wettest time of the year.

NEAREST AIRPORT Berlin International Airport is in the northern suburb of Tegel, about 5 miles (8 km) northwest of the city center, with easy access into Berlin.

ACCOMMODATION Visitor numbers are rapidly increasing, but new hotels are keeping pace, and you will find every option you might want.

The Reichstag (**5**) is the most potent political building in Berlin, and is where the reunification ceremony was held on October 3, 1990.

THE CASTLES OF THE RHINE

As the "Romantic Rhine" flows through the Rhine Gorge, it passes more medieval castles than any other river valley in the world. Little wonder it is a World Heritage Site.

THE RHINE IS ONE OF THE WORLD'S great rivers, flowing through Europe a distance of about 825 miles (1,328 km) from its source high in the Swiss Alps until it reaches the sea at Rotterdam in the Netherlands. Although there are many magnificent stretches of the river, there is one in particular that has been singled out by UNESCO and made a World Heritage Site. It is a 41-mile (65-km) part of the Upper Middle Rhine Valley, where the banks are lined with vineyards, historic towns, and medieval castles.

Roughly from Bingen to Koblenz, the Rhine is at its narrowest and the banks are at their deepest, so the water rushes by and every mile or so, it seems, a new castle emerges to overlook the river. It is here that it is known as the "Romantic Rhine," and on a fine sunny day when the skies are blue, the waters are sparkling, the countryside is lush, and the castles are at their magnificent best, no one could possibly argue. Certainly not UNESCO, who said of here that "The 40½-mile (65-km) stretch of the Middle Rhine Valley, with its castles, historic towns, and vineyards, graphically illustrates the long history of human involvement with a dramatic and varied natural landscape. It is intimately associated with history and legend, and for centuries has exercised a powerful influence on writers, artists, and composers."

Lorelei Rock

One of those writers influenced by the dramatic beauty of this part of the river was Heinrich Heine (1797–1856). He was typical of the nineteenth-century Romantic movement of poets and painters who found inspiration in the Rhine, in the same way the British Romantic poets were stimulated by the English Lake District (see pages 20–23). Heine's verse *Die Lorelei* was set to music, as many of the Romantic poems were, and celebrated the famous Lorelei Rock.

Castle Pfalz (1) sits on a rock and was once used to extract tolls from the passing river traffic: A chain stretched across the Rhine prevented boats from passing by freely.

It isn't known when Stahleck Castle (2) was built, but it was being lived in by the end of the 12th century, and is still inhabited today—as a youth hostel.

-> **FACT FILE**

CURRENCY Euro

CLIMATE Along the Rhine the climate is agreeable, with mild winters and summers that are warm but not too hot. Rainfall is not high, but it falls pretty evenly throughout the year. Summer daytime temperatures average about 68°F (20°C), and in the coldest months of December and January it is usually around freezing.

WHAT TO TAKE An umbrella, just in case.

BEST TIME Any time from spring to fall. Even in winter on bright days the castles look their picturesque best.

NEAREST AIRPORT Cologne

ACCOMMODATION Plentiful, all along the river, from expensive hotels to cozy inns and guesthouses.

The Lorelei or Loreley Rock is near the little town of St. Goarshausen in the part of the river that goes through the Rhine Gorge. The rock towers 394 feet (120 m) above the water, at the point where the river is at its narrowest and the currents are most fierce. This has caused ships to run aground, an event that is often attributed to the seductive song of the Rhine Maidens. Like the Greek Sirens, the Rhine Maidens lure sailors to their doom, and they also inspired Wagner to feature them in his operas *Der Ring des Nibelungen* (*The Ring of the Nibelung*).

The Castles

It is the plentiful castles along this part of the Rhine, though, rather than rocks and Rhine Maidens, that make it such an extraordinary place. There is said to be a castle every mile (1.6 km) or so, and more medieval castles here than along any other river in the world—including even the Loire in France, which is famed for its plentiful châteaux.

The castles may look romantic and appealing today, but the reason for their existence is a long way from that. They were built by local feudal lords who wanted to control their particular piece of this busy trading river. By building castles and manning them, they could control the passing traffic here where the river is narrow. Their men could prevent boats from passing if they did not agree to pay the tolls, so navigating this stretch of water was a slow and costly business. Today the castles can be equally lucrative, as they are very popular with visitors, but at least the tolls today are voluntary.

Cat and Mouse Games

To show what life was like in the days when the castles were built, two of them close to each other near the Lorelei Rock are now better known by their nicknames: Katz (Cat) Castle and Maus (Mouse) Castle. Katz Castle was built in the late fourteenth century, and part of its purpose was to keep a wary eye on its near neighbor, the Maus

The River Rhine curves gracefully through the Rhine Gorge (3), near St. Goarshausen, with the Lorelei Rock on the right of the picture.

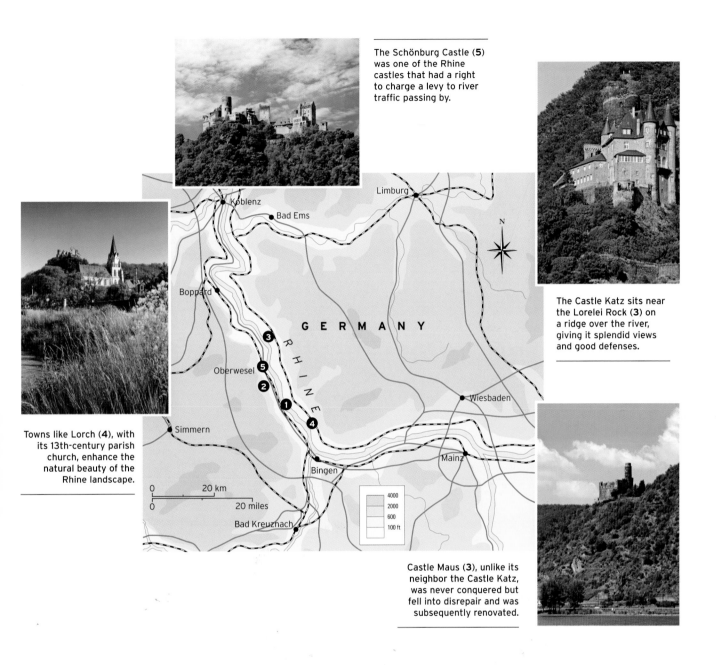

The Schönburg Castle (**5**) was one of the Rhine castles that had a right to charge a levy to river traffic passing by.

The Castle Katz sits near the Lorelei Rock (**3**) on a ridge over the river, giving it splendid views and good defenses.

Towns like Lorch (**4**), with its 13th-century parish church, enhance the natural beauty of the Rhine landscape.

Castle Maus (**3**), unlike its neighbor the Castle Katz, was never conquered but fell into disrepair and was subsequently renovated.

Castle, built at roughly the same time. Hence the buildings were nicknamed Cat and Mouse.

South of here the Schönburg Castle is now a luxury hotel. First mentioned way back in the tenth century, it was destroyed by French soldiers in 1689 but then rebuilt in the late nineteenth century. Stahleck Castle was also destroyed by the French but was rebuilt, and today it is one of the most stylish youth hostels in the world. The Brömserburg Castle in Rüdesheim was built in the year 1000 and still survives, today housing a museum devoted to wine and local history. It is therefore a summing up of what this area's main attractions are—castles, vineyards, and centuries of history. It is indeed the Romantic Rhine.

-> **What's in a Name?**

The River Rhine is not known as the Rhine in Germany, but as the Rhein—pronounced the same but spelled differently. As it crosses the border into the Netherlands, it becomes the River Rijn. When it flows through France, it is the River Rhine, and in Switzerland it depends whether you are a French Swiss or a German Swiss speaker.

BUDA AND PEST: TWO SIDES OF A CITY

Once hidden behind the Iron Curtain, Budapest has now blossomed and can show itself to be one of the most beautiful cities in Europe.

PARIS HAS THE LEFT BANK and the right bank, Londoners are either from north of the river or south of the river, Istanbul is divided by water between two continents—and in Hungary's capital there is Buda and there is Pest. In fact before unification in 1873 there were three towns, which were united into a single city, at first called Pest-Buda. As well as Buda and Pest there was Óbuda, or Old Buda, and the three came together to give birth to what many people regard as one of the most beautiful cities in Europe—East or West.

Four parts of Budapest have been distinguished as UNESCO World Heritage Sites: the banks of the Danube, the area around Buda Castle, Andrássy Avenue, and even its Millennium Underground Railway. This dates back to 1896 and was the first Metro system on the European continent, second in the world after London. It was built so efficiently that its trains ran every two minutes and its one line was carrying thirty-five thousand passengers a day.

Andrássy Avenue

Even when you are traveling below ground in Budapest, you are in a site that is of cultural importance to the whole world. And when you are above ground, you realize why so much of the city has been picked out by UNESCO for special protection. One reason for the subway's existence was that the city was opposed to above-ground transport, especially on its grand street, Andrássy Avenue, where they wanted nothing to mar its classical beauty. But they did want some means of taking people to Budapest City Park to enjoy the millennium celebrations. As Andrássy Avenue had also been built in 1870 as a means of getting to the City Park, the transport system had to be taken underground.

Andrássy Avenue is lined with trees and elegant buildings. For sheer jaw-dropping beauty it can rival any street anywhere, even those of Paris. It was Paris that inspired the street, as the Hungarian Count Gyula Andrássy had spent some time living there, and was impressed by the Champs-Élysées and other wide Parisian boulevards. When he returned to Hungary to live, he thought Budapest needed something similar. Many people think it even surpasses the streets that gave Andrássy his ideas.

The Hungarian State Opera House was added to Andrássy Avenue in 1884, and its imposing exterior

Vajdahunyad Castle (1) in the City Park was originally built of wood and cardboard for an exhibition in 1896, but it was so well liked that it was pulled down and rebuilt properly.

–> FACT FILE

POPULATION 1,700,000

CURRENCY Forint

CLIMATE Budapest's temperate climate brings summers that are warm but not too hot, and chilly winters with some sub-zero days and nights. Rainfall is fairly consistent throughout the year.

WHAT TO TAKE Warm clothing and wet-weather clothing, a phrase book.

BEST TIME July–September gives the best chance of blue skies and sunshine to enhance Budapest's buildings.

NEAREST AIRPORT Budapest Ferihegy International Airport is about 10 miles (16 km) southeast of the center, with an airport bus and taxis linking it to the city.

ACCOMMODATION Boutique hotels are opening in Budapest to cater to the increasing numbers of international visitors, but there is still a shortage of beds in the city, so plan ahead.

The Emperor Franz Joseph financed the building of the opulent State Opera House **(2)** in the late 19th century, with more than 15 pounds (7 kg) of gold used in the auditorium. Performances are still held there today.

The imposing Buda Castle (3) has withstood sieges, neglect, fire, and bombardment through the centuries, proving its worth as Budapest's most prominent building.

conceals a fantastic, swirling, glittering interior, worth seeing on a guided tour if you are not able to get tickets for a performance. Opposite is another magnificent building, the Dreschler Palace, now the Ballet Institute.

Buda Castle

Magnificent buildings are everywhere in Budapest, facing you at almost every turn. Of all the buildings, though, none can match Buda Castle for its impact. All you can do when you get your first sight of it is stand and stare, and wonder if it can be real. It is monumental. It gives some indication of the wealth and power of the Hungarian kings and princes who built it, lived in it, enlarged it, and later rebuilt it completely, over the centuries.

Castle Hill was chosen as the site of a royal residence as long ago as 1245, when the first castle here was built. Some parts of the present building go back to the fourteenth century, when Italian artisans were brought to Buda to help create a Renaissance city to rival—or even surpass—Florence or Venice. Sadly their superb creation was left to decay when Buda became part of the Ottoman Empire, although it was Christians who destroyed the building completely during the siege of 1686.

In 1715 the castle had to be cleared away and a new smaller palace built, though thankfully some parts of the original were able to be rescued from the rubble. As if all this were not enough, the new palace was burned down again in 1849, and rebuilt once more between 1850 and 1856.

Even then, its story was far from finished and still is not. In the late nineteenth century a much bigger palace was commissioned, and took forty years to build. Then this, too, was destroyed during a more recent siege of Budapest, when the city was bombarded in 1944-45 as World War II drew to its climax. The builders had to be brought in once more to rebuild the castle, but in the 1950s the new Communist regime destroyed the palace, as a symbol of royal repression. In the 1960s it was rebuilt, but it was recently thought that the events of the 1950s and '60s caused irreparable damage, and parts are going to have to be reconstructed.

Meanwhile, the River Danube flows gently by, beneath the castle's gaze, as it has done since the arrival of humankind in Europe, its curving shape at this point helping to make Budapest what it is, one of the most beautiful cities in Europe.

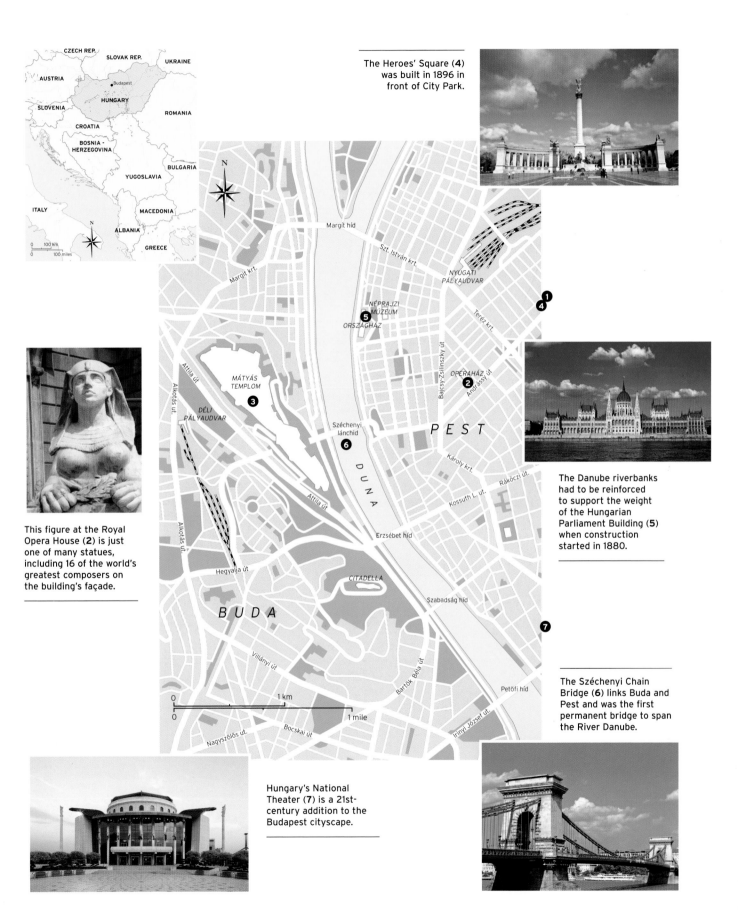

The Heroes' Square (**4**) was built in 1896 in front of City Park.

This figure at the Royal Opera House (**2**) is just one of many statues, including 16 of the world's greatest composers on the building's façade.

The Danube riverbanks had to be reinforced to support the weight of the Hungarian Parliament Building (**5**) when construction started in 1880.

The Széchenyi Chain Bridge (**6**) links Buda and Pest and was the first permanent bridge to span the River Danube.

Hungary's National Theater (**7**) is a 21st-century addition to the Budapest cityscape.

POLAND'S BIALOWIEZA FOREST

Which traveler's pulse would not race at the thought of visiting a primeval forest, where European bison, wolves, and wild boar still roam?

THE BIALOWIEZA FOREST, which includes one of the first national parks in Europe, is about ten thousand years old. At one time woodland like this would have stretched across the Great European Plain, from the Pyrenees to the Urals, and would have been filled with herds of bison, packs of wolves, lynxes, wild boars, deer, elks, foxes, beavers, wild horses, eagles, and owls. It was the kind of forest described in fairy tales, where usually a woodcutter appears, though it was the cutting of the wood for fuel, houses, cathedrals, and castles that contributed to the forests' disappearance. But here, where the Polish border meets that of Belarus, the last of the forest survives.

On the Border
It is at the border where you question what humans have contributed to the forest, and the way we live. Bialowieza is that kind of place. It prompts you to ask serious questions, and to make you wonder what you want from life. The border is an ugly strip of plowed-up land and barbed-wire fences, and although it comes as no surprise that people cannot cross from one country to the other—not even if you have your passport—the restrictions apply to animals, too. One justification for this ruling is to prevent the genetic mixing of the small numbers of European bison (three hundred in the whole forest), but the fences mean that no other large animals can move freely either, animals which know nothing of artificial barriers and borders, but would go only where their instincts take them.

History and Facts
The forest covers about 617 square miles (1,598 sq km). The oldest parts have been dated back to about 8000 B.C., and it owes its survival in part to the fact that it was once a hunting forest, preserved for the use of the kings. The first record of its being protected dates back to 1538, when the Polish King Zygmunt Stary introduced the death penalty for the

There are walkways through parts of the Bialowieza National Forest (1), to educate visitors on the trees and wildlife.

-> FACT FILE

CURRENCY Polish złoty

CLIMATE The forest has a temperate continental cool climate, which means warm summers but very cold winters. There will be snow on the ground for about three months of the year, with a January average temperature of 23ºF (-5ºC). Summer averages are about 64ºF (18ºC), but that is the average, so there are many pleasant, fairly dry and warm days. Most of the precipitation falls as snow.

WHAT TO TAKE Insect repellent, binoculars, a good wildlife guide, phrase book.

BEST TIME Spring and fall are good times for bird activity, summer is beautiful, and even in winter the park has a majestic beauty and some wildlife activity.

NEAREST AIRPORT Warsaw is about 120 miles (193 km) southwest of the forest.

ACCOMMODATION There is a good choice in the village of Bialowieza, from hostels and guesthouses to four luxury hotels, but visiting the park is popular, so book ahead. There are also guest rooms in the Hunter's Lodge and in a hotel within the national park that is run by the park authorities.

The sun sets over the magnificent Bialowieza National Forest (1), but thankfully not on the remaining European bison that still live there.

At one time much of Europe looked like the Bialowieza National Forest (1), though the trees that stand outside the protected national park are still being logged commercially.

poaching of bison in the forest. In the modern era it was protected as a national reserve in 1921. The European bison, known as the wisent, which had died out, were reintroduced in 1929, and the national park was created in 1932. The national park is only one small central area, about 10 percent of the vast forest, and there is an ongoing campaign to make the whole forest into a protected national park, to prevent the logging that continues to eat away at the survival of this rare and magnificent forest.

European Bison

There are only two types of bison left in the world today, the American bison and the European bison, and both are the largest land mammals in their respective continents. The former is regarded as conservation dependent, i.e., there are reasonable numbers but without protection they would not survive. The European bison is now officially endangered, which is why the three hundred or so in the national park are so important.

This is a contrast to the situation some two thousand years ago, when wisent were common throughout most of the European continent. They spread from Spain to Scandinavia, and from Siberia even onto the island of Britain. They are huge creatures, weighing up to 2,000 pounds (907 kg), and apart from occasionally being killed by packs of wolves they have no predators except for humans. By the fourteenth century they were extinct in Western Europe, and the last wild wisent in Poland was killed—by a hunter—in 1919. By 1927 they were totally extinct in the wild, with only fifty or so remaining in zoos. From the descendants of these zoo animals, the wisent has been reintroduced into the wild in several protected areas, the most significant of which is here at Bialowieza.

The Forest

Although the bison bring many visitors to the national park (which sees about one hundred thousand visitors a year), the forest itself is naturally a major attraction. There are trails to take you to some of the most significant trees, some of which have been given grand names like the Emperor of the South, the Tsar Oak, and the Guardian of Zwierzyniec. Some of these are huge and ancient trees that make you feel humble at their great age and immense size, like meeting a gentle giant who is a few hundred years old.

The Jagiello Oak is one of the most famous in the whole forest, as it is said to be where the Polish King Wladyslaw II Jagiello rested before going on to the Battle of Grunwald in 1410. However, legend gets the better of fact, as the tree was no more than about 450 years old when it blew down in a storm in 1974. The tree known as the Great Mamamuszi is the thickest oak in the forest, with a circumference of 22 1/2 feet (6.9 m) and is still very much alive.

These venerable trees have seen humans and beasts, princes and peasants, come and go, and still they stand. It is to be hoped that the forest will stand forever, regenerating itself year after year, as a moving reminder of the way things used to be.

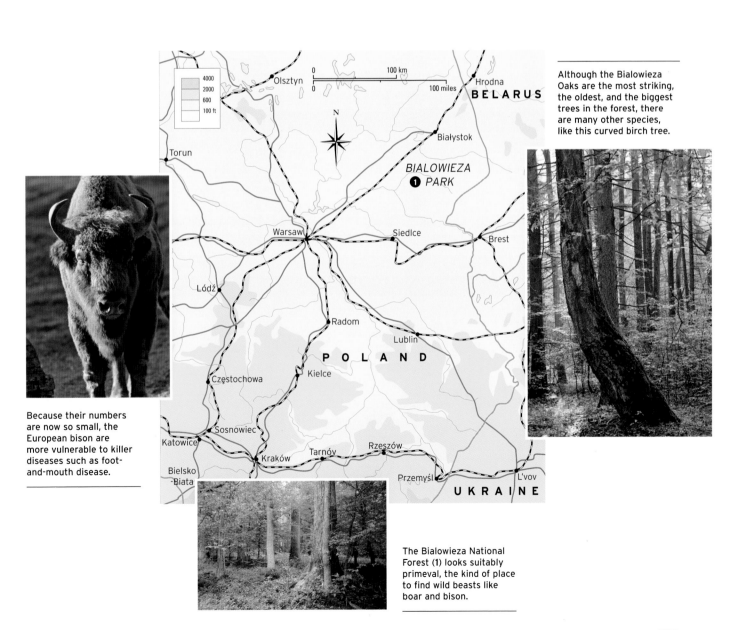

Because their numbers are now so small, the European bison are more vulnerable to killer diseases such as foot-and-mouth disease.

Although the Bialowieza Oaks are the most striking, the oldest, and the biggest trees in the forest, there are many other species, like this curved birch tree.

The Bialowieza National Forest (1) looks suitably primeval, the kind of place to find wild beasts like boar and bison.

Map labels: Olsztyn, Hrodna, BELARUS, Torun, Białystok, BIALOWIEZA ① PARK, Warsaw, Siedlce, Brest, Łódź, Radom, Lublin, POLAND, Częstochowa, Kielce, Sosnowiec, Katowice, Tarnóv, Rzeszów, Kraków, Bielsko-Biata, Przemyśl, L'vov, UKRAINE

Scale: 0 — 100 km, 0 — 100 miles

Elevation key: 4000, 2000, 600, 100 ft

ST. PETERSBURG'S ARCHITECTURE

It has been called the Paris of the East and the Venice of the North, but Russia's St. Petersburg has a charm and beauty of its own, as well as one of the greatest art museums in the world.

FOUNDED IN 1703, AND GOING FIRST by the rather dour names of Petrograd and Leningrad, Russia's second city has flourished since it changed its name back to St. Petersburg after a referendum in 1991. It still lags behind Moscow, its rival city about 400 miles (644 km) away to the southeast, when it comes to an economic boom, but it has never lagged behind Moscow in style.

An important event happened in 1990, when UNESCO placed the "Historic Center of St. Petersburg and Related Groups of Monuments" on its list of World Heritage Sites. It was an acknowledgment of the significance–and sheer beauty–of its baroque and neoclassical styles of architecture, shown especially in such buildings as the Winter Palace, the Marble Palace, the Admiralty, and the Hermitage.

The foundations for the city, and for its style, were laid in 1703 when Peter the Great built the Peter and Paul Fortress as the first building in his proposed exciting new city. Its first name, Peter, was for Peter the Great's patron saint, St. Peter, and not for the tsar himself. Later, the city of St. Petersburg in Florida would be named after the Russian original. Tsar Peter commanded that there should be canals in the new city, and so began the network of canals, crossed today by more than 400 bridges, which give St. Petersburg part of its appeal.

The Palaces

One of the city's most notable buildings was added between 1754 and 1762 when the Winter Palace was built for Peter the Great's daughter, Empress Elizabeth. Sadly she died before it was completed and its first occupant was instead Catherine the Great. It became, as the name suggests, the winter residence of the Russian tsars, and is a unique and striking structure. From the front on Palace Square the Winter Palace stops you in your tracks. It is huge, everything a palace should be, and indeed it boasts 1,945 windows and 1,057 rooms, many of which are now open to the public. Its principal

This Grand Staircase of the Hermitage Museum was built from white marble in the 18th century and extends for the full height of the Winter Palace (1).

Winter temperatures in St. Petersburg are fierce, but the snow they bring only adds to the enchantment of the Winter Palace (1).

-> FACT FILE

POPULATION 4,700,000

CURRENCY Russian ruble

CLIMATE St. Petersburg's average annual temperature is just 39ºF (4ºC), a low average caused by the extreme cold of midwinter and the fact that summers are cooled by winds from the Baltic. The average temperature in January–February is 13ºF (-10ºC), and in July, the hottest month, it is 72ºF (22ºC). Rain falls lightly but steadily throughout the year, with July and August being the wettest months and February–May the driest. In winter expect long periods of snow, and there is higher than average humidity all year-round.

WHAT TO TAKE A raincoat at any time of year, and warm clothing in winter. Dress in layers, as buildings can be stifling inside.

BEST TIME Winters can be beautiful if you are prepared for the weather, but summer is usually the safest bet.

NEAREST AIRPORT St. Petersburg Pulkovo Airport is 10 miles (16 km) south of the city center.

ACCOMMODATION Traditionally the best choice was expensive 5-star hotels, which were not necessarily good by Western standards. They have improved a lot, however, and there is also an increasing number of midrange hotels, though budget ones need to be checked out carefully in advance. If visiting in summer, it is best to book well ahead.

The palace at Peterhof (**2**) on the edge of St. Petersburg was founded by Peter the Great, who planned it to be the greatest summer palace ever built.

colors of pastel green and white make it stand out from any other building in the world, whether in the dazzling light of high summer or on a cold snowy winter's day.

The Winter Palace is now part of one of the world's biggest museums, the Hermitage Museum. There are said to be almost three million items in its collection, of which only a small part can be displayed at any one time. It is estimated that if you spent just one minute looking at every item on display in the Hermitage, it would take you eleven years to get around.

For many it is the priceless works by the famous artists and sculptors that make the Hermitage one of the world's unmissable collections. There are works by Renoir, Rodin, Van Gogh, Gauguin, Cézanne, Manet, Monet, and Matisse. There are rooms filled with the creations of Rubens and Rembrandt—more than twenty of Rembrandt's powerful works, along with twenty-two paintings and nineteen sketches by Rubens. There are works by Canaletto, Van Dyck, and Michelangelo, and two by Leonardo da Vinci. There are thirty rooms just on Italian art, and works by Velázquez, El Greco, Murillo, and Goya.

And those are just some of the major artists, before you get to the prehistoric art, the fine collections from ancient Egypt, Greece, and Rome, the Oriental art, the collections of stained glass, the Fabergé jewelry, and, of course, the Russian collections. When you explore what is inside the Hermitage you realize that the stunning outside view is merely the tip of the iceberg.

The comparative modesty of the tsars' Summer Palace shows that not everything was done on a vast scale. It is an attractive building of just fourteen rooms, in the Summer Garden, and the interior has been sympathetically restored so visitors can see what it was like when Peter the Great lived here, after the palace's construction from 1710 to 1712. Before this he lived in an even more modest wooden cabin, which was the first domestic building put up in St. Petersburg in 1703 and that still survives as a museum.

Russian Admiralty

The Russian Admiralty Board was created by Peter the Great in 1718, both to govern the Russian Navy as it helped to control the mighty Russian Empire of the time and to oversee the building of new ships in the dockyards. In 1806 work began on the Admiralty Building, to house the Admiralty Board. It is a graceful and grand building in Russian Empire style, and today it is a naval college at the end of one of the city's main streets—Nevsky Prospekt. This street was built by Peter the Great, too, as the St. Petersburg road that would go all the way to Moscow, but the thoroughfare developed and instead it became the heart of the city.

St. Petersburg has not yet had the renaissance that has been seen in other Eastern European destinations, such as Moscow, Prague, and the Baltic States. When it does happen, and it will, St. Petersburg will be an even more exciting city to visit.

St. Isaac's Cathedral (**3**) took 40 years to construct in the early 19th century, and was the biggest church in Russia at that time.

The Spas-na-krovi Cathedral (**5**), also known as the Cathedral of Spilled Blood, the Church of the Savior on Spilled Blood, and the Cathedral of the Resurrection of Christ.

The gardens at the Peterhof Palace (**2**) contain numerous fountains, including the Grand Cascade, with its golden figures.

The Gothic Chapel of St. Alexander Nevsky is in Alexandria Park, Peterhof (**2**).

First-class ballet performances are held at the historic Mariinsky Theater (**4**), built in 1860.

MOSCOW: RED SQUARE AND MORE

Moscow is the heart and soul of Mother Russia. With great changes still sweeping the country, it remains one of the most fascinating cities in the world.

THE IRON CURTAIN MAY HAVE PARTED, but there is still the feeling that it is not yet open all the way. Some have flooded through the widening gap, going in both directions, to embrace the new freedoms and opportunities, but people who have spent lifetimes living under a strict system do not change overnight. It is what makes Moscow so fascinating and so frustrating. Alongside the booming Moscow of millionaires and the Mafia (often one and the same) is still the Moscow of peasants and poverty, and people for whom secrecy and wariness of the foreigner is a way of life.

The Kremlin

The Cathedral of the Annunciation in the Kremlin (1) was originally the royal chapel of the tsars and was built in the late 15th century.

It is significant that the seat of government for Russia is inside the Kremlin, the Russian word for "fortress." For most of the twentieth century the "fortress" was a secretive place, behind whose walls the lives of millions of people were controlled. If few

Westerners went there, it was not because the place was totally shut off behind locked doors; it was simply that few tourists went to Moscow. Much of the Kremlin is open, as it is a huge 69-acre (28-hectare) complex of buildings that today draws people like a magnet.

The Kremlin is a part of the history of Moscow. Many Russian towns and cities have kremlins. This one happens to be in the country's capital, and what was formerly the capital of the vast U.S.S.R. (Union of Soviet Socialist Republics), an empire that covered over 8,200,000 square miles (over 21,000,000 sq km)—over twice the size of the United States today.

Cathedrals and Churches

The Kremlin was originally a wooden fortress, built in the twelfth century, replaced with stone walls in the 1360s. In the 1490s the Kremlin was surrounded

POPULATION 10,400,000

CURRENCY Russian ruble

CLIMATE Moscow has a continental climate, with warm summers and bitterly cold winters. July is the hottest month with a maximum average temperature of 75ºF (24ºC), but in winter–which can start as early as October and last six months–there will be long periods of below-zero temperatures, and often severe snowstorms. There is comparatively little rainfall.

WHAT TO TAKE Several layers of warm clothing in winter, a phrase book, a good and up-to-date guidebook.

BEST TIME July and August for summer sun and blue skies.

NEAREST AIRPORT Sheremetyevo International Airport is about 20 miles (32 km) northwest of the city center. Allow plenty of time to get to and from the airport, as traffic is notoriously bad.

ACCOMMODATION There are several good, reliable hotels, including the Sheraton, Radisson, and Holiday Inn, but they are expensive. Cheaper tends to mean basic, so do some research before booking.

The "onion domes" of St. Basil's Cathedral on Red Square (2) are the most familiar image of Moscow, though its official name is the grand-sounding Cathedral of the Intercession of the Virgin by the Moat, as there was once a moat here by the Kremlin.

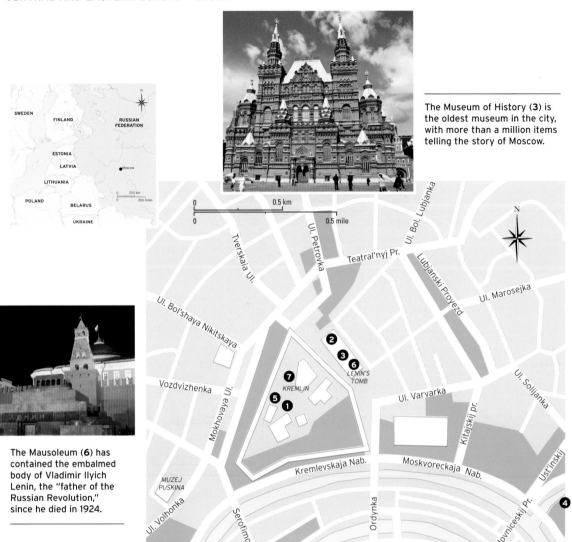

The Museum of History (**3**) is the oldest museum in the city, with more than a million items telling the story of Moscow.

The Mausoleum (**6**) has contained the embalmed body of Vladimir Ilyich Lenin, the "father of the Russian Revolution," since he died in 1924.

The Kremlin's Taynitskaya Tower (**5**), or Secret Tower, was built in 1485 as a defense, and harbors two secrets: an underground tunnel to provide access, and a well to provide water.

The 18th-century Kuskovo Estate (**4**) used to be the summer residence of the Sheremetyev Counts and is now a retreat for the people of Moscow.

–> Fabergé Eggs

Only sixty-nine Fabergé eggs were ever made, of which sixty-one have survived. Most are now in museums, with Moscow's Armory Museum having the greatest collection. The first egg was of simple white enameled gold, which opened like a Russian doll to reveal a yolk of pure gold. The yolk opened to show a golden hen, which in turn opened to reveal a tiny golden crown with a ruby attached.

The Great Kremlin Palace (7)—the ceremonial residence of the president—is suitably imposing, with its main façade facing the Moscow River.

by thick walls of distinctive red brick, most of which remain today to give it that imposing look. The walls run for about 1½ miles (2.5 km) around, and contain within them several cathedrals, churches, museums, and squares, and even residential buildings as well as government offices. Anywhere else in the world this would be called the Old Town, but in Moscow it remains the Kremlin.

The Cathedral of the Annunciation dates back to 1482 and is where the pre-Communist Russian tsars were christened and married. They were crowned in the Cathedral of the Assumption, a light and airy building from about the same period, in contrast to the gloom and severity of most of the other churches and cathedrals here. For about 350 years tsars were buried in the Cathedral of the Archangel Michael, built in 1505 and still showing today its somber collection of tombs and coffins.

Armory Museum
One of the Kremlin's greatest attractions is the Armory Museum, whose military-sounding name conceals one of the finest museums in the whole of Russia, containing much more than merely arms and armor. The present building dates from the nineteenth century, when it was opened as a museum, and it was built on the spot where the treasures of the Russian royal families have always been kept. And what treasures they are, including the wedding dress of Catherine the Great, a gold and turquoise throne that was given to Boris Godunov, the sixteenth-century regent of Russia, by the shah of Persia, and the carved ivory throne of Ivan the Terrible. Most fabulous of all is the priceless collection of Fabergé eggs, which the tsar and tsarista gave each other as gifts each Easter. It was Tsar Alexander III who commissioned the first-ever Fabergé egg, the symbol of ultimate luxury, as a present for his wife in 1885. The Kremlin may seem a dour and forbidding place from the outside, but inside there are countless treasures.

Red Square
Outside the Kremlin it was a very different story, and one that helps visitors understand why the Russian Revolution happened. It was a similar story in France—starving people aware that their rulers lived lives of almost obscene luxury. Red Square was originally a slum outside the Kremlin walls, where beggars, drunks, criminals, and prostitutes all lived. It was cleared at the end of the fifteenth century, but it remained a place of unruly gatherings and demonstrations, and the site for public executions.

St. Basil's Cathedral was built on the square and finished in 1560, and for 450 years has stood as the most recognizable visual symbol of Moscow, like London's Big Ben or the Eiffel Tower in Paris. The cathedral is as extraordinary inside as it is outside, with a soaring roof and strange passageways and staircases that you wander to visit the nine different churches that make up the building.

With only a day or two in Moscow you can at least explore these two fascinating parts of the city, the Kremlin and Red Square. They only touch the surface of this intriguing city, but are guaranteed to make you want to come back for more.

TATRA MOUNTAINS OF SLOVAKIA

The Tatra Mountains are the Alps of Eastern Europe, with dramatic scenery for walkers and skiers, and a sense of wildness for the traveler.

The High Tatra Mountains as seen from Tatranská Lomnica (1), the largest town in the Tatra region and a popular resort for hiking and skiing.

THE TATRA MOUNTAINS form a natural barrier and border between Poland to the north and Slovakia to the south, but perhaps because Slovakia is less well known, it is on this side of the mountains that there is more of a feeling of magic and mystery. In Poland the popular city of Kraków is a gateway to the mountains and busy resorts like Zakopane, but Slovakia is a newer name, coming into existence only in 1992 when the country of Czechoslovakia was divided.

Slovakia's Tatra National Park is much older than Slovakia itself, having been created on January 1, 1949. It covers an area of 285 square miles (738 sq km), and contains within its boundaries the highest mountain in Slovakia, Gerlachovský Peak. At 8,711 feet (2,655 m), it is also the highest peak in the whole Carpathian Mountains chain, of which the Tatra form a part. Another of the Tatra mountains, Mount Krivan (8,186 feet/2,495 m), has become a symbol of the country, and the Slovak coat of arms and the national flag both show three mountain ranges on them—Fatra, Tatra, and Matra. The last is actually now in Hungary, but the symbol has been used to indicate the region where the Slovak people have lived since at least the fourteenth century. Therefore, the Tatra Mountains are far more than merely a beautiful area of their country; they have a symbolic importance to the Slovaks, forming part of their identity. It is this reverence for the mountains, and the way in which they draw people to enjoy them, that help make the area special for visitors, too.

Hiking and Biking

Although the mountains offer skiing in winter and challenges for climbers, as well as gliding and paragliding, it is the simple act of walking in the National Park that brings many people to the region. There are more than 375 miles (604 km) of hiking trails and sixteen cycling trails marked in the park, which are easy to follow through color-coded symbols. Be sure to get a map when you set off and it will be virtually impossible to get lost. As you walk along the trails, and at every junction of paths, you will find somewhere a marker showing which color trail goes in which direction. Just as important, both the distance and the estimated walking time to the next major junction of paths will be indicated.

The High Tatra Mountains cover a vast area of about 290 square miles (750 sq km) and have a special place in the hearts of the Slovak people.

–> **FACT FILE**

CURRENCY Euro

CLIMATE The climate is generally mild, with plenty of snowfall in winter and temperatures around freezing, though on the high peaks it is below zero for more than half the year. It can be hot in summer, with temperatures in the upper 80sºF (low 30sºC) and beyond. Rain can fall any time, and there are occasional storms, as in any mountain region.

WHAT TO TAKE Sunscreen, walking boots, a Slovak phrase book, a raincoat, a good day pack, binoculars, a cell phone and water bottle.

BEST TIME Unless you specifically want to go skiing, the mountains are best explored in summer, though spring and fall can also be beautiful. Some of the mountain hiking trails are closed from November 1 through to June 15, both for safety reasons and to protect the environment.

NEAREST AIRPORT Poprad-Tatry Airport.

ACCOMMODATION Starý Smokovec is one of the most popular bases for exploring the mountains, and has hotels and guesthouses, but booking ahead is recommended.

The city of Poprad (**2**), the tenth largest in Slovakia, stands out against the snow in a plain at the foot of the Tatra Mountains.

The joy of walking in the Tatra Mountains is that they are so accessible. If you stay in one of the small towns on the lower slopes, such as the popular Starý Smokovec (see next page), you can be out of the town and walking through hushed woodlands within a couple of minutes. These lower wooded slopes are like a fairy-tale forest, sometimes filled with an early-morning mist, and often the only sounds you will hear will be your own breathing, birdsong, or the occasional snap of a twig to indicate you are not alone.

Wildlife

You need to take care when walking in the Tatra, even when close to busy towns. There are European brown bears here, and whereas in many places your chance of seeing one might be a million to one, here in the Tatra it is a reasonable possibility. It takes you back to a time when a walk in the woods was sometimes the only way people could get about, foraging for food and wood for their fires, and they had to be attuned to the other creatures that lived there. Today you need to be aware of the bears' presence, and if that makes you at all nervous, you should walk with at least one

In spring and summer in the Tatra Mountains the white of winter gives way to a variety of colors.

When storm clouds gather, walkers should take care in these wild mountains, where deaths are not unknown.

The brown bear is one of the largest creatures found in the region.

other person. Bears are usually more scared of you than you are of them, and the only danger is when a mother is with her cubs.

There are many other birds and animals in the woods and on the mountain slopes. You are far more likely to see the Alpine marmot than a brown bear, and the Tatra chamois, although endangered, can still be seen. You are also very likely to hear the *tok-tok-tok* of woodpeckers building a nest or tapping for insects under the bark of trees.

Starý Smokovec
Starý Smokovec is one of the most popular towns to use as a base for exploring the Tatra Mountains

on foot. It is a charming little place, with hiking trails starting right in the town and some good Alpine-style accommodation and friendly bars and restaurants. It is also conveniently placed, being on the Tatra Railway, which links it with Poprad, where the nearest airport is, and with other towns and villages in the foothills of the mountains. It is the kind of place where you wake up and smell the clean fresh air, and you cannot wait to get out into those woods and hike into the mountains beyond

THE SWISS ALPS

Born five hundred million years ago, the Swiss Alps are Central Europe's biggest and most dramatic mountain range, covering more than half the country.

THE ALPS SPREAD THEMSELVES across five countries, but it is in Switzerland where most of the highest peaks are and where they dominate land and life. They cover more than 60 percent of the country, rising to the highest point in the Swiss Alps, Dufourspitze (15,202 feet/4,634 m). That is bigger than Mount Whitney in California, the highest point in the contiguous United States, but in a country that is smaller than forty-one of the states in the United States.

Five hundred million years ago, there was not even a speck of this country called Switzerland. Then much of the area around what is now the Mediterranean was covered by the immense Tethys Sea, beneath which the vast deposits of granite, limestone, and marble were being formed. About one hundred million years ago, the shifting of the earth's tectonic plates forced the bottom of the sea upward to form the Alps and other landmasses, and the Tethys Sea was split and drained away to become the Mediterranean, the Black Sea, the Caspian Sea, and the Aral Sea.

The Highest

Those immense eruptions and violent movements on the earth's surface resulted in the Dufourspitze being the highest point in Switzerland, though the highest in the whole Alpine range is Mont Blanc on the French/Italian border, at 15,774 feet (4,808 m) high. As well as France and Italy, the Alps spread across Austria and Liechtenstein, but they are so associated with Switzerland that the whole range is often mistakenly called the Swiss Alps. Sometimes shrouded in cloud and covered in ice and snow, the Dufourspitze is an almost perfect peak. It looks like a mighty mountain should look, like a pyramid rising out of the surrounding peaks, and like a captain being hoisted on his team's shoulders to show respect for the boss.

Ibex, Bears, Lynx, and Wolves

Unlike the Pyrenees (see pages 128–131) where brown bears do just about cling on, all the major mammals, including bears, became extinct in the Swiss Alps, although there are endeavors to reintroduce some of them. The ibex lived on in the Pyrenees until the year 2000, but it had died out in the Swiss Alps more than a hundred years earlier,

-> FACT FILE

CURRENCY Swiss franc

CLIMATE Temperatures naturally vary widely in this mountainous region. At lower elevations you might get summer temperatures from about 65 to 80ºF (18 to 27ºC) and a winter range from about 35 to 45ºF (2 to 7ºC). At higher elevations you can expect it to be a few degrees cooler. Rain can fall any time, and the weather can change quickly as in all mountain areas, so take care.

WHAT TO TAKE Sunscreen whatever time of year, something warm to wear even on summer nights, good walking boots, day pack, cell phone, and all your credit cards.

BEST TIME Spring and summer for walking, winter for the skiers, though in some resorts, such as Zermatt, the skiing continues on into the summer.

NEAREST AIRPORT The international airport at Zürich provides good access to the main resorts of the Swiss Alps.

ACCOMMODATION There is a good choice all year-round in the main resorts, but prices—in the Alpine resorts especially—are higher than average.

The unmistakable shape of the Matterhorn (1), with its four faces on the four points of the compass.

The resort of Flumserberg (2) stands high above Lake Walen, or Walensee, one of the biggest and most beautiful lakes in Switzerland.

Lake Brienz (4) is noted for its steep sides, which extend below the surface so that there are hardly any shallow areas in the lake.

Alpine ibex live at heights up to about 15,000 feet (4,572 m).

Klosters (3) is one of the most famous ski resorts in the Alps, although in summer it is also a beautiful area for hiking.

in 1894, and by 2000 had in fact been very successfully reintroduced. As long ago as 1906 the Alpine ibex was brought back into the Swiss Alps, though not in the usual manner. A poacher, with the permission of the Swiss authorities, took two young kids from a royal hunting ground in northwest Italy, where the last few ibex were living, brought them back to Switzerland, and started breeding them. In the hundred years since then, the ibex has firmly established itself again, and today there are more than fourteen thousand of them.

The European gray wolf also became extinct in the Swiss Alps about a hundred years ago, but recently individuals have started making their own way into Switzerland from Italy, where they

are more protected. There are thought to still be only a handful of wolves in Switzerland, but signs are that they might spread and breed in a place where the conditions are quite natural to them. Their main danger comes from farmers and hunters.

The lynx is slightly more prevalent here, though there are still only a hundred or so thought to exist in the wild. Sightings are very rare, and you could wander in the Swiss Alps for a year without coming anywhere near signs of a lynx or a wolf. They are, naturally, very nervous of humans. So too, normally, are bears, the last one of which was killed in the Swiss Alps in 1904. That meant the death of the animal after which the Swiss capital Bern was named, and that appears on the city's flag and coat of arms. Now the European brown bear, too, has been extending its range from Italy into Switzerland, with isolated sightings in the last few years. However, one of only two bears known to exist in the wild in the Swiss Alps was killed by order of the government, as it seemed to have lost its natural fear of humans and was becoming dangerous. So at last count, there was one brown bear hiding somewhere in Switzerland.

The Best of the Swiss Alps

Visitors to the Swiss Alps started to come in increasing numbers in the mid-nineteenth century, thrilled by accounts of the first conquering of some of the famous peaks with their evocative names, including the Jungfrau in 1811 and the Matterhorn in 1856. In winter, resorts like St. Moritz, Zermatt, and Klosters are known worldwide for their skiing, and après-ski, but the Alps are perhaps even better appreciated in summer. There are hundreds of marked mountain trails that enable visitors to appreciate the Alpine air and views up close and on foot. It is one kind of thrill to zoom through this amazing scenery on skis, but quite another to stand before a solid mountain and try to take it in, or to sit and think that the great natural beauty before you was thrust violently up out of the sea about one hundred million years ago.

St. Moritz (**5**) was one of the first ski resorts in Switzerland, and has been attracting visitors since the mid-19th century.

DIRECTORY OF USEFUL ADDRESSES

Bruges
www.brugge.be
Toerisme Brugge
P.O. 744
B-8000 Brugge, Belgium
Email: toerisme@brugge.be
Tel: + 32 50 44 46 46

London
www.visitlondon.com
Britain and London Visitor Centre
1 Lower Regent Street
London SW1 4XT, U.K.
Tel: +44 (0)8701 566 366

Lake District
www.golakes.co.uk
Cumbria Tourism
Windermere Road, Staveley
Kendal, Cumbria LA8 9PL, U.K.
Email: info@golakes.co.uk
Tel: +44 (0)1539 82222

Stonehenge and Avebury
www.visitwiltshire.co.uk/salisbury/home
Salisbury & Stonehenge Tourism Partnership
3 Rollestone Street, Salisbury
Wiltshire SP1 1DX, U.K.
Email: salisburytourismpartnership@salisbury.
gov.uk
Tel: +44 (0)1722 434373

Cornwall
www.visitcornwall.com
Cornwall Tourist Board
Email: enquiries@visitcornwall.com
Tel: +44 (0)1872 322900

Finnish Lapland
http://tourism.rovaniemi.fi
Rovaniemi Tourist Information
Sampo Shopping Centre, Lordi's Square
Maakuntakatu 29-31
96200 Rovaniemi, Finland
Email: travel.info@rovaniemi.fi
Tel: +358 (0)16 346 270

Iceland
www.icetourist.is
Icelandic Tourist Board
Lækjargata 3
101 Reykjavík, Iceland
Email: info@icetourist.is
Tel: +354 535 5500

Cork and Kerry
www.discoverireland.ie
Ireland Tourist Board
Fáilte Ireland South West
Áras Fáilte, Grand Parade
Cork City, Ireland
Email: corkkerryinfo@failteireland.ie
Tel: +353 (0) 21 4255100

Antrim
www.discovernorthernireland.com
Northern Ireland Tourist Board
59 North Street, Belfast BT1 1NB
Email: info@nitb.com
Tel: +44 (0)28 9023 1221

Amsterdam
www.holland.com/amsterdam
Amsterdam Tourist Board
VVV Stationsplein (KCS)
Stationsplein 10
1012 AB Amsterdam, The Netherlands
Email: info@atcb.nl
Tel: +31 (0)20 625 28 69

Norway West Coast Fjords
www.visitnorway.com
Norwegian Tourist Board
Akersgata 13
0158 Oslo, Norway
Email: info@visitnorway.com
Tel: +47 22 00 25 00

Scottish Highlands and Scottish Islands
www.visitscotland.com
Scottish Tourist Board
Ocean Point One, 94 Ocean Drive
Edinburgh EH6 6JH, U.K.
+44 0131 343 1608

Edinburgh
www.edinburgh.org
Edinburgh and Lothians Tourist Board
Fairways Business Park, Deer Park Avenue
Livingston EH54 8AF, U.K.
Email: info@visitscotland.com
Tel: +44 (0) 1506 832 121

Sweden
www.visitsweden.com
Visit Sweden
Box 3030
103 61 Stockholm, Sweden
Email: info@visitsweden.com
Tel: +46 8789 1000

Wales: Snowdonia
www.visitwales.com
Wales Tourist Board
Email: info@visitwales.com
Tel: +44 (0) 8701 211 251

Dubrovnik
Dubrovnik Tourist Board
C. Zuzoric 1/2
Dubrovnik, Croatia
Email: tzgd@du.tel.hr
Tel: +385 20 323 88

Croatian Islands
www.htz.hr
Croatian National Tourist Board
Iblerov trg 10/IV, 10000 Zagreb
Hrvatska, Croatia
Email: info@htz.hr
Tel: +385 (1) 4699 333

Athens, Delphi, Meteora
www.gnto.gr
Greek National Tourism Organisation
Tsoha 24
11521 Athens, Greece
Email: info@gnto.gr
Tel: +30 210 8707000

Santorini
www.gnto.gr
Greek National Tourism Organisation
Fira
84 700 Thira, Greece
Email: info@gnto.gr
Tel: +30 22860 27199

Venice
www.turismovenezia.it
Venice Tourist Board
APT Venezia, Castello 5050
30122 Venezia, Italy
Email: info@turismovenezia.it
Tel: +39 041 529 8711

Cinque Terre
www.enit.it
Italian Government Tourist Board
Riomaggiore Office
c/o Stazione FF. SS.
19017 Riomaggiore, Italy
Tel: +39 018 776 2187

Rome
www.enit.it
Italian Government Tourist Board
Rome Office
Via Parigi 11
00185 Roma, Italy
Tel: +39 064 88991

Florence
www.enit.it
Italian Government Tourist Board
Florence Office
Via A. Manzoni 16
50121 Firenze, Italy
Tel: +39 055 23320

Siena
www.enit.it
Italian Government Tourist Board
Siena Office
Via dei Termini 6
53100 Siena, Italy
Tel: +39 0577 42209

Istanbul and Ephesus
www.tourismturkey.org
Turkish Culture and Tourism Office
Ismet Inonu Bulvan 91 Sokak No. 5
Ankara, Turkey
Tel: +90 312 212 8300

Andorra
www.andorra.ad
Andorra Ministry of Tourism and Culture
Prat de la Creu, 62
Andorra la Vella, Andorra
Tel: +376 875700

Paris
www.parisinfo.com
Paris Tourist Office
25, Rue des Pyramides
75001 Paris, France
Email: agenda@parisinfo.com
Tel: (0) 892 68 3000

Bordeaux
www.bordeaux-tourisme.com
Bordeaux Tourist Office
12 Cours du XXX Juillet
33080 Bordeaux Cedex, France
Email: otb@bordeaux-tourisme.com
Tel: +33 (0)5 56 00 66 00

Loire Valley
www.loirevalleytourism.com
Loire Valley Tourism
37 Avenue de Paris
45000 Orléans, France
Tel: +33 02 38 24 05 05

Provence
www.visitprovence.com
Visit Provence and Office de Tourisme d'Aix-en-Provence
2, Place Du Général de Gaulle
BP 160, 13605 Aix-en-Provence CEDEX 1
Email: infos@aixenprovencetourism.com
Tel: +33 04 42 16 11 61

River Douro
www.visitportugal.com
Portuguese National Tourist Office
Avenida Antonio Augusto de Aguiar, 86
1004 Lisboa Codex, Portugal
Email: info@visitportugal.com
Tel: +351 357 50 86

Madeira
www.madeiratourism.org
Madeira Tourism
Email: info@madeiratourism.com
Tel: +351 291 211 900

Moorish Spain
www.andalucia.org
Turismo de la Junta de Andalucía
Avda. de la Constitución, 21 B
41001 Sevilla, Spain
Email: otsevilla@andalucia.org
Tel: +34 954 221404

Barcelona
www.barcelonaturisme.com
Barcelona Tourist Office
Plaza Catalunya
17-S-08002 Barcelona, Spain
Email: info@barcelonaturisme.com
Tel: +34 932 853834

Jerez
www.turismojerez.com
Jerez Tourism
Alameda Cristina
11403 Jerez de la Frontera, Spain
Email: turismoinfo@aytojerez.es
Tel: +34 956 338874

Seville
www.turismo.sevilla.org
Seville Tourism
Naves del Barranco
c/Arjona, 28
41001 Sevilla, Spain
Email: barranco.turismo@sevilla.org
Tel: +34 954 221714

Vienna
www.wien.info
Vienna Tourist Board
Wien Hotels & Info
1020 Vienna, Austria
Email: info@wien.info
Tel: +43 124 555

Prague and the Castles of Bohemia
www.czechtourism.com
Czech Tourism
Vinohradská 46
120 41 Praha 2, Czech Republic
Email: info@czechtourim.cz
Tel: +420 221 580 445

Berlin
www.visitberlin.de
Berlin Tourism Marketing
Am Karlsbad 11
D-10785 Berlin, Germany
Email: information@visitberlin.de
Tel: +49 (0)30 264 7480

Castles of the Rhine
www.germany-tourism.de
German National Tourist Board
Beethovenstraße 69
60325 Frankfurt/Main, Germany

Budapest
www.budapestinfo.hu
Budapest Tourism Office
Március 15. tér 7
1056 Budapest, Hungary
Email: info@budapestinfo.hu
Tel: +36 126 60479

Polish Bialowieza National Park
www.polandtour.org
Polish National Tourist Office
39 Rue Krakowskie Przedmiescie
00 142 Warszawa, Poland
Email: info@polandtour.org
Tel: +48 226 351 881

St. Petersburg
www.visitrussia.com
Visit Russia
Michurinskaya st. 19
St. Petersburg, Russia
Email: info@visitrussia.com
Tel: +7 812 325 4044

Moscow
www.visitrussia.com
Visit Russia
Kuznetsky most st. 21/5, suite 626
Moscow, Russia
Email: moscow@visitrussia.com
Tel: +7 495 626 0391

Slovakia Tatra Mountains
www.slovakia.travel

Slovak Tourist Board
Námestie Ľ. Štúra 1
P.O. Box 35
974 05 Banská Bystrica, Slovak Republic
Email: sacr@sacr.sk
Tel: +421 48 413 6146

Swiss Alps
www.myswitzerland.com
Swiss National Tourist Office
Tödistrasse 7
CH 8027 Zürich, Switzerland
Email: postoffice@switzerlandtourism.ch
Tel: +41 01 288 1111

INDEX

INDEX

CREDITS

Quarto would like to thank the following agencies for supplying images for inclusion in this book:

l = left; r = right; b = bottom; t = top

4Corners www.4cornersimages.com
pages 52, 68, 83, 84-85t, 146, 191, 200-201t, 209, 212

Getty www.gettyimages.com
pages 36, 37, 87, 106l, 124, 141, 145, 148, 151, 159b

Robert Harding www.robertharding.com
pages 1, 2-3, 13, 20b, 22, 23t, 24, 25, 29, 38t&b, 44-45, 49, 53, 56, 57, 60-61, 63, 73, 74-75t, 90, 92, 95, 97, 99, 102b, 103, 106r, 107, 113b, 117, 132-133, 134b, 135, 143, 146, 149, 152, 157, 158, 159t, 162t, 176b, 185, 188, 203, 204, 206-207, 210, 214-215

Alamy www.alamy.com
pages 8-9, 12, 14, 21, 26, 28, 31-33, 35, 40-41, 42b, 43b, 46, 48, 51, 55, 58, 64-65, 67, 69, 70b, 72, 78-79, 81, 82, 85b, 86b, 88, 89tr, 91, 100-101, 104b, 105, 109, 110b, 111, 112, 114-115, 118, 120-121, 122, 131, 140, 144, 153, 154t, 160b, 161, 163, 164-165, 167, 168b, 169, 170b, 171, 174-175, 178-179, 180, 182-183, 186, 187, 190, 192, 184-195, 196, 198-199, 211, 217

Corbis www.corbis.com
pages 18-19, 123, 137

We would also like to thank the following:

Shutterstock
iStock
Dreamstime
Flickr
Moira Clinch

All other images are the copyright of Quarto Publishing plc. While every effort has been made to credit contributors, Quarto would like to apologize should there have been any omissions or errors, and would be pleased to make the appropriate correction for future editions of the book.